Tobias Hanning

High Precision Camera Calibration

VIEWEG+TEUBNER RESEARCH

Tobias Hanning

High Precision Camera Calibration

VIEWEG+TEUBNER RESEARCH

Bibliographic information published by the Deutsche Nationalbibliothek
The Deutsche Nationalbibliothek lists this publication in the Deutsche Nationalbibliografie;
detailed bibliographic data are available in the Internet at http://dnb.d-nb.de.

Habilitation thesis University of Passau, 2009

1st Edition 2011

All rights reserved
© Vieweg+Teubner Verlag | Springer Fachmedien Wiesbaden GmbH 2011

Editorial Office: Ute Wrasmann | Sabine Schöller

Vieweg+Teubner Verlag is a brand of Springer Fachmedien.
Springer Fachmedien is part of Springer Science+Business Media.
www.viewegteubner.de

No part of this publication may be reproduced, stored in a retrieval system or transmitted, in any form or by any means, electronic, mechanical, photocopying, recording, or otherwise, without the prior written permission of the copyright holder.

Registered and/or industrial names, trade names, trade descriptions etc. cited in this publication are part of the law for trade-mark protection and may not be used free in any form or by any means even if this is not specifically marked.

Cover design: KünkelLopka Medienentwicklung, Heidelberg
Printed on acid-free paper
Printed in Germany

ISBN 978-3-8348-1413-5

Contents

List of symbols xi

1 Introduction   **1**
  1.1 Motivation 1
  1.2 Outline 2
  1.3 Contribution 4

2 Modelling the camera mapping   **5**
  2.1 Geometric optics for computer vision 5
      2.1.1 The "thin lens" assumption and first order optics 5
      2.1.2 The circle of confusion 8
      2.1.3 Image acquisition 9
            2.1.3.1 The sensor array 9
            2.1.3.2 A simplified sensor model 11
            2.1.3.3 The sensor array as coordinate system 12
  2.2 The pinhole camera model 13
  2.3 Third order optics and thick lenses 15
  2.4 The pinhole camera model with distortion 17
      2.4.1 Definition 17
      2.4.2 Radial distortion 18
      2.4.3 Radius transformations 19
      2.4.4 Other distortion functions 21
            2.4.4.1 Misaligned thin lens 21
            2.4.4.2 Misaligned lens systems 22
  2.5 Inverting the camera mapping 23
  2.6 The pinhole camera model in homogeneous coordinates 25

3 Error functions for camera calibration and 3D reconstruction — 27
- 3.1 Introduction — 27
- 3.2 Projective and re-projective error — 27
- 3.3 Euclidean error — 29
- 3.4 Error functions for camera calibration and 3D-reconstruction — 34
  - 3.4.1 Calibration error functions — 34
  - 3.4.2 Reconstruction error functions — 37
- 3.5 Non-linear optimization — 38

4 Initial values for camera calibration problems — 40
- 4.1 Introduction — 40
- 4.2 The two stage method of Tsai — 42
- 4.3 An initial image transformation by direct linear transformation — 47
- 4.4 An initial image transformation from homographies — 50
  - 4.4.1 Introduction — 50
  - 4.4.2 Two necessary conditions for planar targets — 50
  - 4.4.3 Zhang's initial value — 52
  - 4.4.4 An initial image transformation with known center and zero skew — 54
  - 4.4.5 An initial image transformation with known aspect ratio and no skew — 55
  - 4.4.6 An initial image transformation with known aspect ratio and unknown skew — 56
  - 4.4.7 An initial image transformation with no skew — 58
    - 4.4.7.1 A straight forward constraint — 58
    - 4.4.7.2 A solution by a linear least squares problem with Cholesky decomposition — 59
  - 4.4.8 Experimental results — 60
    - 4.4.8.1 Overview — 60
    - 4.4.8.2 Simulations — 61
- 4.5 An initial value for the extrinsic camera parameters — 64
  - 4.5.1 Introduction and problem statement — 64
  - 4.5.2 Standard pose estimation — 64
  - 4.5.3 An algebraic re-projective approach for regular grids — 65
  - 4.5.4 An optimal solution w.r.t. Euclidean error for 1D targets — 70
- 4.6 An initial solution for the distortion — 72
  - 4.6.1 Introduction — 72
  - 4.6.2 Zhang's initial solution for the radial distortion — 72

		4.6.3	An optimal initial solution for all distortion parameters	74

	4.7	Camera calibration with distortion as a semi-linear problem	77
		4.7.1 Parameter reduction by semi-linear optimization	77
		4.7.2 Experimental results	78
		4.7.2.1 Results for the normal setup	79
		4.7.2.2 Results for the webcam setup	85
		4.7.2.3 Results for the wide angle setup	89

5 Calibration of a stereo camera system — 91

- 5.1 Introduction 91
- 5.2 Epipolar geometry 91
- 5.3 Epipolar Curves 95
- 5.4 Stereo camera calibration with multiple targets 97
- 5.5 Extrinsic stereo camera calibration with generalized epipolar constraints 98
  - 5.5.1 A two step algorithm 98
  - 5.5.2 A one step algorithm 100
  - 5.5.3 Application and results 101
- 5.6 Extrinsic stereo camera calibration with respect to the projective error 103
- 5.7 Extrinsic and intrinsic stereo camera calibration 105

6 Non-standard camera models — 107

- 6.1 Introduction 107
- 6.2 Feature point extraction 110
  - 6.2.1 Standard feature point extraction 110
  - 6.2.2 Model based extraction of isolated squares 113
  - 6.2.3 Appropriability of the feature point extraction methods 117
    - 6.2.3.1 Appropriability with respect to the sensor model 117
    - 6.2.3.2 Appropriability with respect to the camera model 117
- 6.3 The residual distortion 119
  - 6.3.1 The point spread function by first order optics 119
  - 6.3.2 Other sources of residual distortion 126
  - 6.3.3 Experimental results 126
- 6.4 Spline correction 134
  - 6.4.1 Motivation and related work 134
  - 6.4.2 A depth-dependent distortion term 134

- 6.4.3 Depth-dependent distortion correction for the projective and re-projective error function 135
- 6.4.4 The tensor spline space 135
- 6.4.5 Tensor splines for the re-projective depth-dependent distortion 137
- 6.4.6 Spline correction for the Euclidean error 138
- 6.4.7 The viewing ray for spline corrected cameras 139
- 6.4.8 Spline correction for stereo reconstruction 139
- 6.4.9 Disadvantages of the spline correction 140
- 6.5 A two-plane distortion model 144
  - 6.5.1 Motivation and related work 144
  - 6.5.2 The plane $\{z = -1\}$ 145
  - 6.5.3 Distortion mappings in $\{z = 1\}$ and $\{z = -1\}$ 146
  - 6.5.4 The re-projection w.r.t. the two-plane distortion 147
  - 6.5.5 Error functions for the two-plane distortion model 148
    - 6.5.5.1 The projective error 149
    - 6.5.5.2 The Euclidean error 149
    - 6.5.5.3 The projected Euclidean error 150
    - 6.5.5.4 The normalized Euclidean error 150
    - 6.5.5.5 Depth-dependence of the two-plane distortion model 153
  - 6.5.6 Calibration algorithm 155
- 6.6 A generic multi-plane camera 156
  - 6.6.1 Introduction and related work 156
  - 6.6.2 From the image to a reference coordinate system 156
  - 6.6.3 Tensor spline approximation of the coordinate transformation 159
  - 6.6.4 A calibration setup for the generic multi-plane camera . . 159
- 6.7 Experimental results 161
  - 6.7.1 Setup 161
    - 6.7.1.1 Calibration setup for the standard camera model 161
    - 6.7.1.2 Calibration setup for the spline correction . . . 161
    - 6.7.1.3 Calibration setup for the two-plane distortion model 161
  - 6.7.2 Results for spline corrected cameras 162
    - 6.7.2.1 Prototype reconstruction 162
      - 6.7.2.1.1 In-plane spline correction 162
      - 6.7.2.1.2 3d spline correction 164

		6.7.2.2	Stereo reconstruction 171
	6.7.3	Results for the two-plane distortion model 173
		6.7.3.1	Stereo reconstruction 173
		6.7.3.2	Point to point error 173
		6.7.3.3	Angles of reconstructed planes 177
		6.7.3.4	Other test series 180
		6.7.3.5	Planarity test 187
		6.7.3.6	Prototype reconstruction 192

7 Conclusions   **197**

Abstract

The main purpose of this work is to determine the camera mapping for optical measurement objectives. The standard approach models the camera mapping as a pinhole camera with distortion. We formulate different error functions for the pinhole camera model. Minimizing all error functions introduces a non-linear optimization. Therefore, we present initial values for the intrinsic and extrinsic camera parameters including distortion. In particular, the distortion can be determined by a linear least squares problem. This yields a semi-linear approach to camera calibration.

Stereo camera calibration introduces an additional constraint, which is used as epipolar line constraint in the literature. We extend this constraint to epipolar curves and present some calibration approaches for a stereo camera setup. These include the epipolar curve constraint.

When modelling the camera as a pinhole with distortion, we observe a residual error. We show that this error depends on the depth of the observed object. Thus, we present two approaches to introduce a depth-dependent distortion model: First, we propose a spline correction of the residual error, second, we suggest a two-plane distortion model. Several experimental results support both approaches.

Symbols

$A_{i,j}$	the element of the i-th row and j-th column of a matrix $A \in \mathbb{R}^{n \times m}$
$\operatorname{argmin}_{x \in X} g(x)$	$:= \{x_0 \in X : g(x_0) = \min\{g(x) \mid x \in X\}\}$
$\mathcal{C}_\infty(E, F)$	the set of functions from E to F which are differentiable for all degrees of differentiation
CCS	camera coordinate system
$\operatorname{dist}_d(A, B)$	$:= \inf\{\|a - b\| \mid a \in A, b \in B\}$ for $A, B \subset \mathbb{R}^d$
ICS	image coordinate system
$\mathcal{K}$	the set of all pinhole cameras
$\mathcal{K}_\Delta$	the set of all pinhole cameras with distortion model Δ
$\mathcal{L}^2(E, F)$	the set of all integrable functions $f : E \to F$ with $\int |f|^2 d\lambda < \infty$
$\mathcal{L}(\mathbb{R}^3)$	$:= \{l \subset \mathbb{R}^3 \mid l \text{ affin in } \mathbb{R}^3, \dim(l) = 1\}$ the set of all lines in $\mathbb{R}^3$
$\mathcal{L}(o)$	$:= \{l \in \mathcal{L}(\mathbb{R}^3) \mid o \in l\}$ the set of all lines in $\mathbb{R}^3$ containing the point $o \in \mathbb{R}^3$
$l(p, q)$	$:= \{x \in \mathbb{R}^n \mid \exists \lambda \in \mathbb{R} : x = q + \lambda(q - p)\}$ the line defined by two point $p, q \in \mathbb{R}^n$
$\tilde{p} := (p_x, p_y, 1)^t \in \mathbb{R}^3$	for a point $p = (p_x, p_y) \in \mathbb{R}^2$
$\tilde{p}^1 := (p_x, p_y, -1)^t \in \mathbb{R}^3$	for $p = (p_x, p_y) \in \mathbb{R}^2$ (see page 146)
O_3	orthogonal group in $\mathbb{R}^{3 \times 3}$
$\mathbb{P}^n$	the (real) projective space $\mathbb{R}^{n+1} \setminus \{O\}/\sim$ with $p \sim q \Leftrightarrow \exists \lambda \in \mathbb{R} \setminus \{0\} : \lambda p = q$
$\hat{p} = \begin{pmatrix} u \\ v \end{pmatrix}$	with $(u, v, 1)^t = \Pi_z(p)$ for a point $p = (x, y, z) \in \mathbb{R}^2 \times \mathbb{R} \setminus \{0\}$

$\mathcal{P}(\mathbb{R}^2, \mathbb{R}^2)$	the vector space of all polynomials from $\mathbb{R}^2$ to $\mathbb{R}^2$
P	a finite set of points in $\mathbb{R}^3$ determining a calibration pattern ("model")
$\mathrm{Proj}_L p$	the orthogonal projection of $p \in \mathbb{R}^3$ on the line L
$Q_t := \begin{pmatrix} 0 & -t_3 & t_2 \\ t_3 & 0 & -t_1 \\ -t_2 & t_1 & 0 \end{pmatrix}$	matrix with $Q_t x = t \times x$ for all $x \in \mathbb{R}^3$ with $t = (t_1, t_2, t_3)^t \in \mathbb{R}^3$
$\mathbb{R}_+ := [0, \infty[$	non-negative real numbers
$\mathbb{R}_+^* :=]0, \infty[$	positive real numbers
RCS	reference coordinate system
$\begin{pmatrix} R & t \end{pmatrix} \in \mathbb{R}^{3 \times 4}$	matrix where the first three columns equal the columns of $R \in \mathbb{R}^{3 \times 3}$ and the last column equals $t \in \mathbb{R}^3$
SO_3	special orthogonal group in $\mathbb{R}^3$ (rotation group)
$\mathcal{T}(\mathbb{R}^3, \mathbb{R}^3)$	isometric coordinate transformations in $\mathbb{R}^3$
$u \times v$	the cross product of two vectors $u, v \in \mathbb{R}^3$ for $u = (u_x, u_y, u_v)^t = (v_x, v_y, v_z)^t$ it is $u \times v = \begin{pmatrix} u_y v_z - u_z v_y \\ -(u_x v_z - u_z v_x) \\ u_x v_y - u_y v_x \end{pmatrix}$
$\mathrm{span}(v_1, \ldots, v_n)$	$\{\lambda_1 v_1 + \cdots + \lambda_n v_n \mid \lambda_1, \ldots, \lambda_n \in \mathbb{R}\}$ the linear span of $v_1, \ldots, v_n$
w.r.t.	with respect to
$\{z = 0\}$	$:= \{(x, y, z) \in \mathbb{R}^3 \mid z = 0\}$
$\{z = 1\}$	$:= \{(x, y, z) \in \mathbb{R}^3 \mid z = 1\}$

Chapter 1

Introduction

1.1 Motivation

As indicated by its name most tasks in computer vision deal with an imaging device. If this imaging device is a camera, it performs a mapping from a 3D world to a 2D image. Determining the parameters of this mapping is called camera calibration. This problem also includes the modeling and parametrization of the observed imaging process.

Long before the computer vision community addressed the modeling and to determination the camera mapping, it was investigated by photogrammetry. Photogrammetry began nearly in parallel to the rise of the photography in the middle of the 19th century in France and Prussia. The name "photogrammetry" was established by Albrecht Meydenbauer (*1832, †1921), who published a procedure to measure buildings by photographies. He also founded the Königliche Preußische Messbild-Anstalt, the first administration for photogrammetric research. The main objective of photogrammetry is accuracy. Therefore, long and tedious calibration routines are taken into account to obtain all parameters of an observed camera mapping. Classic photogrammetry works on photographs. Nowadays, digital image sensors replace the classic cameras and introduce some other problems like the modeling of the digitization, which are yet not fully covered by the photogrammetric community.

On the other hand, the digitization of continuous signals is a well known object of research in computer vision. Many applications of computer vision do not need a high accuracy in reconstruction as photogrammetry provides. In robotics or driving assistance it is sometimes necessary to obtain information from an unknown environment. It is often more important to estimate a self-orientation of the sensor by coarse data than to measure exact distances (*e.g.* to obtain the egomotion of an autonomous system). Moreover, self-calibration defines an important task in computer vision. Self-calibration of a camera means to gather as much information from images of a more or less unknown nature as one can. If one assumes that a camera behaves like a pinhole camera, one can formulate the camera mapping as projective mapping. This opens the whole world of projective geometry for camera calibration and allows a boost in results since the 1990ies (summarized *e.g.* in [HZ00]).

To adjust the pinhole camera model for quality assurance in dimensional accuracy the model is augmented with a distortion mapping which is defined in the image plane. However, like every model, the model of a pinhole camera with distortion is only an approximation to the real behavior of a camera. In particular, most monochromatic aberrations of a lens system (*i.e.* the first four of the five Seidel aberrations: spherical aberration, coma, astigmatism and curvature of field) can not be modeled in a plane (see [Hec87]). Modelling the distortion as an in-plane mapping assumes that the observed distortion of a point does not depend on its distance to the lens plane. In photogrammetry it is well known that for the pinhole camera model the observed distortion varies not only with focusing the lens but also within the depth of field for a fixed focus (see *e.g.* [Atk96]).

In this work we address camera calibration particularly with regard to metric reconstruction. Since projective geometry is non-metrical, we only apply some results of the projective geometry to obtain initial solutions for problems w.r.t. a metric. We share the emphasis on the metric reconstruction with photogrammetry, therefore, we also use some results of the photogrammetric community. In particular, we use some results to motivate a dependence on depth in reconstruction.

1.2 Outline

In the following chapter we derive the camera mapping from geometric optics based on Snell's law. If we simplify Snell's law to first order optics we obtain the classic formulation of the camera mapping by the pinhole equation. The first order optics are only a rough approximation of the observed camera mapping. Any observed deviation to the pinhole camera model must be modeled additionally. The standard way to deal with aberrations is to introduce a distortion mapping in the image plane.

Camera calibration means to determine the camera model parameters which fit best to the observed behavior of the actual camera. Therefore, we have to measure the distance of an observation to a given camera model. In the third chapter we introduce four approaches to define such a distance. The determination of the optimal camera mapping w.r.t. each of these distance functions defines a non-linear optimization problem.

Since the result of every non-linear optimization algorithm depends on the initial value, we address the problem to obtain such an initial value in the fourth chapter. We present some additional constraints for the starting solution according to Zhang ([Zha98]). These additional constraints allow a valid solution for the initial value problem.

The calibration of a stereo camera system is more than calibrating two camera separately: An additional constraint for the stereo camera system can be applied, since a calibration target is observed by both cameras. In the fifth chapter we extend the classic constraint (the so-called epipolar constraint) and present some results for this extension.

The limitations of the pinhole camera model with distortion become visible when it has to deal with blurring. The pinhole camera model depends on the lens maker's equation, which states that there is a determined object plane where the observation of an object appears sharp in the image. All objects outside this object plane appear blurred in the image. In the sixth chapter we analyze the blur induced by first order optics. As a main result will show that even in first order optics the blur depends not only on the depth of an object but also on its position in a fixed depth. Furthermore, the blur is not rotationally symmetric. Therefore, every point extraction method which assumes a rotationally invariant blur which is identical for each pixel, must be erroneous. Also, as experiments show, this error depends on the depth of the observed points. Thus, for a camera calibration which should provide a high precision, we need a component of the camera mapping which depends on the depth of the observed object. We present two approaches for a depth-dependent camera model in the last section. Several experimental results support the proposed non-standard camera models.

1.3 Contribution

This work contributes some new results in the following areas of camera calibration:

- Initial values for non-linear optimization

  Camera calibration is a non-linear problem. However, every non-linear optimization algorithm needs adequate initial values for an optimal performance. Thus, we present several methods to obtain initial values. In particular, we revisit Zhang's method to obtain initial values for the pinhole camera parameters and propose several ways to apply additional constraints which improve the result. Furthermore, we show that the determination of the distortion is a linear least squares problem provided that all other camera parameters are known.

- Semi-linearity in camera calibration

  Since the determination of the distortion forms a linear least squares problem, a part of the camera calibration error function can be minimized by linear methods in closed form. We call such a non-linear problem, which includes a linear part, a semi-linear problem. In the case of camera calibration we can decouple the calculation of the distortion parameters from the non-linear optimization. Thus, the number of parameters in the non-linear minimization will be reduced.

- Stereo camera calibration

  A stereo camera setup introduces additional constraints for the calibration. The well known epipolar constraint is extended to a generalized epipolar constraint. We present several approaches to calibrate a stereo camera w.r.t. this constraint instead of calibrating two single cameras.

- Non-standard camera models

  For the pinhole camera with distortion we observe a residual distortion which depends on the depth of the observed object. The standard camera misses a depth-dependent distortion model. Thus, we present two approaches to include the depth into the distortion model: First a correction by splines which depends on the depth of the observed object, second a novel two-plane distortion model which dissolves the pinhole assumption.

Chapter 2

Modelling the camera mapping

2.1 Geometric optics for computer vision

For our considerations we analyze the optical system by geometric optics. Since the effects are negligible for our purposes, we do not apply wave optical phenomena like diffraction of light. Furthermore, we assume that the lens is rotationally symmetric about a straight line which is called *the optical axis of the lens*.

2.1.1 The "thin lens" assumption and first order optics

Geometric optics are based on the refraction law (also known as Snell's law). Given two media with refraction indices n_1 and n_2 and a light ray, which passes from media one to media two, the refraction law states that the angles θ_1, θ_2 of the light beam to the normal of the interface of the medias obeys

$$n_1 \sin(\theta_1) = n_2 \sin(\theta_2) \tag{2.1}$$

(see Figure 2.1).

In computer vision it is widely accepted that the refraction index of air is so close to 1 that it can be treated as 1 [1]. A (spherical) lens has two media interfaces (air to lens, lens to air) which are described by two spheres with the same radius r (see Figure 2.2). Following Snell's law one can reconstruct the refraction of each light ray emitted from an object through the lens.

---

[1] In fact the refraction index of air is 1.0002926, whereas vacuum has index 1 for light with a wavelength of 589.3nm

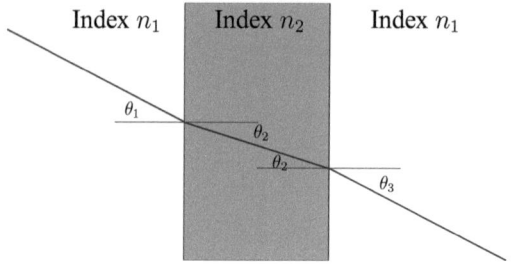

Figure 2.1: Illustration of Snell's law for parallel surfaces.

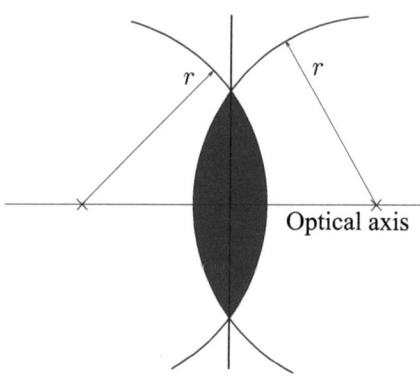

Figure 2.2: Sketch of two spheres with radius r defining a spherical lens (blue).

In first order optics it is assumed that all rays, which are considered in the camera model, are nearly parallel to the optical axis. Such rays are also called *paraxial*. Thus, we assume that there are only small angles to the normals of the lens surfaces and therefore the sine can be approximated by $\sin(x) \approx x$. Since this is the first term of the Taylor approximation of the sine at the origin, the derivations following this assumption are also called *first order optics*.

The second assumption in computer vision is called the *thin lens assumption*: the lens is assumed to be infinitesimally thin. From the refraction point of view the thin lens behaves like a spherical lens. Yet, the distance which a light ray covers inside the lens is infinitesimally small. Thus, from a localization point of view the lens is a plane. This plane is called *principal plane*. A light ray passing the thin lens is refracted at the surface air/lens and immediately after that at the surface lens/air. An immediate consequence of the thin lens assumption is that any light ray passing the thin lens at the optical axis will not be refracted, since both surfaces of the thin lens are parallel in this point (see Figure 2.1). Another consequence of the thin lens model combined with the paraxial optics simplification is that all (paraxial) light rays emitted at a point p at one side of the lens, which pass the lens, meet in one point i_p at the other side of the lens such that

$$\frac{1}{d_p} + \frac{1}{d_i} = \frac{1}{f} \tag{2.2}$$

holds, with $f = \frac{r}{2(n_l-1)}$ and d_p resp. d_i being the distance of the object p resp. the image point i_p to the principal plane and n_l the refraction index of the lens (see [Hec87] for more details). This equation is often called *lens maker's equation*. This means that there is a relation between the object and the image and that this relation depends only on the distance of the object to the principal plane, but not on its distance to the optical axis. There is a determined distance behind the principal plane, denoted as d_i in Figure 2.3, at which an observation of a point from the object side will become a sharp image. On the other hand, any object plane determines a so-called *focal plane* behind the lens where the points in the object plane appear sharp. In Figure 2.3 three principal ways for (paraxial) rays from an object to its image passing through a thin lens model are displayed. Namely, these are

i. A ray that comes in parallel to the optical axis on one side proceeds towards a certain particular point F at a distance f to the principal plane on the other side. F is called *focal point*. The distance f to the principal plane is called *back focal length*.

ii. A ray that passes through the center of the lens will not change its direction. This ray is called *center ray*. The center of the lens is called *optical center*.

iii. A ray that arrives at the lens from the focus F (also at distance f to the principal plane) on one side goes out parallel to the axis on the other side. The distance of F' to the principal plane is called *front focal length*.

In this work we assume a spherical lens there the back focal length equals the front focal length. For the first order optics with the thin lens assumption, the focal length is independent from the distance of the ray to the optical axis.

2.1.2 The circle of confusion

In general, the image acquisition is performed by a planar imaging device (see section 2.1.3.1). In the following we call the plane where the image is acquired *image plane*. It is obvious that in general the image plane does not coincide with the focal plane. Therefore, not all light rays emitted from an observed object meet in a point in the image plane. Let us now consider a point light source in the object plane. All light rays, which are emitted from this light source and pass the lens, form a cone on the image side of the lens (in first order optics). The intersection of this cone with the image plane is called *circle of confusion*.

The three principal ways of the light ray through the lens can be used to determine the circle of confusion (see Figure 2.3). If the circle of confusion is smaller than the size of one element of the imaging device objects in the computer image appear sharp. The area where this is true is called *depth of field*.

The dependency of sharpness and depth can be used to estimate the depth of an object, *i.e.* the distance of the object to the principal plane, (known as "depth from focus", (see *e.g.* [AFM98], [SG87] or [Gro87], or "depth from de-focus", see [CR99] or [Asl03]).

The blurring effect of the first order optics should also be handled by the camera mapping. The common way to handle this is to convolute the "ideal image" with a kernel (see [HS92] or [FP02]).

The "ideal image" g_{ideal} is the image of the objects obtained by the center ray only. Of course, this image can not be observed anywhere. The input function g for the imaging device, which is sometimes called *sensor input function*, becomes

$$g = g_{\text{ideal}} * k \qquad (2.3)$$

for a mollifier $k \in \mathcal{L}^2(\mathbb{R}^2, \mathbb{R}) \cap \mathcal{C}_\infty(\mathbb{R}^2, \mathbb{R})$. The center ray function g_{ideal} may be not continuous, but piecewise continuous. For mathematical reasons we assume

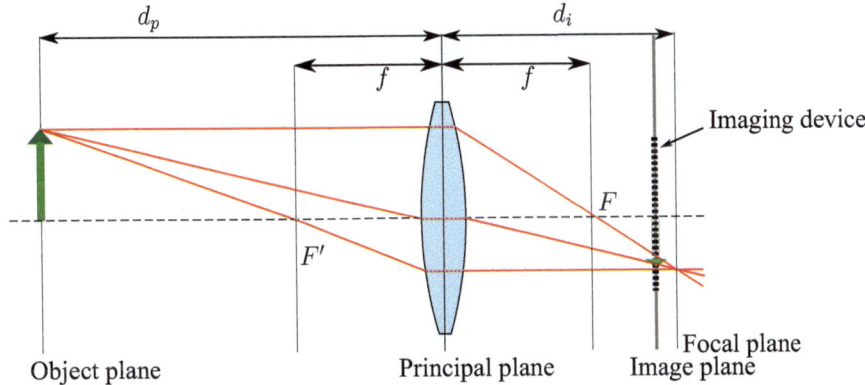

Figure 2.3: Sketch of the three main rays of the thin lens model (for the thin lens assumption the dashed red lines are assumed to have zero length).

that g_{ideal} is twice integrable. Note that the input function for the sensor array g is continuous as a convolution of a $\mathcal{L}^2$-function with a smooth function.

In computer vision the mollifier k is often called *point spread function* (PSF). The PSF can also been seen as the impulse response of the optical system (see *e.g.* [Goo96]). There are numerous ways to estimate the PSF assuming a symmetrical and identical kernel (at least for pixels in a local area) (see *e.g.* [BW93]) or almost without these assumptions (see [Pis06], see also section 6.2.3.1).

2.1.3 Image acquisition

2.1.3.1 The sensor array

Typical cameras use image sensors as imaging device in the image plane. An *image sensor* is a device that samples the sensor input function and converts it to an electric signal. The image sensor itself is a rectangular grid of photo-sensitive sensors. It can be an array of charge-coupled devices (CCD) or complementary metal–oxide–semiconductors (CMOS) sensors. The arrangement of the sensor array introduces a canonic coordinate system for the image.

Each sensor in the sensor array determines the value of the corresponding picture element (short: pixel). Therefore, a pixel represents in fact a rectangular area. Let $d_{p_u} \times d_{p_v}$ be the size of the photosensitive area of one sensor and d_{i_u} resp.

d_{i_v} be the distance between two sensors in the horizontal resp. vertical direction (see Figure 2.4). Then the distance between two pixel centers is $d_u := d_{i_u} + d_{s_u}$ in horizontal and $d_v := d_{i_v} + d_{s_v}$ in vertical direction.

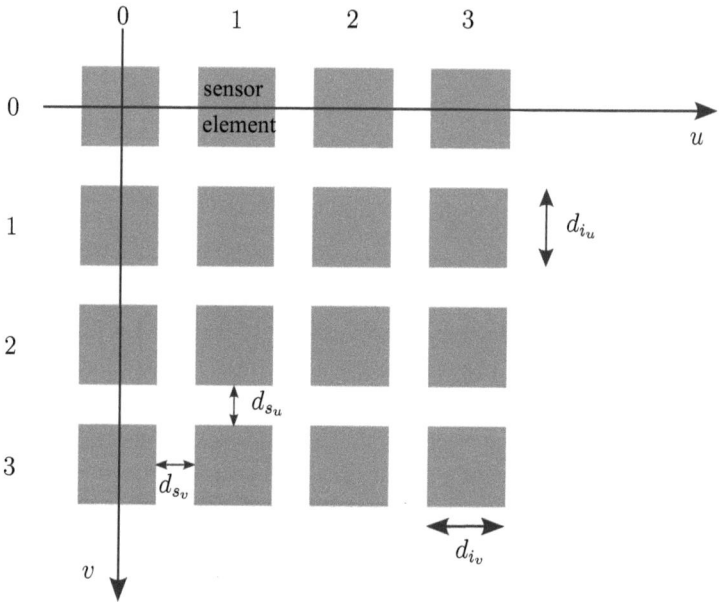

Figure 2.4: Sketch of the elements of an array of photosensitive sensors.

The value of a pixel is obtained by integrating the light intensity function over the area of the corresponding sensor of the sensor array: Let $g \in \mathcal{L}^2(\mathbb{R}^2 \times \mathbb{R}, \mathbb{R})$ be the light intensity function at the sensor array. Then the value $g_{i,j}$ of the sensor (i,j), which is also the value of the pixel (i,j), is

$$g_{i,j} = Q\left(\int_{\Delta t}\int_{A_{i,j}} g(x,t)s_{i,j}(x,t)\,\mathrm{d}x\,\mathrm{d}t\right) \qquad (2.4)$$

Whereas

- $Q : \mathbb{R} \to G$ is a quantization function (which also corrects the characteristic line of the sensor element) for a finite set of gray-values G, and

- Δt is the exposure time of the whole optical device, and

- $A_{i,j}$ is called the *aperture* of the sensor (i,j). If $p_{i,j} = [ip_u - \frac{d_{pu}}{2}, ip_u + \frac{d_{pu}}{2}] \times [jp_v - \frac{d_{pv}}{2}, jp_v + \frac{d_{pv}}{2}]$ is the area of the element (i,j) w.r.t. the coordinate system of the sensor array, then obviously $p_{i,j} \subset A_{i,j}$ should hold. However, since the sensor elements in a typical CCD sensor neighbored sensor elements may interact with each other, we also may choose an aperture $A_{i,j}$ which is superset of $p_{i,j}$. Finally

- $s_{i,j} \in \mathcal{L}^2(\mathbb{R}^2 \times \mathbb{R}, \mathbb{R})$ is the sensor specific density function. It is a characteristic of the sensor element at the position (i,j) in the sensor array. The characteristic has a time component to model each influence on the sensor element which varies with time. This can be any physical influence of the whole device (like dark current, effects of the A/D converting, etc.).

2.1.3.2 A simplified sensor model

Since it is almost impossible to determine the time varying component of $s_{i,j}$, it is often replaced by a random variable ν which implements an additive noise (see [Pis06] or [För00]). The additive noise contains electronic noise, being independent on the intensity. Some authors (see [DS74]) claim that the noise characteristics is dominated by the Poisson distribution of the photon flux.

The most commonly accepted simplifications to the sensor model are that the light intensity function g does not change during Δt, and that the sensor characteristic $s_{i,j}$ is the same for every sensor of the array. Moreover, it is common that $s_{i,j}$ is constant on $p_{i,j}$ and zero on $A_{i,j} \setminus p_{i,j}$. With all these simplifications it is no longer necessary to model the sensor characteristic as a density function. It can be transformed to the discretization function:

$$g_{i,j} = \text{round}(r(\int_{p_{i,j}} g(x)\, dx + \nu(i,j))) \tag{2.5}$$

The bijective function $r : \mathbb{R} \to \mathbb{R}$ is often called radiance function and is generally not linear. It represents a characteristic of the whole sensor array. Typical radiance functions are logarithmic, piecewise linear or have a linear and a logarithmic part. The most significant non-linearity on the response curve is at its saturation point, where any pixel with a radiance above a certain level is mapped to the same maximum image gray-value. However, for practical applications we assume that the camera system is well adjusted to the lighting situation. Therefore, we can assume that r is strictly increasing on the provided data, so its inverse r^{-1} can be defined for a suitable domain of r (see [DM97] for determining r^{-1}).

2.1.3.3 The sensor array as coordinate system

The simplified sensor model neglects

 i. the non-photosensitive areas between the photosensitive areas of the sensor array,

 ii. the arrangement of the elements may vary between two lines (odd- and even-field, see [Atk96]), and

 iii. that there often is a physical interaction between neighboring sensor elements. Effects like "vertical smear" caused by the simple read out of low cost CCD cameras, or blooming are not represented in the simplified model.

In the next section we will define a coordinate system by the canonical coordinate system of the sensor array. It is the coordinate system which can be observed by looking at a discrete computer image. However, one should keep in mind that this coordinate system is based on the simplified sensor model and consequently inherits its drawbacks.

2.2 The pinhole camera model

The pinhole camera model is based on the center ray of the thin lens model. Since the center ray passes through the center of the lens for every object position, it can be modeled like a camera obscura with the optical center as the pinhole.

For real camera setups there might be more than one lens, *i.e.* that is a system of lenses. But, commonly the optical properties of such a lens system are are approximated by one virtual thin lens. The *camera coordinate system* (CCS) is a Cartesian coordinate system defined by the principal plane: The $\vec{x}$- and $\vec{y}$-axis of the CCS determine the principal plane, the $\vec{z}$-axis is given by the optical axis. The optical center of the lens determines the origin $(0, 0, 0)$ of the CCS. Thus, in the camera coordinate system the principal plane becomes $\{z = 0\}$.

The *image coordinate system* (ICS) is the canonic coordinate system of the sensor array. In computer vision the coordinate transformation of the CCS to the ICS assumes that the first axis of the image coordinate system is parallel to the first axis of the camera coordinate system.

The pinhole assumption leads to an upside down image of the observed image, when the image is observed in an image plane behind the pinhole. Since all lines from the object to its image intersect in one point, we obtain the mirrored image in a virtual image plane before the pinhole. Thus, w.r.t. the CCS the central projection becomes

$$\Pi_z : \begin{array}{c} \mathbb{R}^3 \setminus \{z = 0\} \to \{z = 1\} \\ \begin{pmatrix} x \\ y \\ z \end{pmatrix} \mapsto \begin{pmatrix} \frac{x}{z} \\ \frac{y}{z} \\ 1 \end{pmatrix} \end{array} . \qquad (2.6)$$

The plane defined by $\{z = 1\}$ has no physical interpretation. It could be any plane, but obviously the choice $z = 1$ leads to a very handy treatment of the pinhole camera in terms of projective geometry for many useful purposes like robot vision, self calibration, etc. (see [HZ00], [Fau93]).

The intersection of $\{z = 1\}$ with the optical axis, *i.e.* the point $(0, 0, 1)$ w.r.t. the CCS, is called the *principal point*. The coordinate transformation from the $\{z = 1\}$-plane w.r.t. CCS to the ICS can be described by a 2×2-matrix encoding a shearing, a scaling in two directions, and a translation.

Definition 2.2.1
For the camera model of a pinhole camera the coordinate transformation P from

the $\{z = 1\}$-plane w.r.t. the CCS to the ICS is parameterized by

$$P : \begin{array}{c} \{z=1\} \to \mathbb{R}^2 \\ \begin{pmatrix} u \\ v \\ 1 \end{pmatrix} \mapsto A \begin{pmatrix} u \\ v \end{pmatrix} + \begin{pmatrix} u_0 \\ v_0 \end{pmatrix} \end{array} \tag{2.7}$$

with $\alpha, \beta \in \mathbb{R}_+^*$ and $\gamma, u_0, v_0 \in \mathbb{R}$ in

$$A = \begin{pmatrix} \alpha & \gamma \\ 0 & \beta \end{pmatrix}. \tag{2.8}$$

We call P the image transformation.

The translation part (u_0, v_0) is the principal point w.r.t. the image coordinate system. If f is the focal length of the lens and $d_u \times d_v$ is the dimension of one photosensitive element on the sensor array, the parameters α and β can be interpreted as $\alpha = \frac{d_p}{d_u}$ and $\beta = \frac{d_p}{d_v}$. Some authors (e.g. [Tsa87]) prefer this more physical exemplification of the matrix A. γ describes the skewness between the coordinate axes of the ICS. If γ is zero, the coordinate axes of the image coordinate system are perpendicular. If the angle between the image coordinate system axes is ϕ, it is $\gamma = \frac{f \cot(\phi)}{d_v} = \beta \cot(\phi)$.

Since P can be described by

$$P \begin{pmatrix} x \\ y \\ 1 \end{pmatrix} = \begin{pmatrix} \alpha & \gamma & u_0 \\ 0 & \beta & v_0 \end{pmatrix} \begin{pmatrix} x \\ y \\ 1 \end{pmatrix}, \tag{2.9}$$

we sometimes identify the mapping P by this matrix.

Definition 2.2.2 (Pinhole camera)
Let T be a 3D movement (i.e. a rotation R followed by a translation t). Set $D := \mathbb{R}^3 \setminus T^{-1}[\{z = 0\}]$. Then a mapping $C : D \to \mathbb{R}^2$ is called a camera mapping with respect to the pinhole camera model, *if and only if there exists a coordinate transformation P from the $\{z = 1\}$-plane to the image coordinate system such that $C = P \circ \Pi_z \circ T$ holds, whereas Π_z as defined as in (2.6). All parameters describing the mapping $P \circ \Pi_z$ are called* intrinsic camera parameters. *The parameters describing the movement T are called* extrinsic camera parameters. *We denote $\mathcal{K}$ as the set of all camera mappings and $\mathcal{I}$ as the set of all camera mappings where the extrinsic parameters define the identity.*

2.3 Third order optics and thick lenses

The simplification $\sin(x) \approx x$ is only applicable for small angles. A step forward to a more realistic refraction model is to truncate the Taylor series of the sine at the third order term: $\sin(x) \approx x - \frac{1}{6}x^3$ This leads to so-called third order optics. It is easy to see that in third order optics the refraction of a light ray depends on its distance to the optical axis (see *e.g.* [FP02]).

Also, the assumption of a thin lens can be expanded to the so-called thick lens, which can be modeled by two parallel thin lenses. Third order optics with the thick lens model allows to model monochromatic aberrations in an optical system. The so-called *five Seidel aberrations* can all be modeled and derived by these model's assumptions (see [Hec87]). The Seidel aberrations are (in this particular order):

i. Spherical aberrations

Rays that hit the surface of a spherical lens at a greater distance to the optical axis will be more focused to the apex than rays at a lower distance. This leads to a circle of confusion even in the focal plane. This aberration can be eliminated totally by using a Cartesian oval instead of a spherical lens. Since the fabrication of aspherical lenses is expensive, most lenses in computer vision are spherical.

ii. Coma

Rays coming from an object not on the optical axis, will be focused on point off the optical axis. In non-optimal system the focusing can be asymmetric. Instead of a circle, the image of a point appears as a spot with a tail (Coma is Greek for "hair"). Coma is mainly an effect in telescopes, but it should be noted that it transforms the circle of confusion into an asymmetric figure.

iii. Astigmatism

A pencil of rays emitted from an object at a great distance to the optical axis will hit the surface of the lens not symmetrically. This also causes a deformation of the circle of confusion. Modern lenses suppress astigmatism.

iv. Field curvature

The refraction behavior of the third order optics also impacts the relationship of object and image points. For a given object plane, parallel to the lens plane, the area of focused image points is not a plane but a curved surface. This aberration is sometimes called Petzval field curvature, in honor of Josef Petzval (1807-1891) who was the first to analyze the field curvature.

Only for points near the optical axis can it be approximated by a plane. Thus, given a planar imaging device, it is theoretically not possible to get a sharp image in every pixel. Since the sensor array is usually very small in comparison to the object, this effect does not appear significantly in most computer vision applications.

v. Distortion

In third order optics the transversal magnification in the image plane becomes a function of the distance of the observed image to the optical axis. Instead of the aberrations above, the distortion also effects the center ray. The distortion as described by Seidel is completely determined by its observation in the image plane. Therefore, it can be modeled as a function in $\{z = 1\}$ in the pinhole camera model.

It should be noticed that only the fifth aberration, the distortion, has an effect on the center ray. Therefore, only the distortion needs to be considered in the pinhole camera model. Nonetheless, these aberrations have an influence on each observation and consequently on the feature point extraction. We will return to this influence in chapter 6.

Remark 2.3.1 (Chromatic aberrations)
Since the refraction index depends on the wavelength of the applied light, every lens system also introduces chromatic aberrations. In fact, these chromatic aberrations can be used for distance measuring (see e.g. [Lüc06]). However, this work is limited to achromatic aberrations. In all our experiments in this work we use gray-value images. Therefore, the chromatic aberrations are negligible.

2.4 The pinhole camera model with distortion

2.4.1 Definition

Since we consider the center ray only, the pinhole camera model remains valid for third order optics, if we introduce a distortion mapping $\tilde{\delta}$ in the $\{z = 1\}$-plane. An analytical function $\tilde{\delta} : \{z = 1\} \to \{z = 1\}$ is in fact a 2D-function. It is

$$\tilde{\delta} = \begin{pmatrix} \delta \\ 1 \end{pmatrix} \tag{2.10}$$

for an analytical function $\delta : \mathbb{R}^2 \to \mathbb{R}^2$. Therefore, we define a distortion as a function in $\mathbb{R}^2$. Furthermore, in order to parametrize the whole camera model the set of distortion mappings must be adjustable.

Definition 2.4.1 (Distortion model)
Let for $k \in \mathbb{N}$ the set $D \subset \mathbb{R}^k$ be compact and not empty. A set $\Delta \subset \mathcal{C}_\infty(\mathbb{R}^2, \mathbb{R}^2)$ of analytic functions is called distortion model (with k parameters), if there exists a bijective, continuously differentiable mapping $\Phi : D \to \Delta$. A function $\delta \in \Delta$ is called distortion mapping. For a function $\delta = \Phi(c_1, \ldots, c_k)$ the parameters $c_1, \ldots, c_k$ are called distortion parameters of δ.

Remark 2.4.2
The postulation that the domain D of the parameters is compact is left out in most applications. In fact, we only demand the compactness to ensure a global minimum of the error functions we will introduce in section 3.

In section 4.6 we additionally demand that the distortion model is a linear space. In this case it must be $D = \mathbb{R}^k$, which is not compact. However, we derive a least squares solution for the optimal distortion mapping provided all other camera parameters are known.

Definition 2.4.3 (Pinhole camera with distortion)
Let Δ be a distortion model. Let T be an isometric coordinate transformation and set $D_T := \mathbb{R}^3 \setminus T^{-1}[\{z = 0\}]$. Then a mapping $C : D_T \to \mathbb{R}^2$ is called a common camera mapping with respect to the pinhole camera model with distortion model Δ, if and only if there exists a distortion mapping $\delta \in \Delta$ and an image transformation P such that $C = P \circ \tilde{\delta} \circ \Pi_z \circ T$ holds. All parameters which describe the mapping $P \circ \tilde{\delta} \circ \Pi_z$ are called intrinsic camera parameters, all parameters describing T are called extrinsic camera parameters. We denote $\mathcal{K}_\Delta$ as the set of all

camera mappings with a distortion mapping $\delta \in \Delta$ and $\mathcal{I}_\Delta$ as the set of all camera mappings in $\mathcal{K}_\Delta$ with $T = \text{id}$.

For every $K \in \mathcal{K}_\Delta$ there exists a $B \in \mathcal{I}_\Delta$ and a $T \in \mathcal{T}(\mathbb{R}^3, \mathbb{R}^3)$, the isometric coordinate transformations in $\mathbb{R}^3$, such that $K = B \circ T$ holds. Depending on the distortion model this decomposition may not be unique, since definition 2.4.3 allows the distortion function to contain a rotation around the principal point which is the intersection of the optical axis with the image plane.

In the following P is always an image transformation and $\tilde{\delta}$ a distortion mapping, where we denote $B \in \mathcal{I}_\Delta$ with $B = P \circ \tilde{\delta} \circ \Pi_z$.

2.4.2 Radial distortion

Most lenses in computer vision applications are rotationally invariant. We assume that there exists a rotation axis - the optical axis - which is also the rotation axis of the actual lens. Therefore, it is obvious that aberrations caused by a lens depend only on the distance to the rotation axis.

Let for each point $p \in \mathbb{R}^2$ the direction be defined as $n_p := \frac{1}{\|p\|} p$. The radial distortion functions are mappings that map

$$p = \|p\| n_p \mapsto c(\|p\|) n_p \tag{2.11}$$

for an analytical function $c : \mathbb{R}_+ \to \mathbb{R}_+$. They therefore depend only on the distance of p to the origin. Since the distortion functions are defined as analytical, they can be formulated as a Taylor series. With respect to the camera coordinate system, the radius correction function $c : \mathbb{R}_+ \to \mathbb{R}$ becomes

$$c(r) = \sum_{i=0}^{\infty} c_i r^i \tag{2.12}$$

with coefficients $(c_i)_{i \in \mathbb{N}}$.

Obviously, any constant and linear part in c could also be parametrized in the image transformation P. Therefore, there should be no constant or linear part in c yielding $c_0 = 0$. Furthermore, the linear part should be fixed, since $c_1 = 0$ would exclude the identity from the set of radial distortion functions. Hence, we set $c_1 = 1$.

With the previous remarks it is $c(r) = r + \sum_{i=2}^{\infty} c_i r^i = r \left(1 + \sum_{i=1}^{\infty} c_{i+1} r^i\right)$

and thus

$$c(\|p\|)n_p = \|p\|\left(1 + \sum_{i=1}^{\infty} c_{i+1}\|p\|^i\right)n_p \qquad (2.13)$$

$$= \left(1 + \sum_{i=1}^{\infty} c_{i+1}\|p\|^i\right)p \qquad (2.14)$$

$$= p + p\sum_{i=1}^{\infty} c_{i+1}\|p\|^i \qquad (2.15)$$

Obviously, there are only positive radii to be considered in the correction function c. We assume that c can be approximated by an odd function. This has the advantage that we only have to look at even exponents in the power series $\sum_{i=1}^{\infty} c_{i+1}r^i$. Therefore, in practical applications we avoid the square root to determine $r = \|p\|$ for $p \in \mathbb{R}^2$.

Definition 2.4.4 (Radial distortion)
For $D \in \mathbb{N}, c_1, \ldots, c_D \in \mathbb{R}$ the mapping

$$\delta_{rad} : \mathbb{R}^2 \longrightarrow \mathbb{R}^2 : p \mapsto p + \left(\sum_{i=1}^{D} c_i \|p\|^{2i}\right)p \qquad (2.16)$$

is called *radial distortion function with D coefficients*. We denote $\Delta_{r,D}$ for the set of all radial distortion functions with D coefficients.

For most purposes taking the first two to four coefficients only leads to satisfactory results for off-shelf cameras. It is reported *e.g.* in [Tsa87, Zha98, WM94], or [Zha96b] that more than two or four coefficients (depending on the author and/or the camera) may lead to numerical instabilities.

2.4.3 Radius transformations

Wide-angle lenses that take in an extremely wide hemispherical image are called fish-eye lenses.

Fish-eye projections are a class of projections where the distance of a projected point to the principal point is nearly proportional to the angle of the viewing ray to the optical axis:

For a pinhole camera without distortion and focal length f the radius r of an observed point is related to the angle θ of its viewing ray to the optical axis by

$$r = f \tan(\theta) \qquad (2.17)$$

while for a fish-eye camera it is

$$r \approx f \sin\left(\frac{\theta}{2}\right) \text{ or even } r \approx f\theta. \qquad (2.18)$$

Therefore, the image of a camera with a fish-eye lens can not be modeled as a pure pinhole camera.

A radial distortion function with a finite number of coefficients does not cover the radial distortion of a fish-eye camera. To overcome this problem for computer vision purposes, many authors propose radius transformations which can been seen as a limit of a power series, instead of a truncated power series.

- Fish-eye model

  A characteristic feature of fish-eye cameras is that there is great difference in resolution near the principal point and the corners of the observed image. Therefore, Shah and Aggarwal [SA96] formulate a logarithmic approach to the change of the radius. The transformation $c : \mathbb{R}_+ \to \mathbb{R}$ with

  $$c(r) = s \log(1 + \lambda r) \qquad (2.19)$$

  is called *fish-eye transformation* parametrized by $\lambda \in \mathbb{R}_+ \setminus \{0\}, s \in \mathbb{R}_+ \setminus \{0\}$. One advantage of this transformation is that its inverse mapping can be determined easily. It is

  $$c^{-1}(r) = \frac{1}{\lambda} \left(e^{\frac{r}{s}} - 1\right). \qquad (2.20)$$

  However, Shah and Aggarwal admit that their polynomial fish-eye transformation with

  $$c(r) = \sum_{i=1}^{n} c_i r^i \qquad (2.21)$$

  leads to better results, since it has more parameters.

- Field of view

Devernay and Faugeras introduce another radius transformation called *field of view*. In [DF01] they set

$$c(r) = \frac{1}{\omega} \arctan\left(2r \tan \frac{\omega}{2}\right),$$

where ω is the distortion parameter.

For many applications, the inversion of the distortion mapping is important (see also 2.5). Thus, for some distortion models the reversibility is a strong motivation. For the field of view transformation it is very easy to achieve the inverse mapping

$$c^{-1}(r) = \frac{\tan(r\omega)}{2\tan\frac{\omega}{2}}. \quad (2.22)$$

- Division model

  In [Fit01] the inverse of the distortion function $c(r) = (1 + c_1 r^3)$ is approximated by $c^{inv}(r) = \frac{r}{|1+c_1 r^2|}$.

2.4.4 Other distortion functions

Roughly speaking, the concept of a radial distortion models the manufacturing of a lens by a rotating device (see *e.g.* [SZH05]). The majority of authors on camera calibration for computer vision agree that the distortion function in the image plane is completely dominated by the radial components. In particular, any more elaborated modeling may lead to numerical instabilities as postulated for example by [Tsa87, WM94, Zha98, Zha96b] or [Zha96a].

The alignment of a lens in an optical system can also lead to distortions, which can not be described as functions depending only on the distance to the principal point.

2.4.4.1 Misaligned thin lens

The camera model as described in section 2.2 assumes that the image plane and the camera plane are parallel. Therefore, any misalignment of these planes should be treated by the distortion mapping. For lenses which are tilted,w.r.t. an axis of the image plane, the radial distortion will become elliptical. Therefore, the distortion

$$\delta_{\text{ell}}(u, v) = \begin{pmatrix} u \\ v \end{pmatrix} + \begin{pmatrix} u \sum_{i=1}^{\infty} c_{i,u}(u^2 + v^2)^i \\ v \sum_{i=1}^{\infty} c_{i,v}(u^2 + v^2)^i \end{pmatrix} \quad (2.23)$$

is called *elliptical distortion*. However, in practical applications the elliptical distortion series in (2.23) will also be truncated.

2.4.4.2 Misaligned lens systems

As mentioned in section 2.2, real lens systems in cameras are often combinations of two or more lenses. Ideally the elements of such a lens system share the same optical axis. However, during the manufacturing small aberrations may occur.

A characteristic of these aberrations is that the (calculated) optical axis may not be the center of the radial distortion. Consequently, these distortions are mostly called *decentering*. In the literature two approaches to handle this distortion have been accomplished.

- thin prism distortion

  One way to model the decentering distortion is to put a thin prism before the lens virtually. The mapping

  $$\delta_{\text{thp}}(u, v) := \begin{pmatrix} s_1(u^2 + v^2) \\ s_2(u^2 + v^2) \end{pmatrix} \quad (2.24)$$

  with $s_1, s_2 \in \mathbb{R}$ is called *thin prism distortion* and is supposed to model this effect. Obviously, the thin prism distortion is the first summand of the elliptical distortion. See e.g. [WCH92] for more details.

- tangential distortion

  The *tangential distortion* is defined by

  $$\delta_{\text{tan}}(u, v) = \begin{pmatrix} t_1(3u^2 + v^2) + 2t_2 uv \\ t_2(u^2 + 3v^2) + 2t_1 uv \end{pmatrix}, \quad (2.25)$$

  with t_1 and t_2 as distortion parameters. See [Atk96] for more information.

Different distortion models are usually added to the radial distortion term. However, one has to be careful that the parameters defining the complete distortion mapping remain independent.

An overview of more distortion functions can be found in [Sla80, Atk96] or [Luh03].

2.5 Inverting the camera mapping

Let $B \in \mathcal{I}_\Delta$ be a camera mapping with $B = P \circ \tilde{\delta} \circ \Pi_z$. To solve Euclidean reconstruction problems (see section 3.3) we are also interested in an inverse camera mapping. For the camera mapping of a pure pinhole camera the inverse relation maps points to lines (which exclude one point). This inverse relation can be obtained simply by inverting the mapping P. When a distortion is considered the problem becomes more complicated: definition 2.4.3 allows non-injective distortion functions. In particular, the set of radial distortion mappings $\Delta_{r,D}$ contains non-injective functions.

Therefore, for an observation $i_p \in \mathbb{R}^2$ the set $\vec{i}_{p,B} := \{x \in \mathbb{R}^3 | B(x) = i_p\}$ is in general a set of straight lines (excluding the origin), whose closure contains the origin. On the other hand, the actual codomain observed in images of a real camera mapping is a bounded subset of $\mathbb{R}^2$. Therefore, we may restrict the codomain of each distortion mapping such that the distortion mapping becomes injective: In the following we only consider points $p \in \mathbb{R}^3$ as input for any camera which can actually be observed by the camera. Thus, there exists a bounded and closed set $I \subset \mathbb{R}^2$ such that

$$B(p) \in I \tag{2.26}$$

holds for all p observed by the camera. We call such an I *image of the camera mapping B*. Additionally we assume that there is a $D \subset \{z = 1\}$ with $\delta|_D$ is injective and $\delta[D] = P^{-1}[I]$. Therefore, $\delta|_D : D \to P^{-1}[I]$ is invertible.

Definition 2.5.1 (undistortion, re-projection)
With the premises above we call $(\tilde{\delta}|_D)^{-1}$ the un-distortion mapping. Furthermore, we call the mapping $i_p \mapsto \vec{i}_{p,B}$ the re-projection of the camera mapping. For a simpler notation we identify $\vec{i}_{p,B}$ with $B^{-1}[\{i_p\}]$.

Remark 2.5.2
To keep a simple notation we omit the restriction of δ to the compact domain D in the following. Note that this is in fact a constraint for the observed points.

For the pinhole assumption the closure of all sets $B^{-1}[\{i_p\}]$ (for $i_p \in I$) intersect in the origin. For some notational aspects we are interested in a distinguished representative of $B^{-1}[\{i_p\}]$. As for $i_p = (u,v)^t \in I$ it is

$$B^{-1}[\{(u,v)\}] = \left\{ \lambda \left(\tilde{\delta}^{-1} \circ P^{-1} \right) \begin{pmatrix} u \\ v \end{pmatrix} \, \bigg| \, \lambda \in \mathbb{R} \setminus \{0\} \right\}, \tag{2.27}$$

we choose $B^{-1}(i_p) := \left(\tilde{\delta}^{-1} \circ P^{-1}\right)(i_p) \in \{z = 1\}$ as the canonical representative of $B^{-1}[\{i_p\}]$.

In real camera parametrizations a difficulty in inverting the camera mapping from the distortion function $\tilde{\delta}$ arises. For a set of distortion functions Δ and a distortion $\delta \in \Delta$ the inverse mapping δ^{-1} may not be in Δ (take $\Delta = \Delta_{r,D}$ as an example).

Let $\mathbf{P} \subset \mathbb{R}^3$ be a finite set of points fulfilling (2.26), such that for each $p \in \mathbf{P}$ it is $i_p = B(p)$. With (2.27) we can restrict our considerations to $\hat{\mathbf{P}} := \{\Pi_z(p) \mid p \in \mathbf{P}\} \subset \{z = 1\}$. Then we are interested in a mapping $\delta^* \in \Delta$ with

$$\forall \hat{p} \in \hat{\mathbf{P}} : \left(\tilde{\delta}^* \circ \tilde{\delta}\right)(\hat{p}) = \hat{p}. \tag{2.28}$$

Obviously, if such a $\tilde{\delta}^*$ exists, it needs not to be the inverse of $\tilde{\delta}$. Furthermore, such a $\delta^* \in \Delta$ may not exist. Therefore, we are interested in $\delta^* \in \Delta$ minimizing

$$\sum_{\hat{p} \in \hat{\mathbf{P}}} \| \left(\tilde{\delta}^* \circ \tilde{\delta}\right)(\hat{p}) - \hat{p}\|^2. \tag{2.29}$$

This approximation can be done in an iterative process (see [Mel94] or [PWH97]).

For the ideal camera mapping it is $i_p = P(\tilde{\delta}(\hat{p}))$, and (2.29) becomes

$$\sum_{\hat{p} \in \hat{\mathbf{P}}} \|\tilde{\delta}^*(P^{-1}(i_p)) - \hat{p}\|^2. \tag{2.30}$$

One should keep in mind that $\tilde{\delta}$ itself is the result of an approximation. A determination of $\tilde{\delta}^*$ should avoid the use of an approximated function. Therefore, we prefer the minimization of (2.30) to determine the un-distortion function $\tilde{\delta}^*$ (see also [TYO02] or [WM94]).

2.6 The pinhole camera model in homogeneous coordinates

The transition from a Euclidean reference coordinate system to a projective coordinate system allows us to denote changes of coordinate systems as matrices. Since the camera mapping consists of coordinate system transformations, except the distortion, nearly the whole camera mapping can be described by a matrix.

For a rotation matrix $R \in \mathbb{R}^{3\times 3}$ and a translation $t \in \mathbb{R}^3$ we define

$$\tilde{T} = (R \; t) \in \mathbb{R}^{3\times 4}. \tag{2.31}$$

Using the notation of Zhang (see [Zha98]) we set

$$\tilde{P} = \begin{pmatrix} \alpha & \gamma & u_0 \\ 0 & \beta & v_0 \\ 0 & 0 & 1 \end{pmatrix}, \tag{2.32}$$

with $\alpha, \beta \in \mathbb{R}_+^*$ and $u_0, v_0, \gamma \in \mathbb{R}$. Assuming an ideal camera without distortion we define

$$\tilde{K} = \tilde{P}\tilde{T} \in \mathbb{R}^{3\times 4} \tag{2.33}$$

to describe the camera mapping. $\tilde{K}$ is the matrix of a projective mapping from $\mathbb{P}^3$ to $\mathbb{P}^2$. Therefore, the projection $(u,v)^t$ of a world point $(x,y,z)^t$ by the camera mapping fulfills

$$s \begin{pmatrix} u \\ v \\ 1 \end{pmatrix} = \tilde{K} \begin{pmatrix} x \\ y \\ z \\ 1 \end{pmatrix}, \tag{2.34}$$

for a scalar $s \in \mathbb{R}$. Equation 2.34 is called *pinhole model equation*. Thus, for every world point $p = (x,y,z)^t$ the projection i_p of p by the camera K can be obtained by setting $(\tilde{u}, \tilde{v}, \tilde{w}) = \tilde{K}(x,y,z,1)^t$ and $i_p = (\frac{\tilde{u}}{\tilde{w}}, \frac{\tilde{v}}{\tilde{w}})^t$, if $\tilde{w} \neq 0$. Otherwise, the world point has no image point and accordingly is mapped on a point at infinity in the projective sense.

Remark 2.6.1
i. In the textbook of Hartley and Zisserman the matrix $\tilde{P}$ is called calibration matrix, while K is called camera matrix (see [HZ00]). We mention this because many publications in the area of camera calibration adopted the notation of this popular book.

ii. Note that the decomposition $\tilde{K} = \tilde{P}\tilde{T} \in \mathbb{R}^{3\times 4}$ in Equation 2.33 is unique. This can be shown easily by the uniqueness of the QR-decomposition with positive entries on the main diagonal of the upper triangular matrix (see e.g. [HZ00]).

Remark 2.6.2
In the formulation (2.33) of the camera mapping in a homogeneous frame of reference, the dimension is reduced by the matrix $\begin{pmatrix} R & t \end{pmatrix}$, which describes the 3D movement.

A typical intention for the usage of homogeneous coordinates is to describe affine mappings in matrix notation. For example, a movement $T \in \mathcal{T}(\mathbb{R}^3, \mathbb{R}^3)$ with $\forall p \in \mathbb{R}^3 : T(p) = Rp + t$ can be described by the matrix

$$\begin{pmatrix} R & t \\ 0 & 1 \end{pmatrix} \in \mathbb{R}^{4\times 4} \tag{2.35}$$

Therefore, one may want to encode the coordinate transformation from the RCS to the CCS in the camera matrix by this matrix. With

$$\hat{P} = \begin{pmatrix} \tilde{P} & 0 \end{pmatrix} \in \mathbb{R}^{3\times 4} \tag{2.36}$$

we obtain an equivalent formulation of the camera mapping in a projective frame of reference by

$$\tilde{K} = \tilde{P}\begin{pmatrix} R & t \end{pmatrix} = \hat{P}\begin{pmatrix} R & t \\ 0 & 1 \end{pmatrix}. \tag{2.37}$$

As stated above, for pure pinhole cameras the camera mapping in a Euclidean frame of reference and in a projective frame of reference are equivalent:

Lemma 2.6.3
Let $K = P \circ \Pi_z \circ T$ be a mapping of a pinhole camera (without distortion). Then for all $p := (x, y, z)^t \in \mathbb{R}^3$ with $T(p) \in \mathbb{R}^2 \times \mathbb{R} \setminus \{0\}$ it is

$$K\begin{pmatrix} x \\ y \\ z \end{pmatrix} = \begin{pmatrix} u \\ v \end{pmatrix} \Leftrightarrow \exists \lambda \in \mathbb{R} \setminus \{0\} : \tilde{K}\begin{pmatrix} x \\ y \\ z \\ 1 \end{pmatrix} = \lambda \begin{pmatrix} u \\ v \\ 1 \end{pmatrix} \tag{2.38}$$

Proof see [Gra08] □

From the projective point of view, the mapping of a pure pinhole camera is well analyzed in the literature. The textbooks of Faugeras ([Fau93]) and of Hartley and Zisserman ([HZ00]) summarize the possibilities and advantages of the projective formulation of the camera mapping.

Chapter 3

Error functions for camera calibration and 3D reconstruction

3.1 Introduction

A central question in camera calibration is how to fit the model of the camera mapping to the observed behavior of an actual camera.

Throughout this section we assume that we have a given finite set of points $\mathbf{P} \subset \mathbb{R}^3$. For each $p \in \mathbf{P}$ we know its observation i_p in the image of the actual camera. Camera calibration means to find the extrinsic and intrinsic parameters of a camera mapping which match the observation. To formulate this problem in mathematical terms we have to propose an error which measures how good a set of parameters describes the reality.

In this section we present three error functions for camera calibration.

3.2 Projective and re-projective error

The projective error is the most common approach to camera calibration in computer vision (see [Tsa87, Zha98, Fau93, HZ00] and many more). It measures the distance of the projected point to the observed point. In a projective frame of reference this error can be seen as the Euclidean distance of the distinguished representative of the image point in homogeneous coordinates $(\tilde{i}_p)$ to the distinguished representative of the projection $(\Pi_z(\tilde{K}(\tilde{p})))$. Since the error is measured in the image plane, the unit of the projective error is pixel. On the other hand, the lack of a metric unit in the calibration error function allows an elegant approach to self-calibration (see *e.g.* [HZ00] and remark 4.4.1).

Definition 3.2.1 (Projective Error)
Let $i_p \in \mathbb{R}^2$ be the observation of a point $p \in \mathbf{P}$ by a camera. Then for $K \in \mathcal{K}_\Delta$ the projective error is defined as

$$dist_2(i_p, K(p)). \tag{3.1}$$

It can be shown that the projective error is optimal in reconstruction (in the sense of a maximum-likelihood function), if the only source of error in the imaging process is distributed normally, identical, and independently in the image plane (see *e.g.* [Zha98]).

The change from the ICS to CCS (defined by the mapping P^{-1}) can also be applied to the observed image point i_p. In this case the error is measured in the plane $\{z = 1\}$. Since the distortion mapping is also defined in the plane $\{z = 1\}$, we can apply B^{-1} instead of P^{-1} to define a re-projective error.

Definition 3.2.2 (Re-projective Error)
Let $i_p \in \mathbb{R}^2$ be the observation of $p \in \mathbf{P}$ by a camera. Let $B \in \mathcal{I}_\Delta$ and $T \in \mathcal{T}(\mathbb{R}^3, \mathbb{R}^3)$ be the intrinsic and extrinsic parameters of a camera mapping $K = B \circ T$. Then the re-projective error is defined as

$$dist_3(B^{-1}(i_p), \Pi_z \circ T(p)). \tag{3.2}$$

For $B = P \circ \delta$ it is

$$dist_3(B^{-1}(i_p), \Pi_z \circ T(p)) = \|\tilde{\delta}^{-1}(P^{-1}(i_p)) - \Pi_z(T(p))\|. \tag{3.3}$$

Since in practical applications δ^{-1} is approximated by a function δ^*, which is not exactly the inverse of δ, a calibration w.r.t. the re-projective error determines the un-distortion as an approximation of the distortion function.

Although a 3D distance is involved in the definition of re-projective error, the error is only measured in $\{z = 1\}$. Therefore, the distance is in fact only a 2D-distance, but is measured in the unit of the reference coordinate system.

For pinhole cameras without distortion the re-projective error can be notated more elegantly in a projective frame of reference: Let $\tilde{K} = \tilde{P}\tilde{T}$ be the camera mapping of $K \in \mathcal{K}$ with $K = P \circ \Pi_z \circ T$ in a projective frame of reference. Then for p and i_p as in definition 3.2.2, the re-projective error is given by

$$\|\tilde{P}^{-1}\tilde{i}_p - (\Pi_z \circ T)(p)\|. \tag{3.4}$$

It is easy to see that for $\tilde{P} = I_3$ the projective error and the re-projective error are the same.

3.3 Euclidean error

The Euclidean error is common in photogrammetric applications (see [Luh03] or [Atk96]).

Definition 3.3.1 (Euclidean error)
Let $i_p \in \mathbb{R}^2$ be the observation of $p \in \mathbf{P}$ by a camera. Let $B \in \mathcal{I}_\Delta$ and $T \in \mathcal{T}(\mathbb{R}^3, \mathbb{R}^3)$ be the intrinsic and extrinsic parameters of a camera mapping $K = B \circ T$. Then the Euclidean error is defined as

$$dist_3(\overline{B^{-1}[\{i_p\}]}, T(p)). \tag{3.5}$$

Obviously, it is $dist_3(B^{-1}(\{i_p\}), T(p)) = dist_3(K^{-1}(\{i_p\}), p)$. If K^{-1} is known, the Euclidean error can be determined without a division.

A great aspect in computer vision is the accuracy of object extraction algorithms. Since computer images are discretized and quantized signals, this accuracy is limited by the actual size of a pixel. Even if one can enhance the subpixel accuracy of the extraction by using gray-value weighted barycenters, line or ellipse fit (see also 6.2), it is commonly accepted that only accuracy of about $\pm\frac{1}{10}$pixel can be achieved ([SCS94]). For lens with a focal length of 8 mm and an actual pixel size of 8 μm this error becomes ± 1 cm in 1 m and ± 10 cm in 10 m distance to the plane $\{z = 1\}$. However, for the projective error the error value remains $\frac{1}{10}$pixel independently from the distance of the object.

To achieve such behavior with respect to a Euclidean distance we introduce the normalized Euclidean error.

Definition 3.3.2 (Normalized Euclidean error)
Let $i_p \in \mathbb{R}^2$ be the observation of $p \in \mathbf{P}$ by a camera. Then for $K \in \mathcal{K}_\Delta$ with $K = B \circ T$ with $B \in \mathcal{I}_\Delta, T \in \mathcal{T}(\mathbb{R}^3, \mathbb{R}^3)$ and $T(p) \neq 0$ the normalized Euclidean error is defined as

$$dist_3(n_{i_p}, n_p) \tag{3.6}$$

with $n_p := \frac{T(p)}{\|T(p)\|}$ and $n_{i_p} := \frac{B^{-1}(i_p)}{\|B^{-1}(i_p)\|}$.

Note that points with the same Euclidean distance to re-projection yield the same normalized Euclidean error if these points have the same Euclidean distance to the camera center. This is a difference to the behavior of the projective error (see Figure 3.1). In fact, the projective error introduces some kind of asymmetric behavior (see Figure 3.2 and 3.3).

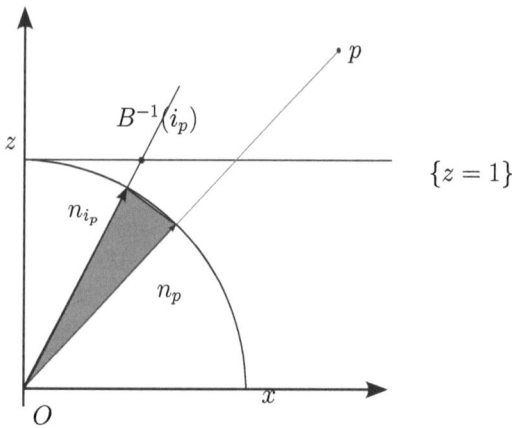

Figure 3.1: Sketch of the normalized Euclidean error: The error measures the distance of $\Pi_z(p)$ to the normalized direction of the re-projected image point.

Remark 3.3.3
Let $\mathcal{L}(0)$ denote all lines in $\mathbb{R}^3$ containing the origin. In [WLD99] Wagner et al. demand two properties for an error $\epsilon : \mathcal{L}(0) \times \mathbb{R}^3 \to \mathbb{R}_+$ of a point p to the re-projection $B^{-1}[\{i_p\}]$ of its observation i_p:

i. The error ϵ should be perspectively invariant:

$$\epsilon(\overline{B^{-1}[\{i_p\}]}, \lambda p) = \epsilon(\overline{B^{-1}[\{i_p\}]}, p) \tag{3.7}$$

should hold for all $\lambda \in \mathbb{R}_+$.

ii. The error ϵ should be independent for all directions with the same angular difference to the re-projected point: In the notation of definition 3.3.2

$$\epsilon(\overline{B^{-1}[\{i_p\}]}, p_1) = \epsilon(\overline{B^{-1}[\{i_p\}]}, p_2) \tag{3.8}$$

should hold for all $p_1, p_2 \in \mathbb{R}^3$ with $\sphericalangle(n_{p_1}, n_{i_p}) = \sphericalangle(n_{p_2}, n_{i_p})$.

Wagner et al. propose $\epsilon(\overline{B^{-1}[\{i_p\}]}, p) = \arccos(\langle n_{i_p} | n_p \rangle)$, which describes the arc-length from n_p to n_{i_p}, as an error function fulfilling their postulations. Since it is $\text{dist}_3(n_{i_p}, n_p)^2 = \langle n_{i_p} - n_p | n_{i_p} - n_p \rangle = 2 - 2 \langle n_{i_p} | n_p \rangle$, the normalized Euclidean error also fulfills the demands of Wagner et al.

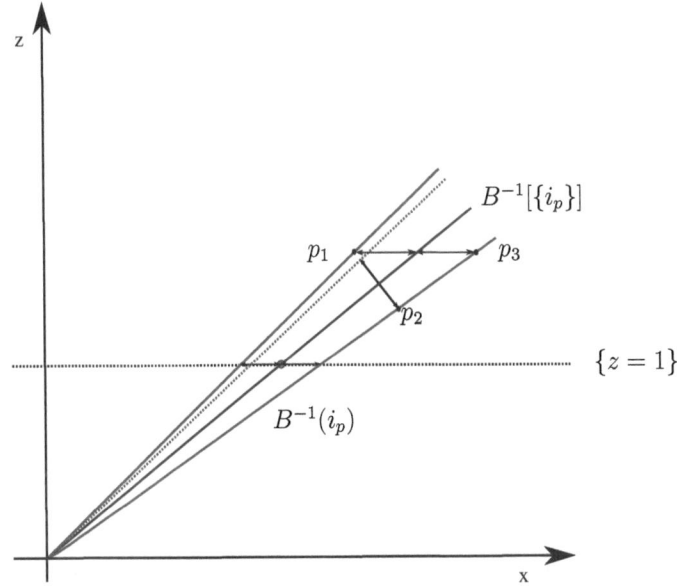

Figure 3.2: Asymmetric behavior of the (re-)projective error: p_1 and p_2 have the same Euclidean distance to $B^{-1}[\{i_p\}]$, but they do not have the same projective distance to i_p. On the other hand, p_1 and p_3 have the same projective distance to i_p, but different Euclidean distances to $B^{-1}[\{i_p\}]$.

Remark 3.3.4 (In front of and behind the camera)
It should be pointed out that - except for the normalized Euclidean error - there is a symmetry in points before and behind the camera. To be more precise, for a $B \in \mathcal{I}$ there is for each point $p = (x, y, z)^t$ with $z > 0$ a point $p' = (x', y', z')$ with $z' < 0$ such that the error between these points is zero. Such a behavior may be justified in the projective sense, since points on a line through the origin form an equivalence class, but it is not feasible for measurement objectives. However, a discrimination between points before and behind the camera leads to algorithmic overhead which is not necessary in most cases.

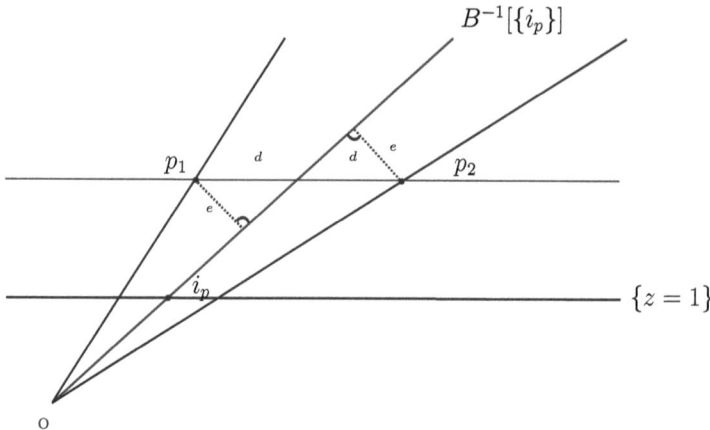

Figure 3.3: Asymmetric behavior of the (re-)projective error: p_1 and p_2 have the same Euclidean distance e to $B^{-1}(\{i_p\})$ and the same projective distance to i_p. They are not at the same distance to the origin, but they are at the same distance to $\{z=1\}$.

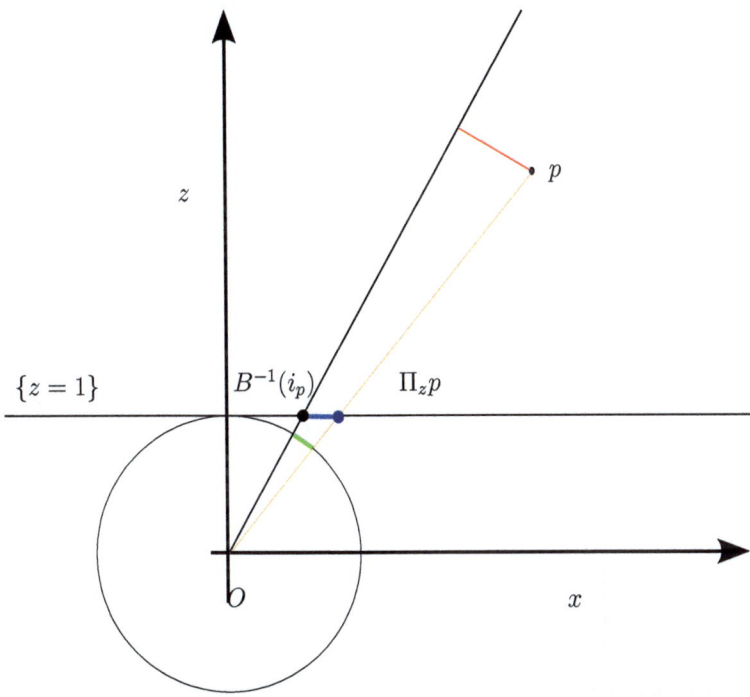

Figure 3.4: Different errors for camera calibration algorithms: The blue line sketches re-projective error, the red line the Euclidean error and the green line the normalized Euclidean error.

3.4 Error functions for camera calibration and 3D-reconstruction

3.4.1 Calibration error functions

To calibrate a camera, *i.e.* to determine which parameters describe the observed camera mapping best, we can apply one of the previous defined error functions. Let $\text{CamError}: \mathcal{I}_\Delta \times \mathcal{T}(\mathbb{R}^3, \mathbb{R}^3) \times \mathbb{R}^3 \times \mathbb{R}^2 \to \mathbb{R}_+$ be one of these functions. For a camera $K = B \circ T$ with image I the CamError may apply

- the projective error:

$$\text{CamError}(B, T, p, i_p) = \begin{cases} \text{dist}_2(i_p, B(T(p))), & i_p \in I, p \notin T^{-1}[\{z = 0\}] \\ \infty & , \text{else} \end{cases} \quad (3.9)$$

- the re-projective error

$$\text{CamError}(B, T, p, i_p) = \begin{cases} \text{dist}_3(B^{-1}(i_p), \Pi_z(T(p))), & i_p \in I, \\ & p \notin T^{-1}[\{z = 0\}] \\ \infty, & \text{else} \end{cases} , \quad (3.10)$$

- the Euclidean error

$$\text{CamError}(B, T, p, i_p) = \begin{cases} \text{dist}_3(\overline{B^{-1}(\{i_p\})}, T(p)), & i_p \in I \\ \infty, & \text{else} \end{cases} , \quad (3.11)$$

or

- the normalized Euclidean error

$$\text{CamError}(B, T, p, i_p) = \begin{cases} \text{dist}_3(\frac{B^{-1}(i_p)}{\|B^{-1}(i_p)\|}, \frac{T(p)}{\|T(p)\|}), & i_p \in I, p \notin T^{-1}[\{0\}] \\ \infty, & \text{else} \end{cases} . \quad (3.12)$$

Then a camera calibration minimizes the function

$$\Phi : \begin{array}{c} \mathcal{I}_\Delta \times \mathcal{T}(\mathbb{R}^3, \mathbb{R}^3) \to \mathbb{R}_+ \\ (B, T) \mapsto \sum_{p \in \mathbf{P}} \text{CamError}(B, T, p, i_p)^2 \end{array}, \quad (3.13)$$

where i_p denotes the observation of the $p \in \mathbf{P}$.

Remark 3.4.1 (Root mean square error)
To give comparable results we do not display the value of the camera calibration error function. Instead, we give the root mean square:

$$\epsilon_{rms} = \sqrt{\frac{1}{|\mathbf{P}|} \sum_{p \in \mathbf{P}} \text{CamError}(B, T, p, i_p)^2} \qquad (3.14)$$

Remark 3.4.2 (Existence of an optimal solution)
Note that Φ is continuous for each error function (for suitable $i_p \in I$ and $p \in \mathbf{P}$). Thus, an optimal solution for each error functions exists if the domain of all parameters is compact. Therefore, to ensure an optimal solution in every case, one has to limit the parameters defining the image transformation P to a compact subset of $\mathbb{R}^5$.

For photogrammetric applications, the set of model points $\mathbf{P}$ is supplied by a three-dimensional calibration solid, which has coordinates that are well known w.r.t. to a reference coordinate system. The observations of such a calibration target should fill the whole image of the camera. Since it has to provide a certain depth in the provided coordinates, it sometimes fills a whole room. Therefore, it is expensive and does not allow a calibration on site.

For flexible calibration purposes the set of points $\mathbf{P}$ is often a grid of points on a plane (see Figure 3.5). A planar calibration target is easier to move and much cheaper. It is obvious that all calibration error functions yield no sufficient and no unique result when using only one image of such a planar calibration pattern.[1] Therefore, it needs more than one observation of such a target to calibrate a camera. Hence, its observation does not need to fill the whole image. It allows a cheap calibration on site, but there is no common reference coordinate system for all positions of the calibration plane. Thus, the determination of the pose and orientation of the calibration plane for each observation becomes part of the optimization. As we additionally have to determine the position of every plate w.r.t. the camera coordinate system, with multiple targets the number of parameters in the error function (3.13) rises: For N positions of the calibration plane the error

---

[1] Actually, there are methods to estimate the parameters of a pure pinhole camera by a single view of a planar calibration pattern, see *e.g.* [CRZ99, Cri01] or [WH05], but they need some additional assumptions and do not minimize one of the error functions in (3.13)

functions become

$$\Phi_N : \begin{array}{c} \mathcal{I}_\Delta \times \mathcal{T}^N \to \mathbb{R}_+ \\ (B, T_1, \ldots, T_N) \mapsto \sum_{c=1}^{N} \sum_{p \in \mathbf{P}} \text{CamError}(B, T_c, p, i_{c,p})^2 \end{array} \qquad (3.15)$$

where $i_{c,p}$ denotes the observation of the point $p \in \mathbf{P}$ in the c-th image of the calibration pattern. In (3.15) each calibration plate defines a reference coordinate system. Thus, technically we determine a set of N camera which share the same intrinsic camera parameters.

A more suitable formulation of the problem defines the camera coordinate system as reference coordinate system:

$$\Phi_N^{(id)} : \begin{array}{c} \mathcal{I}_\Delta \times \mathcal{T}^N \to \mathbb{R}_+ \\ (B, T_1, \ldots, T_N) \mapsto \sum_{c=1}^{N} \sum_{p \in \mathbf{P}} \text{CamError}(B, \text{id}, T_c(p), i_{c,p})^2 \end{array} \qquad (3.16)$$

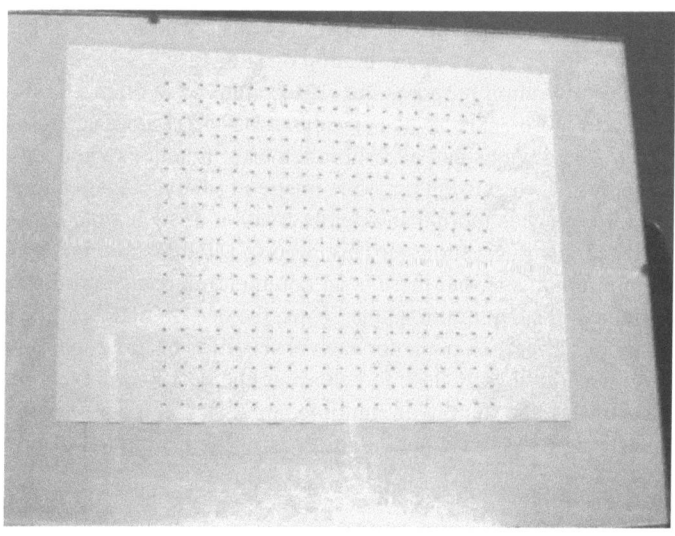

Figure 3.5: Calibration grid of 20×19 points.

Remark 3.4.3 (Complete Calibration)
A calibration w.r.t. the re-projective, the Euclidean, and the normalized Euclidean error determines the un-distortion δ^* instead of the distortion δ which is determined in the case of the projective error. We already stated in section 2.5 that δ^* is only an approximation of the inverse of δ. A complete camera calibration should include the determination of δ and δ^*. Depending on the error function which is applied to calibrate the camera, one should apply (2.30) or the result we present in section 4.6 to obtain δ^* and δ after the calibration.

3.4.2 Reconstruction error functions

The error functions, which we introduced in section 3.4.1 can not only be used to calibrate the camera, but also to reconstruct the position of an observed object. If the camera mapping $B \in \mathcal{I}_\Delta$ is known, we can apply the error function to determine the pose and orientation of a model $\mathbf{P}$ by its observation $(i_p)_{p \in \mathbf{P}}$: a *prototype reconstruction* minimizes the function

$$\Phi : \begin{array}{l} \mathcal{T}(\mathbb{R}^3, \mathbb{R}^3) \setminus \{T \in \mathcal{T}(\mathbb{R}^3, \mathbb{R}^3) \mid \exists p \in \mathbf{P} : T(p) \in \{z = 0\}\} \to \mathbb{R}_+ \\ T \mapsto \sum_{p \in \mathbf{P}} \operatorname{CamError}(B, \operatorname{id}, T(p), i_p)^2 \end{array},$$

(3.17)

where id denotes the identity in $\mathcal{T}(\mathbb{R}^3, \mathbb{R}^3)$. In fact, the prototype reconstruction can be seen as calibration of the extrinsic camera parameters.

To reconstruct a single point by its observation a stereo setup is needed. A stereo setup consists of two calibrated cameras $K_l = B_l \circ T_l$ and $K_r = B_r \circ T_r \in \mathcal{K}_\Delta$. Let i_{p_l} be the observation of a point p in the image of the left camera and i_{p_r} be the observation of p in the image of the right camera. Then a *stereo reconstruction* minimizes the function

$$\Phi : \begin{array}{l} \mathbb{R}^3 \setminus \{(T_l^{-1}[\{z=0\}] \cup T_r^{-1}[\{z=0\}]\} \to \mathbb{R}_+ \\ p \mapsto \operatorname{CamError}(B_l, T_l, p, i_{p_l})^2 + \operatorname{CamError}(B_r, T_r, p, i_{p_r})^2 \end{array}.$$

(3.18)

Remark 3.4.4
It is possible to perform a prototype reconstruction or a stereo reconstruction w.r.t. one error function and a calibration w.r.t. another error function. However, this should be avoided. By choosing an error function we inherently make an assumption about the main origin of the error of the observed camera mapping. This assumption should hold for the calibration and for the reconstruction.

3.5 Non-linear optimization

The minimization of the error functions in section 3.4 defines a non-linear problem: Given an open set $D \subset \mathbb{R}^n$ and a function $f : D \longrightarrow \mathbb{R}_+$ we are looking for a value $x^* \in \mathrm{argmin}_{x \in D} f(x)$.

For differentiable functions f it is $\mathrm{grad}(f)(x^*) = 0$ necessarily. Therefore, a simple approach to solve non-linear minimization problems is given by Newton's method to find roots of the gradients. Another class of algorithms to find a local minimum of a function is given by the *steepest descent method*, where each step of the algorithms is proportional to the negative of the gradient of the function at the current point.

A special case of the non-linear optimization is defined by non-linear least squares problems: Given measured values $y_i \in \mathbb{R}^k$ and functions $g_i : D \longrightarrow \mathbb{R}^k$ let $F_i : D \longrightarrow \mathbb{R}$ be defined as $F_i(x) := \|g_i(x) - y_i\|$ for $i \in \{1, \ldots, m\}$. Then we are looking for a value $x^* \in D$ with $x^* \in \mathrm{argmin}_{x \in D} f(x)$, whereas $f(x) = \sum_{i=1}^{m} F_i(x)^2 = \sum_{i=1}^{m} \|g_i(x) - y_i\|^2$. The number of measured values should be significantly higher than the number of parameters to be determined.

A classic approach to this problem is given by the *Gauss-Newton algorithm* which is a modification of the Newton algorithm such that it does not require second derivatives. This is achieved by linearization by a truncated Taylor expansion of the error function in each step. Such an approach can be an advantage when the calculation of the second derivatives is computationally expensive.

Methods where the Hessian matrix of the second derivatives of the function to be minimized is not computed at any stage are called *Quasi-Newton* methods. The Hessian is updated by analyzing successive gradient vectors. Quasi-Newton methods are a generalization of the secant method to find the root of the first derivative for multidimensional problems. In this case the secant equation has to be constrained to be determined. The Quasi-Newton methods differ in the constraint they apply. The algorithm of Broyden, Fletcher, Goldfarb, and Shanno (BFGS) is one of most popular Quasi-Newton algorithms.

Another approach to solve non-linear least squares problems, which is very popular in camera calibration, is given by the algorithm of Levenberg and Marquardt. The Levenberg-Marquardt algorithm can be seen as an interpolation between the Gauss-Newton algorithm and the method of gradient descent. It is very popular because in many cases it finds a solution even if the initial value is far off the final minimum. In most of these cases it is faster than the Gauss-Newton algorithm. However, for initial values near the optimum other methods may be faster than the Levenberg-Marquardt algorithm.

For a detailed introduction in non-linear optimization of differentiable functions see *e.g.* [Spe93]. An elaborated collection of algorithms can be found in [PTVF92]. A recent introduction of non-linear optimization in bundle adjustment including implementation details on step width prediction, managing sparse matrices, first order adjustment and update strategies can be found in [TMHF00].

Although all error functions in this work are differentiable, we may also apply non-linear optimization algorithms, which do not require a differentiable function. The common approach in this area is the simplex method which is also known as the algorithm of Nelder and Mead ([NM65]). This algorithm works only by comparison of points in the parameter space and therefore needs no gradient. The algorithm tends to be slower than gradient based methods, but is known to be robust (see *e.g.* [LRWW98]).

Chapter 4

Initial values for camera calibration problems

4.1 Introduction

In this chapter we give some initial solutions to support the subsequent non-linear optimization.

In the following two sections we present initial solutions for the image transformation P. For historical reasons we sketch Tsai's method, which needs some information of the image sensor, in the next section.

In the third section we introduce the direct linear transformation to camera calibration. This approach is actually older than Tsai's algorithm. It treats the camera mapping completely as linear mapping in homogeneous coordinates.

The concept of the pinhole camera without distortion as a projective mapping introduces constraints, which allow the estimation of all parameters of the image transformation P by observations of a calibration pattern without user input. In particular, for a planar calibration pattern the mapping of the pattern to its image can be treated as a projective mapping in $\mathbb{P}^2$. In accordance with the literature we call such a mapping a *homography*. In the fourth section, we follow the approach of Zhang, who derives two constraints for a homography introduced by a pinhole camera. We give some additional constraints for his approach which improve the initial value (in particular for cameras with a very low resolution).

In the fifth section we present some approaches to estimate the transformation of an observed model w.r.t. a reference coordinate system to obtain an initial solution for the extrinsic camera parameters. With known parameters of image transformation and coordinate transformation from the RCS to the CCS, we present a closed form solution for the optimal distortion parameters w.r.t. the projective error function in the sixth section. The closed form solution is obtained by a solution of a linear least squares problem.

Since there is a linear solution for the optimal distortion parameters, we are able to decouple the determination of the distortion parameters from the non-linear optimization. In the seventh section we utilize this fact to formulate the camera calibration as a semi-linear problem.

4.2 The two stage method of Tsai

In computer vision the article of R. Y. Tsai defines a first well accepted approach to camera calibration. In [Tsa87] Tsai introduces the *radial alignment constraint* (RAC). For the following we assume that the reference coordinate system is given by the camera coordinate system. Thus, $\{\lambda(0,0,1)^t \mid \lambda \in \mathbb{R}\}$ defines the optical axis. Let $q \in \{z = 1\}$ be the observation of a point $p \in \mathbb{R}^3$ in camera coordinates. For $p = (p_x, p_y, p_z)$ we define $p_0 = (0, 0, p_z)$ as the orthogonal projection of p on the optical axis. Analogously, we set $q_0 = (0, 0, 1)$ as the orthogonal projection of $q = (q_x, q_y, 1)$ onto the optical axis. Then the radial alignment constraint states that the vector $\overrightarrow{p_0p}$ is parallel to $\overrightarrow{q_0q}$ (see Figure 4.1). Note that the radial alignment constraint is invariant to radial distortion.

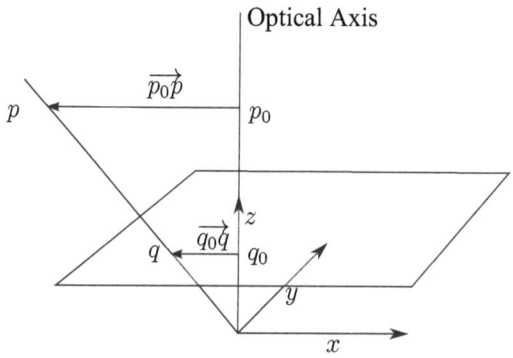

Figure 4.1: Sketch of the radial alignment constraint proposed by Tsai.

In the first stage of his two stage calibration algorithm Tsai deduces a system of linear equations with five parameters from which he derives parts of the extrinsic camera parameters, namely the rotation and the x- and y-part of the translation. Since the radial alignment constraint can be expressed by the direction of $\overrightarrow{pp_0}$ and $\overrightarrow{qq_0}$, the linear equations are independent of the unknown focal length f. In the second stage the focal length f and the z-component of the translation are obtained by applying the central projection mapping.

The algorithm of Tsai initially assumes that the principal point is located in the middle of the image. In [LT88] Lenz and Tsai address this problem and give an algorithm which calculates the principal point in advance. Moreover, Tsai's algorithms demand initial values for the actual size of a photosensitive element.

In the following we sketch the basic equations introduced by Tsai. The reader is referred to the original article [Tsa87] for all details and proofs. Without loss of generality we assume that the the principal point is located in the origin of the image. Then the image transformation considered by Tsai becomes

$$P \begin{pmatrix} x \\ y \\ 1 \end{pmatrix} = \begin{pmatrix} f & 0 \\ 0 & f \end{pmatrix} \begin{pmatrix} x \\ y \end{pmatrix}. \qquad (4.1)$$

Now let $R = \begin{pmatrix} r_1 & r_2 & r_3 \\ r_4 & r_5 & r_6 \\ r_7 & r_8 & r_9 \end{pmatrix}$ be the rotation matrix and $t = \begin{pmatrix} t_x \\ t_y \\ t_z \end{pmatrix}$ be the translation of the extrinsic camera parameters. Then the whole camera mapping of a point $(x, y, z)^t$ to its observation $(u, v)^t$ becomes

$$\begin{pmatrix} u \\ v \end{pmatrix} = (P \circ \Pi_z)(R \begin{pmatrix} x \\ y \\ z \end{pmatrix} + t) \qquad (4.2)$$

$$= \frac{f}{r_7 x + r_8 y + r_9 z + t_z} \begin{pmatrix} r_1 x + r_2 y + r_3 z + t_x \\ r_4 x + r_5 y + r_6 z + t_y \end{pmatrix}. \qquad (4.3)$$

Hence, in homogeneous coordinates there exists a $\lambda \in \mathbb{R} \setminus \{0\}$ such that

$$\lambda \begin{pmatrix} u \\ v \\ 1 \end{pmatrix} = \begin{pmatrix} r_1 & r_2 & r_3 & t_x \\ r_4 & r_5 & r_6 & t_y \\ r_7 & r_8 & r_9 & t_y \end{pmatrix} \begin{pmatrix} x \\ y \\ z \\ 1 \end{pmatrix} \qquad (4.4)$$

holds. For a planar model $\mathbf{P}$ it is $z = 0$ for all $p = (x, y, z) \in \mathbf{P}$. Thus, Equation 4.4 can be simplified to

$$\lambda \begin{pmatrix} u \\ v \\ 1 \end{pmatrix} = \begin{pmatrix} r_1 & r_2 & t_x \\ r_4 & r_5 & t_y \\ r_7 & r_8 & t_y \end{pmatrix} \begin{pmatrix} x \\ y \\ 1 \end{pmatrix}. \qquad (4.5)$$

Now, the radial alignment constraint states that $\begin{pmatrix} u \\ v \end{pmatrix}$ and $\begin{pmatrix} r_1 x + r_2 y + t_x \\ r_4 x + r_5 y + t_y \end{pmatrix}$

are linear dependent. Thus, for $t_y \neq 0$

$$\det \begin{pmatrix} u & r_1 x + r_2 y + t_x \\ v & r_4 x + r_5 y + t_y \end{pmatrix} = 0 \tag{4.6}$$

$$\Leftrightarrow u(r_4 x + r_5 y + t_y) = v(r_1 x + r_2 y + t_x) \tag{4.7}$$

$$\Leftrightarrow u(\frac{r_4}{t_y} x + \frac{r_5}{t_y} y + 1) = v(\frac{r_1}{t_y} x + \frac{r_2}{t_y} y + \frac{t_x}{t_y}) \tag{4.8}$$

holds. Setting $r'_1 := \frac{r_1}{t_y}, r'_2 := \frac{r_2}{t_y}, r'_4 := \frac{r_4}{t_y}, r'_5 := \frac{r_5}{t_y}$ and $t'_x := \frac{t_x}{t_y}$ we obtain an equation which is linear in these parameters:

$$\begin{pmatrix} vx & vy & v & -ux & -uy \end{pmatrix} \begin{pmatrix} r'_1 \\ r'_2 \\ t'_x \\ r'_4 \\ r'_5 \end{pmatrix} = u. \tag{4.9}$$

Since for $t_y \neq 0$ this equation holds for every $p = (x, y, 0) \in \mathbf{P}$ and its observation $i_p = (u, v) \in I$, we obtain a system of $|\mathbf{P}|$ linear equations. Hence, we can determine a least squares solution for $(r'_1 \ r'_2 \ t'_x \ r'_4 \ r'_5)^t$.

The missing parameter t_y is obtained by

$$t_y^2 = \frac{s - \sqrt{s^2 - 4\Delta}}{2\Delta} \tag{4.10}$$

for $s := r'^2_1 + r'^2_2 + r'^2_4$ and $\Delta := r'_1 r'_5 - r'_2 r'_4 \neq 0$. This equation can be derived by the properties of a rotation matrix (see [Tsa87], Appendix V). Tsai obtains the sign of t_y by a stronger formulation of the radial alignment constraint:

$$\left\langle \begin{pmatrix} u \\ v \end{pmatrix} \middle| \begin{pmatrix} r_1 x + r_2 y + t_x \\ r_4 x + r_5 y + t_y \end{pmatrix} \right\rangle > 0 \tag{4.11}$$

should hold as the radial alignment constraint can extended from the directions of $\overrightarrow{p_0 p}$ and $\overrightarrow{q_0 q}$ to the orientation of these vectors. Thus, (4.11) defines a test for the sign of t_y. With r_1, r_2, r_4, r_5 known, we can determine the rotation matrix R (see [Tsa87] for details and ambiguities).

The determination of the rotation matrix and of the translation entries t_x, t_y defines the first stage of the two stage method. In the second stage Tsai considers the central projection for planar models

$$\begin{pmatrix} u \\ v \end{pmatrix} = \frac{f}{r_7 x + r_8 y + t_z} \begin{pmatrix} r_1 x + r_2 y + t_x \\ r_4 x + r_5 y + t_y \end{pmatrix} \tag{4.12}$$

which defines equations that are linear in f and t_z:

$$u(r_7 x + r_8 y + t_z) = f(r_1 x + r_2 y + t_x) \qquad (4.13)$$
$$v(r_7 x + r_8 y + t_z) = f(r_4 x + r_5 y + t_y). \qquad (4.14)$$

Thus, the missing parameters t_z and f can be determined by

$$\begin{pmatrix} u & -r_1 x - r_2 y - t_x \\ v & -r_4 x - r_5 y - t_y \end{pmatrix} \begin{pmatrix} t_z \\ f \end{pmatrix} = - \begin{pmatrix} u(r_7 x + r_8 y) \\ v(r_7 x + r_8 y) \end{pmatrix}. \qquad (4.15)$$

There are many drawbacks of Tsai's approach to obtain an intial value for parameters of the image transformation: First the model of Tsai as sketched in (4.1) is limited. It lacks a parameter for a skewness between the axes of the sensor array and two parameters for the principal point w.r.t. the image coordinate system. Second the algorithm demands information of the actual sensor: the size of a photosensitive element must be provided before the parameters of the projection in (4.1) are estimated. This may be a problem for cheap cameras like web cameras, which are usually sold without such information. For such cameras one must assume that the dimensions of a photosensitive element are 1×1. This leads to another simplification in the camera model. Altogether in the notation of the image transformation in definition 2.2.1 the camera model of Tsai assumes $\alpha = \beta$ and $\gamma = u_0 = v_0 = 0$. This means that there is actually one intrinsic parameter in Tsai's camera model.

A third disadvantage of Tsai's approach can be seen in the two stages itself: In the first stage some extrinsic parameters are estimated. In the second stage the intrinsic and the remaining extrinsic parameter are determined with fixed parameters of the first stage. This means that the robustness of the determination of the intrinsic parameter depends on the first step.

In the next two sections we present approaches which are based on the assumption of a pinhole camera mapping without distortion. In this case the mapping of a model to its observed image is a projective mapping as already stated in section 2.6. A projective mapping can be represented by a matrix which contains information about the extrinsic and intrinsic parameters of the complete camera mapping as defined in section 2.2. Once this matrix is known all parameters can be determined in one step.

In contrast to the projective approach Tsai's method is based on the radial alignment constraint only. It should be emphasized that this constraint holds also for images obtained by cameras with a significant radial distortion, while the pinhole assumption is no longer valid for such cameras. Therefore, the radial alignment constraint and thus the two stage method of Tsai remains a valid tool for camera calibration.

4.3 An initial image transformation by direct linear transformation

Assuming a pure pinhole camera, an image of a calibration object defines a projective mapping from the object's coordinate system to the image coordinate system. For a fixed observation $(i_p)_{p \in \mathbf{P}}$ of a model $\mathbf{P}$ the matrix $H \in \mathbb{R}^{3 \times 4}$ of this projective mapping should minimize

$$\sum_{p \in \mathbf{P}} \|\tilde{i}_p - \Pi_z(H\tilde{p})\|^2. \tag{4.16}$$

With the pinhole equation (2.34) for an ideal observation of the model $\mathbf{P}$

$$\lambda H = \tilde{P}\tilde{T} = \tilde{P}\begin{pmatrix} R & t \end{pmatrix} \tag{4.17}$$

must hold, for a pure pinhole camera $\tilde{P}\tilde{T}$ and a $\lambda \in \mathbb{R}$. Therefore, the camera mapping of a pinhole camera can be described completely by the matrix $A = \begin{pmatrix} \tilde{P}R & \tilde{P}t \end{pmatrix}$ in homogeneous coordinates. It is easy to see that the relation $\tilde{i}_p = \lambda H\tilde{p}$ allows a linear guess for the parameters of $H \in \mathbb{R}^{3 \times 4}$ (see e.g. [HZ00]). This method is called *direct linear transformation* (DLT). However, to avoid the trivial solution, an additional constraint has to be applied. In the first article on direct linear transformation [AAK71] Abdel-Aziz and Karara propose the constraint $H_{3,4} = 1$. Since this introduces a singularity when $H_{3,4}$ is zero, Faugeras and Toscanini suggest $H_{3,1}^2 + H_{3,2}^2 + H_{3,3}^2 = 1$ ([FT87]). Nowadays it is quite common to use $\sum_{\substack{1 \leq i \leq 3 \\ 1 \leq j \leq 4}} H_{i,j}^2 = 1$ as a constraint (see e.g. [HZ00]).

However, it should be noticed that the DLT provides only a linear guess for H, the minimization of (4.16) remains a non-linear problem.

Applying

$$\lambda H = \tilde{P}\begin{pmatrix} R & t \end{pmatrix} = \begin{pmatrix} \tilde{P}R & \tilde{P}t \end{pmatrix} \tag{4.18}$$

the matrix $M := \tilde{P}R \in \mathbb{R}^{3 \times 3}$ can be used to derive the parameters of $\tilde{P}$ by an RQ-decomposition:

Let

$$Q_x(\theta) := \begin{pmatrix} 1 & 0 & 0 \\ 0 & \cos(\theta) & -\sin(\theta) \\ 0 & \sin(\theta) & \cos(\theta) \end{pmatrix} \quad (4.19)$$

$$Q_y(\theta) := \begin{pmatrix} \cos(\theta) & 0 & \sin(\theta) \\ 0 & 1 & 0 \\ -\sin(\theta) & 0 & \cos(\theta) \end{pmatrix} \quad (4.20)$$

$$Q_z(\theta) := \begin{pmatrix} \cos(\theta) & -\sin(\theta) & 0 \\ \sin(\theta) & \cos(\theta) & 0 \\ 0 & 0 & 1 \end{pmatrix} \quad (4.21)$$

be rotation matrices. Then a RQ-decomposition of M consists of three steps:

i. Determine θ_x with $MQ_x(\theta_x) = M'$ and $M'_{3,2} = 0$
ii. Determine θ_y with $M'Q_y(\theta_y) = M''$ and $M''_{3,1} = 0$
iii. Determine θ_z with $M''Q_z(\theta_z) = M'''$ and $M'''_{2,1} = 0$

Set $A = M'''$ and $Q = Q_x(\theta_x)Q_y(\theta_y)Q_z(\theta_z)$ to obtain $M = AQ^t$, where A is an upper triangular matrix and Q a rotation matrix (see e.g. [HZ00]).

Note that this decomposition is not unique. A statement about the uniqueness of a decomposition $M = AQ^t$ can only be made for $Q \in O_3$: In this case the decomposition is unique where A is an upper triangular matrix with positive diagonal entries (see e.g. [GvL96]).

For $Q \in SO_3$ a decomposition where A has only positive diagonal entries can not be guaranteed: Let

$$\lambda M = \underbrace{\begin{pmatrix} a & c & d \\ 0 & b & e \\ 0 & 0 & 1 \end{pmatrix}}_{=:P} \quad Q = \underbrace{\begin{pmatrix} a' & c' & d' \\ 0 & b' & e' \\ 0 & 0 & 1 \end{pmatrix}}_{=:P'} Q' \quad (4.22)$$

with P, P' regular and $Q, Q' \in SO_3$. With $\det(P) = \det(P')$ it is $ab = a'b' \neq 0$. Therefore, there exists a $\mu \in \mathbb{R} \setminus \{0\}$ with $a' = \frac{a}{\mu}$ and $b' = b\mu$. Furthermore, $P'^{-1}P = Q'Q^t$ yields $P'^{-1}P \in SO_3$. Thus, $(P'^{-1}P)^t = (P'^{-1}P)^{-1}$ must hold and hence

$$\begin{pmatrix} \mu & 0 & 0 \\ \frac{\mu c - c'}{a} & \frac{1}{\mu} & 0 \\ \frac{\mu db - c'e + c'e' - d'b\mu}{ab} & \frac{e - e'}{\mu b} & 1 \end{pmatrix} = \begin{pmatrix} \frac{1}{\mu} & \frac{c' - \mu c}{a} & \frac{ce - ce' - db + d'b}{ab} \\ 0 & \mu & \frac{e' - e}{b} \\ 0 & 0 & 1 \end{pmatrix}. \quad (4.23)$$

Thus, $e' = e$ and $d' = d$ and $|\mu| = 1$ follows directly. For $\mu = 1$ we derive $a' = a, b' = b$ and $c' = c$. For $\mu = -1$ it is $a' = -a, b' = -b$ and $c' = -c$. Recapitulating, an RQ-decomposition of M with

$$\lambda M = PQ \tag{4.24}$$

with $Q \in SO_3$ and an upper triangular matrix $P_{33} = 1$ is not unique. In particular two RQ-decompositions of $M = PQ = P'Q'$ with $Q, Q' \in SO_3$ differ in the common sign of the entries P_{11}, P_{12} and P_{22}. From the point of camera calibration this means that such a decomposition determines the principal point w.r.t. the image coordinate system uniquely. However, a decomposition such that the entries α, β on the main diagonal of P are positive can not be guaranteed.

Remark 4.3.1 (negative values for α and β)
It is obvious – under the assumption of correct input data – that a negative value for α or β obtained by a RQ-decomposition with $Q \in SO_3$ indicates a mirrored axis of image coordinate system.

Let now $M = AQ$ be an RQ-decomposition where A has only positive entries and $Q \in SO_3$, then we estimate the matrix $\tilde{P}$ of the image transformation by setting $\tilde{P} = \frac{1}{A_{3,3}} A$. With (4.18) we obtain the translation part as the fourth column of $\tilde{P}^{-1}\tilde{K}$.

Remark 4.3.2
We presented the RQ-decomposition by Givens rotations. Obviously, there are several other methods to obtain such a decomposition like Fast Givens, Householder reflections, or a modified Gram-Schmidt approach (see e.g. [GvL96]). However, in the simple case of a 3×3 matrix Givens rotations are satisfactory in numerical aspects.

4.4 An initial image transformation from homographies

4.4.1 Introduction

As stated in section 3.4.1 a planar target allows a flexible calibration procedure in the sense that such a target is straightforward to produce and easy to handle. The mapping from a planar target to its observation can be described by a projective mapping in $\mathbb{P}^2$. In the following we present two constraints for this mapping by which Zhang derived two constraints for the observed camera mapping ([Zha98]).

From a number of observations of the same model one can derive the matrix of the image transformation by these constraints. The constraints can be transformed into a homogeneous system of linear equations. An additional constraint is needed to avoid the trivial solution. The canonical way is to determine a solution on the unit sphere. Unfortunately, this side condition does not reflect any correlation between the parameters. A solution of the resulting linear least squares problem may not represent a valid image transformation. Therefore, we present some additional quadratic constraints and also closed form solutions for the constrained linear least squares problems, which ensure a valid or do consider side conditions of the camera parameters.

4.4.2 Two necessary conditions for planar targets

In this section we derive two necessary conditions for the parameters of the mapping of a pure pinhole camera which can be derived by the observation of a planar calibration target. Our argumentation follows the introduction of Zhang ([Zha98]).

Let $H = (h_1\ h_2\ h_3\ h_4) \in \mathbb{R}^{3\times 4}$ with columns $h_i \in \mathbb{R}^3$ for $i = 1, \ldots, 4$ be the matrix of the projective mapping minimizing (4.16). A planar model **P** defines a reference coordinate system such that every z-coordinate of a point in the model plane is zero. This means it is

$$H \begin{pmatrix} x \\ y \\ 0 \\ 1 \end{pmatrix} = (h_1\ h_2\ h_4) \begin{pmatrix} x \\ y \\ 1 \end{pmatrix} \qquad (4.25)$$

for every point $(x, y, 0)^t$ within the model plane. Therefore, the column h_3 is not of interest when we observe a planar pattern. In fact, the matrix $H' = (h_1\ h_2\ h_4)$

is the matrix of a projective mapping from $\mathbb{P}^2$ to $\mathbb{P}^2$, *i.e.* the mapping of the points in **P** to the observed image. We call such a mapping *homography*. The determination of the homography H' minimizing (4.16) defines a non-linear optimization problem with 8 degrees of freedom, since H' is determined up to a scale factor. Note that the determination of a homography is not restricted to point-to-point correspondences. Corresponding lines or conics can also be used (see *e.g.* [AJN05] or [KSH06]). A linear estimation of an initial value can be found in [Zha98]. A normalization of the input data as described in [Har97] improves the initial guess.

Let now $r_1, r_2, r_3 \in \mathbb{R}^3$ be the columns of the rotation matrix $R = (r_1 \; r_2 \; r_3)$. For a planar target we derive

$$\lambda \begin{pmatrix} u \\ v \\ 1 \end{pmatrix} = \tilde{P}\tilde{T} \begin{pmatrix} x \\ y \\ 0 \\ 1 \end{pmatrix} = \tilde{P} \begin{pmatrix} r_1 & r_2 & t \end{pmatrix} \begin{pmatrix} x \\ y \\ 1 \end{pmatrix} \qquad (4.26)$$

by the pinhole equation (2.34) for a scalar $\lambda \in \mathbb{R} \setminus \{0\}$. Therefore, with Equation 4.17 and Equation 4.25 $\lambda \begin{pmatrix} h_1 & h_2 & h_4 \end{pmatrix} = \tilde{P} \begin{pmatrix} r_1 & r_2 & t \end{pmatrix}$ follows.

Since the columns r_1 and r_2 of the rotation matrix R are orthonormal, we obtain

$$0 = r_1^t r_2 = \lambda^2 \left(\tilde{P}^{-1} h_1 \right)^t \tilde{P}^{-1} h_2 = \lambda^2 h_1^t (\tilde{P}^{-1})^t \tilde{P}^{-1} h_2 \;. \qquad (4.27)$$

with $\lambda \tilde{P}^{-1} \begin{pmatrix} h_1 & h_2 & h_4 \end{pmatrix} = \begin{pmatrix} r_1 & r_2 & t \end{pmatrix}$. Hence,

$$h_1^t \tilde{P}^{-t} \tilde{P}^{-1} h_2 = 0 \qquad (4.28)$$

holds, where $\tilde{P}^{-t}$ denotes $(\tilde{P}^t)^{-1}$. Analogously, with $r_1^t r_1 = r_2^t r_2 = 1$ we obtain

$$h_1^t \tilde{P}^{-t} \tilde{P}^{-1} h_1 - h_2^t \tilde{P}^{-t} \tilde{P}^{-1} h_2 = 0 \;. \qquad (4.29)$$

Equation 4.28 and Equation 4.29 define two constraints for the image transformation $\tilde{P}$. These are two necessary conditions which a pinhole camera without distortion must fulfill. Note that for real cameras an image transformation which fulfills these constraints may not minimize one of the error functions defined in section 3.4.1.

Remark 4.4.1
$\tilde{P}^{-t}\tilde{P}^{-1}$ is known as the image of the absolute conic under the projective mapping defined by H. The absolute conic is a well researched topic in computer vision (see [HZ00] for an overview). One remarkable result is that (4.28) and (4.29)

must hold for all homographies derived by models **P'** which are related to **P** by a similarity transformation $S = sR + t$, for a rotation matrix R, a factor $s \in \mathbb{R} \setminus \{0\}$ and a translation $t \in \mathbb{R}^2$. This result can be derived by analyzing the image of the absolute conic and the circular points $(1, i, 0), (1, -i, 0)$, where i denotes the imaginary unit. For a detailed introduction of the absolute conic, circular points, and the image of the absolute conic see [HZ00]. A geometric approach to these constraints is presented by Gurdjos et al. ([GCP02]). They characterize the set of all cameras satisfying Zhang's constraints.

An immediate consequence of this result is that someone does not have to know the actual distances of points on the planar model **P** to obtain an initial solution of the inner camera parameters which satisfy the constraints. The location of the model points must only be known up to a similarity. This can be used for a self-calibration of the camera. As self-calibration we consider any algorithm which estimates the camera parameters without a gauged calibration model **P**.

4.4.3 Zhang's initial value

With

$$\tilde{P} = \begin{pmatrix} \alpha & \gamma & u_0 \\ 0 & \beta & v_0 \\ 0 & 0 & 1 \end{pmatrix} \quad (4.30)$$

(see section 2.6) the matrix $B = \tilde{P}^{-t}\tilde{P}^{-1}$ is given by

$$B = \begin{pmatrix} \frac{1}{\alpha^2} & -\frac{\gamma}{\alpha^2\beta} & \frac{v_0\gamma - u_0\beta}{\alpha^2\beta} \\ -\frac{\gamma}{\alpha^2\beta} & \frac{\gamma^2+\alpha^2}{\alpha^2\beta^2} & -\frac{\gamma(v_0\gamma-u_0\beta)+v_0\alpha^2}{\alpha^2\beta^2} \\ \frac{v_0\gamma-u_0\beta}{\alpha^2\beta} & -\frac{\gamma(v_0\gamma-u_0\beta)+v_0\alpha^2}{\alpha^2\beta^2} & \frac{(v_0\gamma-u_0\beta)^2+v_0^2\alpha^2}{\alpha^2\beta^2}+1 \end{pmatrix}. \quad (4.31)$$

B is symmetric, so it can be parametrized by six values: $b = (b_1, b_2, b_3, b_4, b_5, b_6)^t$ with $b_1 := B_{11}, b_2 := B_{12}, b_3 := B_{22}, b_4 := B_{13}, b_5 := B_{23}$, and $b_6 := B_{33}$. Let $h_1 := (h_{11}, h_{21}, h_{31})^t$ and $h_2 := (h_{12}, h_{22}, h_{32})^t$ be the first and the second column of $H' = (h_{ij})_{1 \leq i,j \leq 3}$. Equation 4.28 and Equation 4.29 are linear in b. It is easy to see that

$$\begin{pmatrix} h_{11}h_{12} & h_{12}h_{21}+h_{22}h_{11} & h_{22}h_{21} & h_{12}h_{31}+h_{32}h_{11} & h_{22}h_{31}+h_{32}h_{21} & h_{32}h_{31} \\ h_{11}^2-h_{12}^2 & 2h_{11}h_{21}-2h_{12}h_{22} & h_{21}^2-h_{22}^2 & 2h_{11}h_{31}-2h_{12}h_{32} & 2h_{21}h_{31}-2h_{22}h_{32} & h_{31}^2-h_{32}^2 \end{pmatrix} b = 0 \quad (4.32)$$

holds for every observed homography H. For n observations we get n homographies and hence $2n$ equations which we stack in a matrix V such that $Vb = 0$

must hold. To avoid the trivial solution one can compute $b^* \in \underset{\|b\|=1}{\operatorname{argmin}} \|Vb\|$. A solution can be obtained as the eigenvector associated to the smallest eigenvalue of V^tV or the right singular vector to the smallest singular value of V. A solution b^* encodes B up to a scale factor λ. Note that the constraint $\|b\| = 1$ has no other justification than to avoid the trivial solution. Any other constraint which excludes the trivial solution, e.g. $b_1 = 1$ (since b_1 should not be zero) can also be applied.

From $b^* = \lambda(B_{11}, B_{12}, B_{22}, B_{13}, B_{23}, B_{33})^t$ Zhang ([Zha98]) derives

$$v_0 = \frac{b_2^* b_4^* - b_1^* b_5^*}{b_1^* b_3^* - b_2^{*2}},$$

$$\lambda = b_6^* - \frac{b_4^{*2} + v_0(b_2^* b_4^* - b_1^* b_5^*)}{b_1^*},$$

$$\alpha = \sqrt{\frac{\lambda}{b_1^*}}, \text{ and}$$

$$\beta = \sqrt{\frac{\lambda b_1^*}{b_1^* b_3^* - b_2^{*2}}},$$

$$\gamma = -\frac{b_2^* \alpha^2 \beta}{\lambda},$$

$$u_0 = \frac{\gamma v_0}{\beta} - \frac{b_4^* \alpha^2}{\lambda}. \quad (4.33)$$

It should be noticed that the constraint $\|b^*\| = 1$ guarantees neither that all assignments in (4.33) are well defined, nor that α and β are positive.

Another way to obtain $\tilde{P}$ from b^* is given by the Cholesky factorization of the matrix

$$A := \begin{pmatrix} b_1^* & b_2^* & b_4^* \\ b_2^* & b_3^* & b_5^* \\ b_4^* & b_5^* & b_6^* \end{pmatrix} \quad (4.34)$$

defined by b^* (see e.g. [HZ00]). For a positive definite symmetric matrix A the Cholesky factorization $A = C^tC$ ensures that the diagonal entries in the upper triangular matrix C are positive. The scale factor can be obtained simply by the fact that $\tilde{P}_{33} = 1$ holds for the image transformation. However, a Cholesky factorization requires that b^* encodes a positive definite matrix.

Remark 4.4.2 (Minimal number of observations)
Since every observation of a planar calibration pattern yields two equations which are linear in $b \in \mathbb{R}^6$ (see Equation 4.32), one needs at least three observations of the pattern in general position (mutually not co-planar). However, the knowledge of a parameter (like α, β, u_0, v_0 or $\frac{\alpha}{\beta}$ of the image transformation) yields to a system of linear equations with less unknowns (see [SM99] for more details).

In fact, in section 4.4.8 we apply such adjustments for some known parameters in our experiments.

4.4.4 An initial image transformation with known center and zero skew

To simplify the problem we assume that the principal point w.r.t. the image coordinate system coincides with the center of the image. In this case the parameters u_0 and v_0 of the image transformation are known. Furthermore, we assume that the image sensor is located strictly perpendicular to the optical axis of the lens and that the axes of the imaging device define an orthogonal coordinate system. This yields $\gamma = 0$ in the image transformation. In this case we are able to parametrize B by the use of two variables

$$B = \begin{pmatrix} \frac{1}{\alpha^2} & 0 & -\frac{u_0}{\alpha^2} \\ 0 & \frac{1}{\beta^2} & -\frac{v_0}{\beta^2} \\ -\frac{u_0}{\alpha^2} & -\frac{v_0}{\beta^2} & \frac{u_0^2}{\alpha^2} + \frac{v_0^2}{\beta^2} + 1 \end{pmatrix} = \begin{pmatrix} b_1 & 0 & -u_0 b_1 \\ 0 & b_2 & -v_0 b_2 \\ -u_0 b_1 & -v_0 b_2 & u_0^2 b_1 + v_0^2 b_2 + 1 \end{pmatrix} \quad (4.35)$$

with $b_1 = \frac{1}{\alpha^2}, b_2 = \frac{1}{\beta^2}$. This means that in this case the parameters b_1, b_2 are uncorrelated. The constraints (4.28) and (4.29) yield a system of linear equations, which is not homogeneous since the parametrization of B has a constant entry in $B_{3,3}$. Here, a solution can be obtained by one observation. Otherwise, for $n > 1$ observations we obtain the linear least squares problem $\|V'b - h'\|$. In fact, the closed form solution implemented in the camera calibration routine of Intel's Open Source Computer Vision library [1] is based on this method. To be more precise, the OpenCV uses the operation

$$H' := \begin{pmatrix} 1 & 0 & -u_0 \\ 0 & 1 & -v_0 \\ 0 & 0 & 1 \end{pmatrix} H \quad (4.36)$$

on every observed homography H to obtain a modified problem with $(u_0, v_0) = (0, 0)$. The OpenCV solves the resulting least squares problem by a pseudo-inverse, which may not be numerically stable in every case.

Remark 4.4.3 ($\gamma = 0$)
The assumption that there is no skew between the coordinate axes of the imaging sensor, i.e. $\gamma = 0$ in the image transformation, is quite common in computer vision (see e.g. [Hei97, SM99, GCP02]). In particular, Heikkilä considers a non-zero value for γ as linear distortion term.

---

[1] see http://opencvlibrary.sourceforge.net/ visited on Sep. 12th 2008, or [Bra02])

4.4.5 An initial image transformation with known aspect ratio and no skew

A common assumption for off-the-shelf cameras is that pixels are actually squared areas. However, for special cameras the image sensor may also have a very unusual aspect ratio: In particular, for the imaging device of the Siemens range camera ([MLK⁺06]) the dimensions of one sensor element is $130\mu m \times 300\mu m$.

In this section we assume that we know the dimensions of a sensor element. This means that we know the factor $c \in \mathbb{R}_+$ such that $\beta = c\alpha$ in $\tilde{P}$. Furthermore, we assume $\gamma = 0$ in the image transformation. Therefore, we achieve the restricted matrix of the image transformation

$$\tilde{P} = \begin{pmatrix} \alpha & 0 & u_0 \\ 0 & c\alpha & v_0 \\ 0 & 0 & 1 \end{pmatrix}. \tag{4.37}$$

In this case it is

$$B = \tilde{P}^{-t}\tilde{P}^{-1} = \frac{1}{\alpha}\begin{pmatrix} \frac{1}{\alpha} & 0 & -\frac{u_0}{\alpha} \\ 0 & \frac{1}{c^2\alpha} & -\frac{v_0}{c^2\alpha} \\ -\frac{u_0}{\alpha} & -\frac{v_0}{c^2\alpha} & \frac{u_0^2}{\alpha} + \frac{v_0^2}{c^2\alpha} + \alpha \end{pmatrix}. \tag{4.38}$$

B can be described by $b = (b_1, b_2, b_3, b_4)^t$ with $b_1 := \frac{1}{\alpha}$, $b_2 := -\frac{u_0}{\alpha}$, $b_3 := -\frac{v_0}{\alpha}$, and $b_4 := \frac{u_0^2}{\alpha} + \frac{v_0^2}{c^2\alpha} + \alpha$:

$$\alpha B = \begin{pmatrix} b_1 & 0 & b_2 \\ 0 & \frac{1}{c^2}b_1 & \frac{1}{c^2}b_3 \\ b_2 & \frac{1}{c^2}b_3 & b_4 \end{pmatrix}. \tag{4.39}$$

Again, the constraints (4.28) and (4.29) can be summarized in a system of linear equations, stacked in a $2n \times 4$-matrix V.

However, instead of determining b minimizing $\|Vb\|$ subject to $\|b\| = 1$ we are now able to formulate a meaningful constraint for the solution:

$$\frac{b_2^2}{b_1} + \frac{b_3^2}{c^2 b_1} + \frac{1}{b_1} = \frac{u_0^2}{\alpha} + \frac{v_0^2}{c^2\alpha} + \alpha = b_4 \tag{4.40}$$

must hold for a valid solution of the calibration problem. This means

$$b_2^2 + \frac{1}{c^2}b_3^2 + 1 = b_1 b_4 \Leftrightarrow b_1 b_4 - b_2^2 - \frac{1}{c^2}b_3^2 = 1 \tag{4.41}$$

should be fulfilled by a solution b^*. This can be put into matrix form by

$$b^t \underbrace{\begin{pmatrix} 0 & 0 & 0 & \frac{1}{2} \\ 0 & -1 & 0 & 0 \\ 0 & 0 & -\frac{1}{c^2} & 0 \\ \frac{1}{2} & 0 & 0 & 0 \end{pmatrix}}_{=:C} b = 1. \qquad (4.42)$$

The problem to determine $\underset{\{b \in \mathbb{R}^4 \mid b^t C b = 1\}}{\operatorname{argmin}} \|Vb\|^2 = \underset{\{b \in \mathbb{R}^4 \mid b^t C b = 1\}}{\operatorname{argmin}} b^t V^t V b$ can be solved by the Lagrange approach: A vector b^* which minimizes $b^t V^t V b$ subject to $b^t C b = 1$ must satisfy

$$\left(V^t V - \lambda C\right) b^* = 0 \qquad (4.43)$$

for a Lagrange-multiplier $\lambda \in \mathbb{R}$ (see e.g. [Jah96]). The task to find λ and b^* solving (4.43) defines a generalized eigenvalue problem. As C is regular, we achieve

$$\left(C^{-1} V^t V - \lambda I\right) b^* = 0. \qquad (4.44)$$

Hence, the solution b^* is the eigenvector associated to the smallest non-negative eigenvalue of $C^{-1} V^t V$ (see e.g. [SHZ06]).

4.4.6 An initial image transformation with known aspect ratio and unknown skew

If we want to include the skewness γ into the image transformation with a known aspect ratio c, we obtain

$$\tilde{P} = \begin{pmatrix} \alpha & \gamma & u_0 \\ 0 & c\alpha & v_0 \\ 0 & 0 & 1 \end{pmatrix} \qquad (4.45)$$

and subsequently

$$B = \tilde{P}^{-t} \tilde{P}^{-1} = \begin{pmatrix} b_1 & b_4 & b_2 \\ b_4 & b_5 & b_6 \\ b_2 & b_6 & b_3 \end{pmatrix} \qquad (4.46)$$

with

$$b_1 := \frac{1}{\alpha^2},$$
$$b_2 := \frac{v_0\gamma - u_0 c\alpha}{\alpha^3 c},$$
$$b_3 := \frac{(u_0 c\alpha - v_0\gamma)^2}{\alpha^4 c^2} + \frac{v_0^2}{\alpha^2 c^2} + 1, \text{ and}$$
$$b_4 := -\frac{\gamma}{\alpha^3 c},$$
$$b_5 := \frac{\gamma^2}{\alpha^2 c^2} + \frac{1}{\alpha^2 c^2}, \quad (4.47)$$
$$b_6 := \frac{u_0 c\alpha\gamma - v_0\gamma^2}{\alpha^4 c^2} - \frac{v_0}{\alpha^2 c^2}.$$

A vector b^* minimizing $\|Vb\|$ with $b = (b_1, \ldots, b_6)^t$ and V derived from the constraints (4.28) and (4.29) as in the previous sections should satisfy

$$b_1 b_3 - b_2^2 = \frac{v_0^2}{\alpha^4 c^2} + \frac{1}{\alpha^2} > 0. \quad (4.48)$$

Since b^* defines parameters of $\tilde{P}$ only up to a scale factor, we demand

$$b_1 b_3 - b_2^2 = 1 \quad (4.49)$$

as a constraint for the vector minimizing $\|Vb\|$. This constraint can be expressed by a matrix $C \in \mathbb{R}^{6\times 6}$ with

$$C = \begin{pmatrix} C_1 & 0 \\ 0 & 0 \end{pmatrix} \text{ with } C_1 = \begin{pmatrix} 0 & 0 & \frac{1}{2} \\ 0 & -1 & 0 \\ \frac{1}{2} & 0 & 0 \end{pmatrix} \in \mathbb{R}^{3\times 3}. \quad (4.50)$$

We decompose $V^t V \in \mathbb{R}^{6\times 6}$ into three sub-matrices $S_1, S_2, S_3 \in \mathbb{R}^{3\times 3}$ such that

$$V^t V = \begin{pmatrix} S_1 & S_2 \\ S_2^t & S_3 \end{pmatrix} \quad (4.51)$$

holds. Then, the vector b^* minimizing $\|Vb\|$ subject to $b^t C b = 1$ is the eigenvector to the smallest non-negative eigenvalue of

$$M = C_1^{-1}(S_1 - S_2 S_3^{-1} S_2^t). \quad (4.52)$$

For a detailed derivation of the mathematics see [HF98].

Remark 4.4.4
In [WH05] Wu and Hu propose the constraint

$$\frac{b_5}{b_1} - \left(\frac{b_4}{b_1}\right)^2 = \frac{1}{c^2} \quad (4.53)$$

for this case. They use this constraint for a calibration (w.r.t. an algebraic error) by a single-view. However, they apply this constraint not in a least squares problem, but they use it for substitution.

The constraint can be rewritten as

$$b_1 b_5 - b_4^2 - \frac{1}{c^2} b_1^2 = 0 \tag{4.54}$$

If we assume that there is no skew, i.e. $\gamma = 0$ (i.e. $b_4 = 0$), this constraint becomes very simple. It is

$$b_1 b_5 = \frac{1}{c^2} b_1^2 \tag{4.55}$$

or, even more simpler, $b_5 = \frac{1}{c^2} b_1$.

4.4.7 An initial image transformation with no skew

For an unknown aspect ratio we must estimate both scaling factors α and β of the image transformation. Since γ should be small for actual camera mappings, we assume $\gamma = 0$ and therefore obtain a simpler problem than the one discussed in 4.4.3. With this the matrix $B = \tilde{P}^{-t} \tilde{P}^{-1}$ is given by

$$B = \begin{pmatrix} \frac{1}{\alpha^2} & 0 & -\frac{u_0}{\alpha^2} \\ 0 & \frac{1}{\beta^2} & -\frac{v_0}{\beta^2} \\ -\frac{u_0}{\alpha^2} & -\frac{v_0}{\beta^2} & \frac{u_0^2}{\alpha^2} + \frac{v_0^2}{\beta^2} + 1 \end{pmatrix}. \tag{4.56}$$

4.4.7.1 A straight forward constraint

Setting $b_1 := \frac{1}{\alpha^2}, b_2 := \frac{1}{\beta^2}, b_3 := -\frac{u_0}{\alpha^2}, b_4 := -\frac{v_0}{\beta^2}$, and $b_5 := \frac{u_0^2}{\alpha^2} + \frac{v_0^2}{\beta^2} + 1$ we parametrize

$$B = \begin{pmatrix} b_1 & 0 & b_3 \\ 0 & b_2 & b_4 \\ b_3 & b_4 & b_5 \end{pmatrix}. \tag{4.57}$$

For a valid image transformation, the following inequalities must hold

$$b_1 b_2 > 0, b_1 b_5 > 0, b_2 b_5 > 0, \text{ and } b_3 b_4 > 0, \tag{4.58}$$

because these entries of B have the same sign. Hence, we obtain

$$b_1 b_2 + b_1 b_5 + b_2 b_5 + b_3 b_4 > 0 \tag{4.59}$$

as a necessary condition for an assignment of b. Since the constraints (4.28) and (4.29) define a solution b only up to a scale factor, we demand that

$$b_1 b_2 + b_1 b_5 + b_2 b_5 + b_3 b_4 = 1 \qquad (4.60)$$

should hold for a minimum of $\|Vb\|$. The quadratic constraint in Equation 4.60 can be put into a regular matrix $C \in \mathbb{R}^{5 \times 5}$ with

$$C = \begin{pmatrix} 0 & \frac{1}{2} & 0 & 0 & \frac{1}{2} \\ \frac{1}{2} & 0 & 0 & 0 & \frac{1}{2} \\ 0 & 0 & 0 & \frac{1}{2} & 0 \\ 0 & 0 & \frac{1}{2} & 0 & 0 \\ \frac{1}{2} & \frac{1}{2} & 0 & 0 & 0 \end{pmatrix} \qquad (4.61)$$

by $b^t C b = 1$. Since C is regular, the problem to minimize $\|Vb\|$ subject to $b^t C b = 1$ can be solved by finding the eigenvector to the smallest positive eigenvalue of $C^{-1} V^t V$ (see [SHZ06]).

The eigenvalues of C are $-\frac{1}{2}, -\frac{1}{2}, -\frac{1}{2}, \frac{1}{2}$, and 1, $V^t V$ has only positive eigenvalues. Following [Fit97] it is easy to see there are only two positive eigenvalues of $C^{-1} V^t V$ (see also [SHZ06]). This simple observation can be very helpful in a numerical aspect of the problem: a numerical evaluation may result in a situation with four or two negative eigenvalues. In this case, the second highest eigenvalue represents the solution.

4.4.7.2 A solution by a linear least squares problem with Cholesky decomposition

If we set $\beta = c\alpha$ for an unknown factor $c \in \mathbb{R}_+$, we obtain

$$\begin{aligned} B &= \begin{pmatrix} \frac{1}{\alpha^2} & 0 & -\frac{u_0}{\alpha^2} \\ 0 & \frac{1}{c^2 \alpha^2} & -\frac{v_0}{c^2 \alpha^2} \\ -\frac{u_0}{\alpha^2} & -\frac{v_0}{c^2 \alpha^2} & \frac{u_0^2}{\alpha^2} + \frac{v_0^2}{c^2 \alpha^2} + 1 \end{pmatrix} \qquad (4.62) \\ &= \frac{1}{\alpha^2 c^2} \begin{pmatrix} c^2 & 0 & -c^2 u_0 \\ 0 & 1 & -v_0 \\ -c^2 u_0 & -v_0 & c^2 u_0^2 + v_0^2 + c^2 \alpha^2 \end{pmatrix}. \qquad (4.63) \end{aligned}$$

Since we are only able to determine a solution up to a scale factor, we set $b = (b_1, b_2, b_3, b_4)^t$ with $b_1 := c^2$, $b_2 := -c^2 u_0$, $b_3 := -v_0$, and $b_4 := c^2 u_0^2 + v_0^2 + c^2 \alpha^2$

to parametrize B as

$$\frac{1}{\alpha^2 c^2} \begin{pmatrix} b_1 & 0 & b_2 \\ 0 & 1 & b_3 \\ b_2 & b_3 & b_4 \end{pmatrix}. \tag{4.64}$$

This parametrization of B has a constant entry. Thus, we derive an inhomogeneous system of linear equations by the constraints (4.28) and (4.29). . Since the entries of b are independent, we derive a least squares problem $\|V'b - h'\|$ without additional constraints. A solution b^* of this linear least squares problem can be obtained by Householder transformations. If the matrix λB described by the solution b^* is positive definite, one can derive $\tilde{P}$ by a Cholesky decomposition. If b^* does not describe a positive definite matrix we achieve only $u_0 = -\frac{b_2}{b_1}$ by the definition of the solution vector b^*, since b^* is only defined up to a scale factor λ. To obtain the remaining parameters α, β, and v_0, one has to determine λ.

With $\alpha = \frac{1}{c}\beta$ we derive

$$B = \begin{pmatrix} \frac{c^2}{\beta^2} & 0 & -\frac{u_0 c^2}{\beta^2} \\ 0 & \frac{1}{\beta^2} & -\frac{v_0}{\beta^2} \\ -\frac{u_0 c^2}{\beta^2} & -\frac{v_0}{\beta^2} & \frac{u_0^2 c^2}{\beta^2} + \frac{v_0^2}{\beta^2} + 1 \end{pmatrix} = \frac{c^2}{\beta^2} \begin{pmatrix} 1 & 0 & -u_0 \\ 0 & \frac{1}{c^2} & -\frac{1}{c^2}v_0 \\ -u_0 & -\frac{1}{c^2}v_0 & u_0^2 + \frac{1}{c^2}v_0^2 + \frac{\beta^2}{c^2} \end{pmatrix}$$
(4.65)

and therefore a dual least squares problem. It allows us to determine v_0 instead of u_0 by a solution of this problem. v_0 can now be applied to determine the scale factor λ for b^* to obtain the remaining camera parameters.

4.4.8 Experimental results

4.4.8.1 Overview

In [HS07a] we investigated the additional constraints presented in this section. Some of the presented restrictions (like a known principal point) are quite common or — as in the case of a known aspect ratio — are easy to obtain for special hardware. In particular, for the calibration of a 3D-camera based on the SIEMENS 64×8 Time-Of-Flight range sensor (see [MLK+06]), the approach with a known aspect ratio, as proposed in section 4.4.5, was very stable. For this very low resolution the standard approach of Zhang fails in a significant number of cases. Another application of the additional constraints are wide angle lenses or fisheye optics. The experimental results in [HS07a] show that for these degenerated configurations the additional constraints proposed in section 4.4.4, section 4.4.5, section 4.4.6, and section 4.4.7 yield not only a valid initial solution of the camera calibration problem, but also provides a better initial value for a subsequent non-linear optimization.

4.4.8.2 Simulations

To test the different initial solutions with valid reference data we use simulated data. Given an image transformation and a calibration pattern at different positions, we project the points by the camera mapping and simulate a pixel discretization with distortion. The minimization of $\|Vb\|$ with additional constraints defines an algebraic error. It is merely the attempt to find a camera mapping which fulfills the constraints (4.28) and (4.29). Nonetheless, we apply the projective error function as defined in section 3.4.1 to measure the quality of our proposed closed form solutions.

We refer to the method of Zhang as presented in [Zha98] by **Zhang**. We denote **Zhang5** when we refer to the minimum with no skew (*i.e.* $\gamma = 0$). We denote **Zhang4** when we refer to the minimum with no skew and identical scale factors in the image transformation (*i.e.* $\gamma = 0$, $\alpha = \beta$). For the first configuration the vector b has five entries, for the second there are four entries in b. Both parametrizations of the problem have been proposed by Zhang in [Zha98] to handle degenerate configurations. In [SM99] Sturm and Maybank extended this approach to a known aspect ratio c with $\beta = c\alpha$ and studied the singularities of several degenerated configurations.

We denote **OpenCV** for the closed form solution which is used in the Open Computer Vision Library (Open CV). The sources are available at sourceforge[2]. In contrast to the original code we apply Householder transformations instead of the pseudo-inverse to solve the linear least squares problem. For the method with a known aspect ratio c and no skew as presented in section 4.4.5 we denote **Const4**. For the problem of finding a starting solution with no skew (section 4.4.7) we examine the solution with the necessary condition that some entries share the same sign (section 4.4.7.1) (denoted by **Const5**) and the least squares solution as introduced in section 4.4.7.2. We denote this approach by **LSQ**. In our experiments we always applied the Cholesky decomposition to determine the matrix of the image transformation for this approach.

---

[2]Available at http://opencvlibrary.sourceforge.net/, visited on Sep. 12th 2008

To model a standard VGA camera we set $\alpha = 700, \beta = 600, \gamma = 0, u_0 = 320, v_0 = 240$ and apply an image resolution of 640 × 480 pixels. We assume that we can extract a position of an observation with an accuracy of $\frac{1}{10}$ of a pixel from the pixel image. Each pixel position obtained by an image transformation of a model with 3 × 3 points is distorted by Gaussian noise with mean 0 and variance σ^2.

Figure 4.2 shows the measured errors for increasing variances σ^2. For each value of σ^2 we perform 1000 tests and depict the average value root mean square projective camera calibration error (see definition 3.4.1) in our charts. Each test is performed with the model at three different positions (parallel, tilted at 0.2 rad to the front, tilted at 0.2 rad to the left) at a depth of 1m to the camera (w.r.t. the camera coordinate system). One can see in Figure 4.2 that for increasing noise the

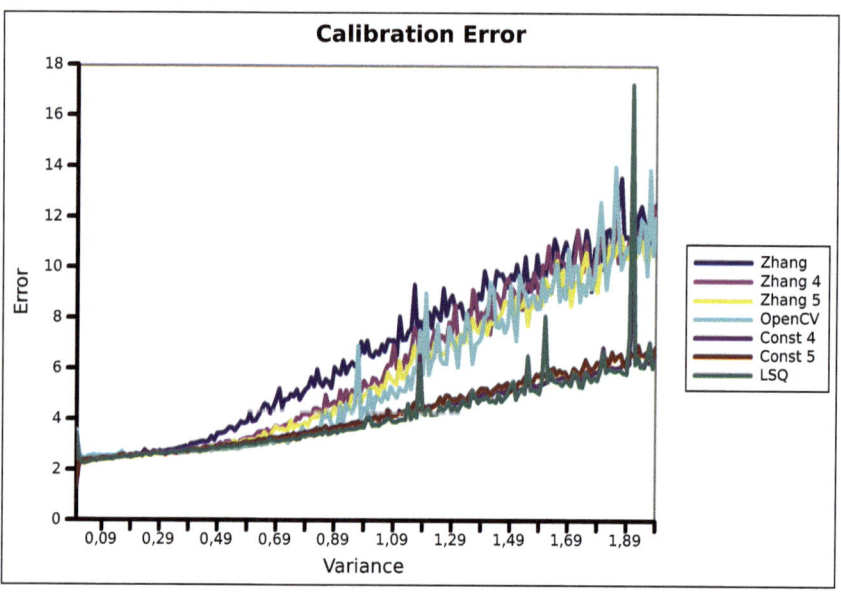

Figure 4.2: Camera calibration error (root mean square) for each initial solution. The x-axis shows the variance of the distortion of the point extraction, the y-axis the average root mean square camera calibration error over 1000 tests.

proposed methods provide better results than the standard approaches (including

OpenCV).

Due to the noise and the discretization not every experiment leads to a valid solution of the calibration problem. In Figure 4.3 we show the number of invalid results w.r.t. to increasing noise for all methods investigated. The results show that all proposed methods supply more stable results than all standard approaches (excluding **OpenCV**). In particular, **OpenCV**, **Const4**, and **LSQ** nearly always deliver a valid solution.

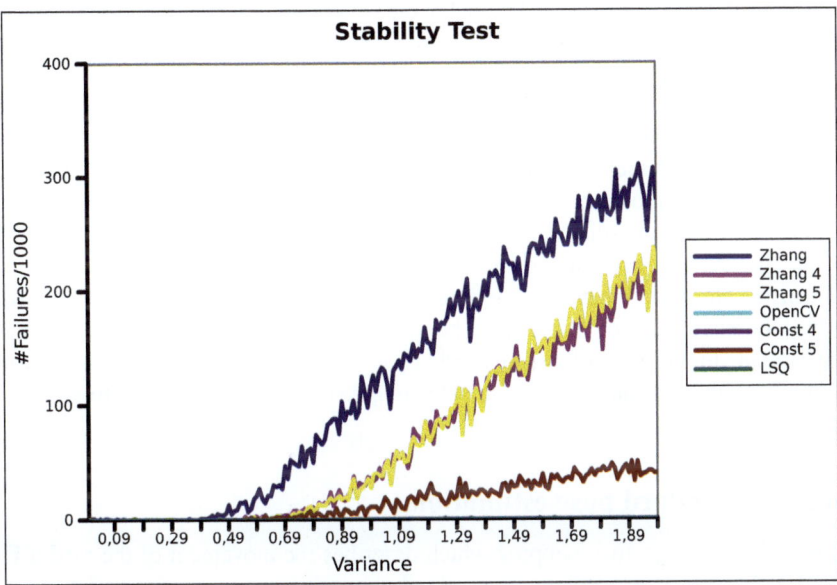

Figure 4.3: Number of invalid results for the camera calibration problem. The abscissa shows the variance of the distortion of the point extraction, the ordinate shows the number of invalid results in 1000 tests.

4.5 An initial value for the extrinsic camera parameters

4.5.1 Introduction and problem statement

The extrinsic camera parameters define the position and orientation of the camera w.r.t. a reference coordinate system. Equivalently, we may estimate the position and orientation of the observed model, which defines the reference coordinate system, w.r.t. to the camera coordinate system. We call this problem *pose estimation*.

In the following we assume that the intrinsic camera parameters are given. The standard approach to pose estimation, which we present in the next section, uses only the parameters of the image transformation P to estimate the position of the observed model by the observed projective mapping. If the distortion is known, one has to un-distort the image before applying the standard pose estimation. However, we present two approaches which treat the mapping defined by the intrinsic camera parameters (including the distortion parameters) as a black box. Only the knowledge of $B \in \mathcal{I}_\Delta$ (to be more precise: we need B^{-1}) is necessary to estimate the position of a regular grid by a re-projective method. Moreover, for a model with collinear points we are able to give a solution which is optimal w.r.t. the Euclidean error.

4.5.2 Standard pose estimation

Let H be the projective mapping which describes the movement of the model $\mathbf{P}$ to the observed image points. For a fixed observation $(i_p)_{p \in \mathbf{P}}$ of a model Γ the mapping $H \in \mathbb{R}^{3 \times 4}$ minimizes

$$\sum_{p \in \mathbf{P}} \|i_p - \Pi_z(H\tilde{p})\|^2 \qquad (4.66)$$

(see also (4.16) in section 4.4).

Obviously H can be determined only up to a scale factor. Moreover, for cameras satisfying the pinhole equation (2.34) on page 25, it is $\lambda H = \tilde{P}\begin{pmatrix} R & t \end{pmatrix}$. For a calibrated camera we know the image transformation $\tilde{P}$ yielding $\begin{pmatrix} R & t \end{pmatrix} = \lambda \tilde{P}^{-1} H =: A$ for the rotation matrix R and translation t. Since the first column of $\begin{pmatrix} R & t \end{pmatrix}$ must be normal and $t_z \geq 0$ should hold, we set $c = \sqrt{A_{1,1}^2 + A_{2,1}^2 + A_{3,1}^2}$

and

$$\tilde{A} = \begin{cases} \frac{1}{c}A & \text{if } A_{3,3} > 0 \text{ holds} \\ -\frac{1}{c}A & \text{otherwise} \end{cases} \quad (4.67)$$

to obtain the extrinsic parameters R and t by $\begin{pmatrix} R & t \end{pmatrix} = \tilde{A}$.

4.5.3 An algebraic re-projective approach for regular grids

In [HSG06] we presented an approach based on the theorem of intersecting lines. For three model points on a single line we test all configurations where the first two points are on their re-projected observations. From all these configurations we choose the one where the third point has the least Euclidean distance to the viewing ray of its observation. This distance can be expressed in a continuous function.

Let $p_1, p_2, p_3 \in \mathbf{P}$ be three equidistant collinear for which their observation $i_{p_1}, i_{p_2}, i_{p_3} \in I$ exists. We define

$$n_j := \frac{B^{-1}(i_{p_j})}{\|B^{-1}(i_{p_j})\|} \quad (4.68)$$

for $j = 1, 2, 3$ and for a direction $n \in \{x \in \mathbb{R}^3 \mid \|x\| = 1\}$ we define

$$L_n := \{\alpha n \mid \alpha \in \mathbb{R}\} \quad (4.69)$$

as the *line with direction n containing the origin*. Then the line L_{n_j} contains p_j for $j \in \{1, 2, 3\}$.

For each point $p \in L_{n_1}$ we determine two points $q_{1,2}$ on the viewing ray L_{n_2} with a fixed given distance (see Figure 4.4). The two points p, q_1, respectively p, q_2, define a line in space. If we now know that a third point r_1, respectively r_2, is collinear to these two points at a given distance, we can determine the distance of this point to its viewing ray L_{n_3} using this collinearity constraint. If we predict the first point along its viewing correctly, this last distance should be zero. For $p = xn_1 \in L_{n_1}$ this distance can be described by a function of the form $F_{1,2}(x) = ax^2 \pm bx\sqrt{-cx^2 + d^2} + e$ (see [HSG06] or algorithm **POSITION ESTIMATION** on page 68 for the actual values of a, b, c, d, e). A root of $F_{1,2}$ indicates a position of $p = xn_1$ where a reconstruction of the model line where all points are on their re-projections is possible.

In [HSG06] we have proven the following lemma:

Lemma 4.5.1
For $a, b, e \in \mathbb{R}$ and $c, d \in \mathbb{R}_+$ set $D := \left\{ x \in \mathbb{R} \,\middle|\, x^2 \leq \frac{d^2}{c} \right\}$ and define the function $f : D \to \mathbb{R}$ by
$$f(x) = ax^2 + bx\sqrt{-cx^2 + d^2} + e.$$
Then it is
$$f(x) = 0 \Rightarrow x_{1,2,3,4} = \pm\sqrt{\frac{d^2b^2 - 2\,ea \pm \sqrt{d^4b^4 - 4\,d^2b^2ea - 4\,e^2cb^2}}{2cb^2 + 2a^2}}$$

Furthermore, for the derivative of f as in 4.5.1 we obtain the following lemma (see [HSG06]):

Lemma 4.5.2
The derivative of the function f defined in lemma 4.5.1 is
$$f'(x) = 2ax + b\sqrt{-cx^2 + d^2} - \frac{bcx^2}{\sqrt{-cx^2 + d^2}},$$
and, furthermore,
$$f'(x) = 0 \Rightarrow x_{1,2,3,4} = \pm\sqrt{\frac{a^2 + cb^2 \pm \sqrt{a^4 + a^2cb^2}}{2c\,(cb^2 + a^2)}}\,d$$
holds.

Therefore, the following algorithm can be used to estimate the pose of a regular grid.

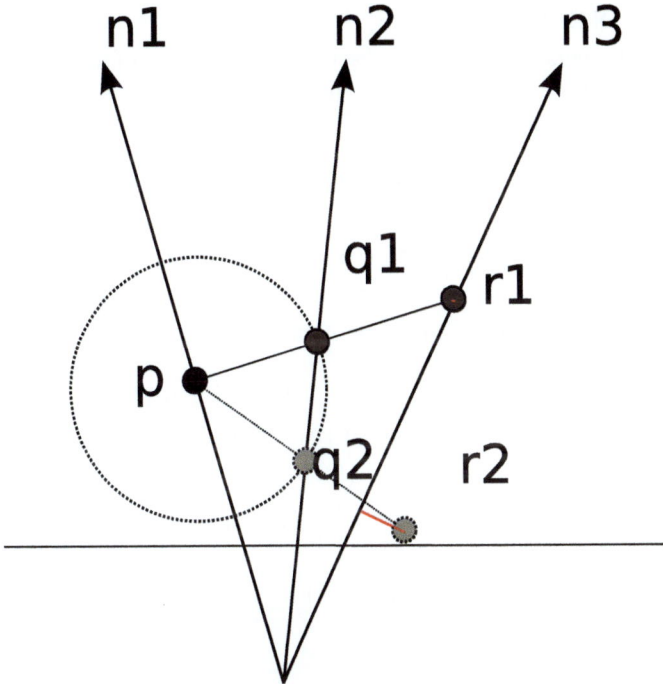

Figure 4.4: Construction of the point $q_{1,2}$ and $r_{1,2}$ for a point p on L_{n_1}. The red lines sketch the distances $\text{dist}(r_1, L_{n_3})$ and $\text{dist}(r_1, L_{n_3})$ which should be minimized.

POSITION ESTIMATION
INPUT: Camera $B \in \mathcal{I}_\Delta$, three observations $i_{p_1}, i_{p_2}, i_{p_3}$ of three equidistant collinear points p_1, p_2, p_3 with $d := \text{dist}(p_1, p_2) = \text{dist}(p_2, p_3)$.
OUTPUT: Estimated positions $\tilde{p}_1, \tilde{p}_2, \tilde{p}_3$ of p_1, p_2, p_3.

i. Determine the re-projections of the observed image points:
$$n_1 := \frac{B^{-1}(i_{p_1})}{\|B^{-1}(i_{p_1})\|}, n_2 := \frac{B^{-1}(i_{p_2})}{\|B^{-1}(i_{p_2})\|}, n_3 := \frac{B^{-1}(i_{p_3})}{\|B^{-1}(i_{p_3})\|}$$

ii. Set the two distance functions: With
$$\begin{aligned} a &:= 1 + 4\left(\langle n_1 | n_2 \rangle^2 - 1\right) - 4\left(\langle n_1 | n_2 \rangle \langle n_2 | n_3 \rangle\right)^2 \\ &\quad + 4 \langle n_1 | n_2 \rangle \langle n_2 | n_3 \rangle \langle n_1 | n_3 \rangle - \langle n_1 | n_3 \rangle^2 \\ &\quad - 4 \langle n_2 | n_3 \rangle^2 \left(\langle n_1 | n_2 \rangle^2 - 1\right) \\ b &:= 4\left(\langle n_1 | n_2 \rangle - 2 \langle n_1 | n_2 \rangle \langle n_2 | n_3 \rangle^2 + \langle n_1 | n_3 \rangle \langle n_2 | n_3 \rangle\right) \\ c &:= 1 - \langle n_1 | n_2 \rangle^2 \\ e &:= 4d^2 \left(1 - \langle n_2 | n_3 \rangle^2\right) \end{aligned}$$

to obtain the functions
$$\begin{aligned} F_1(x) &= ax^2 + bx\sqrt{-cx^2 + d^2} + e \\ F_2(x) &= ax^2 - bx\sqrt{-cx^2 + d^2} + e \end{aligned}$$

iii. Compute the positive roots of F_1 and F_2 (see lemma 4.5.1).
(Note that by the geometric construction only one positive root of F_1 and F_2 exists!).
Set β as the positive root of F_1 or F_2.

iv. Set $\tilde{p}_1 := \beta n_1$, $\tilde{p}_2 := \left(\langle n_2 | \tilde{p}_1 \rangle \pm \sqrt{\langle n_2 | \tilde{p}_1 \rangle^2 - \|\tilde{p}_1\|^2 + d^2}\right) n_2$ and $\tilde{p}_3 := 2\tilde{p}_2 - \tilde{p}_1$.

Algorithm 1: Algorithm to estimate the position of equidistant collinear points.

Algorithm **POSITION ESTIMATION** makes only sense if only one positive root of the distance functions F_1 and F_2 exists. Figure 4.5 sketches such an ideal situation. However, real data is always corrupted by noise and the camera mapping only approximates the real behavior of the imaging device. Therefore, one can not ensure the existence of exactly one positive root of F_1 and F_2. In fact, in real camera setups the situation that no such root exists (see Figure 4.6) or that two roots of F_1 resp. F_2 exist (see Figure 4.7) may occur. Using lemma 4.5.2 instead of lemma 4.5.1 we can change step iii. to obtain the global minimum of the positive part of F_1 and F_2 as a solution for β.

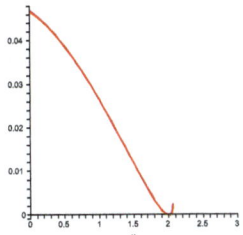

Figure 4.5: Typical graph of an ideal construction of a distance function F_1 (lens with focal length 12 mm and low distortion).

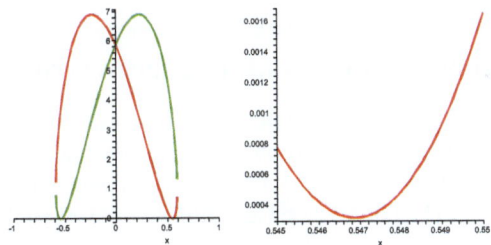

Figure 4.6: Typical graph for F_1 (red) and F_2 (green) based on real data (lens with focal length 4.8 mm and significant distortion). As can be seen in the left image, the positive minimum of these functions is not zero.

Of course, this approach minimizes an algebraic error that may lead to a result which may not be optimal with respect to the Euclidean distance.

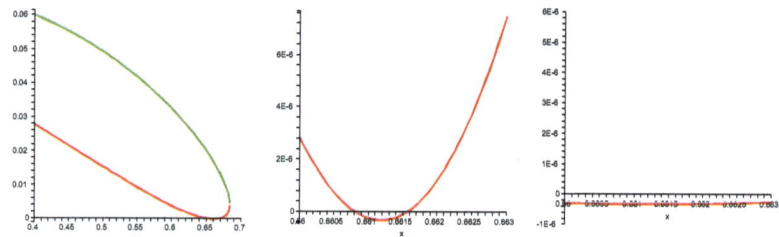

Figure 4.7: Example of the numerical problems in root finding of F_1, F_2 (lens with focal length 4.8 mm and significant distortion). The left image shows F_1 (red) and F_2 (green). The local behavior around the positive minimum of F_1 is shown in the middle image. The right image displays F_1 in a local neighborhood of this minimum.

Remark 4.5.3 (Non equidistant collinear points)
*In algorithm **POSITION ESTIMATION** we sketched the pose estimation for equidistant collinear points. In fact, in [HSG06] the distance functions F_1 and F_2 are derived for equidistant collinear points only. Yet, it is obvious that such distance functions can also be derived in every case when two points determine the position of a third point. The construction as sketched in Figure 4.4 is not limited to collinear points. For the derivation of the distance functions F_1, F_2 in [HSG06] it is necessary that the third point can be expressed as a linear combination of the first two points.*

4.5.4 An optimal solution w.r.t. Euclidean error for 1D targets

For regular 1D targets a solution which is optimal w.r.t. the Euclidean distance of the model points to the re-projected observations was presented in [PH07]. Let $\mathbf{P} = \{p_1, \ldots, p_m\} \subset \mathbb{R}^3$ be a finite set of collinear points with $p_j = (x_j, 0, 0) \in \mathbb{R}^3$ for $j \in \{1, \ldots, m\}$. For every observation $i_{p_j} \in I$ of $p_j \in \mathbf{P}$ we set $n_j = \frac{B^{-1}(i_{p_j})}{\|B^{-1}(i_{p_j})\|}$. We assume that not all i_{p_j} are equal.

For $n \in \{x \in \mathbb{R}^3 \mid \|x\| = 1\}$ and L_n as defined in section 4.5.3 it is easy to see that for every point $p \in \mathbb{R}^3$

$$\text{dist}(p, L_n)^2 = \|(I_3 - N_n)p\|^2 \tag{4.70}$$

holds, where N_n is defined as $N_n = nn^t \in \mathbb{R}^{3 \times 3}$ and I_3 is the 3×3 identity matrix.

The Euclidean pose estimation problem is to determine the parameters $R \in SO_3$ and $t \in \mathbb{R}^3$ which minimize

$$\sum_{j=1}^{m} \text{dist}(Rp_j + t, L_{n_j})^2. \tag{4.71}$$

For our special 1D model we obtain $Rp_j + t = x_j r_1 + t$, where $r_1 \in \mathbb{R}^3$ is the first row of the rotation matrix R. Since it is $N_{n_j} N_{n_j} = N_{n_j}$ and thus $(I_3 - N_{n_j})^2 = (I_3 - N_{n_j})$ for $j \in \{1, 2, 3\}$, applying (4.70) we obtain

$$\sum_{j=1}^{m} \|(I_3 - N_{n_j})(x_j r_1 + t)\|^2$$

$$= \sum_{j=1}^{m} (x_j r_1 + t)^t (I_3 - N_{n_j})(x_j r_1 + t)$$

$$= r_1^t \left(\sum_{j=1}^{m} x_j^2 (I_3 - N_{n_j}) \right) r_1 + 2 r_1^t \left(\sum_{j=1}^{m} x_j (I_3 - N_{n_j}) \right) t$$

$$+ t^t \left(\sum_{j=1}^{m} (I_3 - N_{n_j}) \right) t.$$

Using the abbreviations $M_1 := \sum_{j=1}^{m}(I_3 - N_{n_j})$, $M_2 := \sum_{j=1}^{m} x_j(I_3 - N_{n_j})$ and $M_3 := \sum_{j=1}^{m} x_j^2(I_3 - N_{n_j})$ the Euclidean pose determination problem is to obtain $r_1 \in \mathbb{R}^3$ with $\|r_1\| = 1$ and $t \in \mathbb{R}^3$ minimizing

$$r_1^t M_3 r_1 + 2 r_1^t M_2 t + t^t M_1 t. \tag{4.72}$$

For a fixed vector $r_1 \in \mathbb{R}^3$, the optimal value for t is

$$t = -M_1^{-1} M_2 r_1, \tag{4.73}$$

since M_1 is positive definite (see [PH07] for details).

Given the optimal translation as a function of r_1 (4.72) can be rewritten as

$$\min_{r_1 \in \mathbb{R}^3, \|r_1\|=1} r_1^t (M_3 - M_2 M_1^{-1} M_2) r_1. \tag{4.74}$$

Since M_1, M_2 and M_3 are symmetric matrices, the matrix $M_3 - M_2 M_1^{-1} M_2$ is also symmetric. Therefore, a solution of (4.74) can be obtained by the normalized eigenvector to the smallest eigenvalue of $M_3 - M_2 M_1^{-1} M_2$ (c.f. [GvL96]).

In [PH07] some results of this approach are shown. However, it is limited to 1D targets.

4.6 An initial solution for the distortion

4.6.1 Introduction

As stated in section 2.4, real cameras are modeled with a distortion mapping in $\{z = 1\}$. The last step of classic calibration algorithms is a non-linear optimization including all distortion parameters. Therefore, a suitable initial solution for the distortion is needed. In this section we present a simple method to obtain optimal distortion parameters w.r.t. the projective error given the image transformation P and the transformation T.

Let Δ be a distortion model. Then for a fixed transformation T and image transformation P the optimal distortion mapping minimizes

$$\Psi : \begin{array}{c} \Delta \to \mathbb{R}_+ \\ \delta \mapsto \sum_{p \in \mathbf{P}} \| \left(P \circ \tilde{\delta} \circ \Pi_z \circ T \right)(p) - i_p \|^2 \end{array} . \qquad (4.75)$$

In the following we assume that all camera parameters defining a pure pinhole camera are given. Since the transformation part T of the camera is fixed, we assume w.l.o.g. $T = \mathrm{id}$. Therefore, the problem of (4.76) becomes: determine $\delta_0 \in \Delta$ such that

$$\sum_{p \in \mathbf{P}} \|(P \circ \tilde{\delta}_0 \circ \Pi_z)(p) - i_p\|^2 \qquad (4.76)$$

is minimal under all $\delta \in \Delta$.

Remark 4.6.1 (Initial distortion for the re-projective error)
In the following we determine the optimal distortion w.r.t. the projective error. It should be clear that the determination of an optimal distortion is actually very simple w.r.t. the re-projective error as defined in definition 3.2.2: Determine $\delta_0^* \in \Delta$ such that

$$\sum_{p \in \mathbf{P}} \|\tilde{\delta}_0^*(P^{-1}(\tilde{i}_p)) - \Pi_z(p)\|^2 \qquad (4.77)$$

is minimal under all $\delta^* \in \Delta$. If Δ is a finite dimensional vector space, the determination of δ_0^* is a linear least squares problem.

4.6.2 Zhang's initial solution for the radial distortion

In [Zha98] Zhang presents a method to determine the parameters of a radial distortion with two parameters quite efficiently. In fact, it is the optimal solution if all other camera parameters are fixed. However, this is not shown by Zhang explicitly. Therefore, we sketch a proof for the optimality of his approach:

Let P be the image transformation of the actual camera with

$$P \begin{pmatrix} u \\ v \\ 1 \end{pmatrix} = A \begin{pmatrix} u \\ v \end{pmatrix} + \begin{pmatrix} u_0 \\ v_0 \end{pmatrix}. \tag{4.78}$$

Let $(u, v)^t = \Pi_z(p)$ for a point $p \in \mathbf{P}$ with a corresponding observation $i_p \in \mathbb{R}^2$ in pixel coordinates. For a radial distortion with two parameters k_1, k_2 we obtain

$$\begin{aligned}
& (P \circ \delta) \begin{pmatrix} u \\ v \end{pmatrix} - i_p \\
=\ & P\left(\begin{pmatrix} u \\ v \end{pmatrix} + k_1(u^2+v^2)\begin{pmatrix} u \\ v \end{pmatrix} + k_2(u^2+v^2)^2\begin{pmatrix} u \\ v \end{pmatrix} \right) - i_p \quad (4.79) \\
=\ & A\begin{pmatrix} u \\ v \end{pmatrix} + k_1(u^2+v^2)A\begin{pmatrix} u \\ v \end{pmatrix} + k_2(u^2+v^2)^2 A\begin{pmatrix} u \\ v \end{pmatrix} \quad (4.80) \\
& - i_p + \begin{pmatrix} u_0 \\ v_0 \end{pmatrix} \\
=\ & \underbrace{\left((u^2+v^2)A\begin{pmatrix} u \\ v \end{pmatrix}\ (u^2+v^2)^2 A\begin{pmatrix} u \\ v \end{pmatrix} \right)}_{=:M} \underbrace{\begin{pmatrix} k_1 \\ k_2 \end{pmatrix}}_{=:x} \quad (4.81) \\
& + \underbrace{A\begin{pmatrix} u \\ v \end{pmatrix} - i_p + \begin{pmatrix} u_0 \\ v_0 \end{pmatrix}}_{=:b} \quad (4.82) \\
=\ & Mx - b
\end{aligned}$$

Thus, the determination of k_1, k_2 such that δ minimizes Ψ in (4.76) becomes a linear least squares problem $\|Mx - b\|$. It can be verified by basic calculus that this is the same problem as the one proposed by Zhang in [Zha98].

4.6.3 An optimal initial solution for all distortion parameters

In section 2.4 we introduced a typical distortion mapping containing a radial, tangential and thin prism part. It can be re-written as

$$\tilde{\delta}\begin{pmatrix}u\\v\\1\end{pmatrix} = \begin{pmatrix}u\\v\\1\end{pmatrix} + \begin{pmatrix}\text{rad}\binom{u}{v}\\0\end{pmatrix} + \begin{pmatrix}\delta_{\text{tan}}\binom{u}{v}\\0\end{pmatrix} + \begin{pmatrix}\delta_{\text{thp}}\binom{u}{v}\\0\end{pmatrix} + \begin{pmatrix}r\binom{u}{v}\\0\end{pmatrix} \quad (4.83)$$

where id + rad is the radial distortion δ_r, δ_{tan} the tangential, δ_{thp} the thin prism distortion, and r the residual distortion. It is

$$\text{rad}\binom{u}{v} := \binom{u}{v}\sum_{i=1}^{D} k_i (u^2+v^2)^i \quad (4.84)$$

$$= k_1\binom{u(u^2+v^2)}{v(u^2+v^2)} + k_2\binom{u(u^2+v^2)^2}{v(u^2+v^2)^2} + \quad (4.85)$$

$$\ldots + k_D\binom{u(u^2+v^2)^D}{v(u^2+v^2)^D}$$

and

$$\delta_{\text{tan}}\binom{u}{v} = \binom{t_1(u^2+v^2+2u^2)+2t_2uv}{2t_1uv+t_2(u^2+v^2+2v^2)} \quad (4.86)$$

$$= t_1\binom{3u^2+v^2}{2uv} + t_2\binom{2uv}{u^2+3v^2} \quad (4.87)$$

and

$$\delta_{\text{thp}}\binom{u}{v} = \binom{s_1(u^2+v^2)}{s_2(u^2+v^2)} \quad (4.88)$$

$$= s_1\binom{u^2+v^2}{0} + s_2\binom{0}{u^2+v^2} \quad (4.89)$$

for parameters $k_1, \ldots, k_D, t_1, t_2, s_1, s_2 \in \mathbb{R}$. Thus, the radial, tangential and thin prism part of the distortion define linear function spaces. It is rad $\in V_{\text{rad}}$ with

$$V_{\text{rad}} := \text{span}\left(\binom{u(u^2+v^2)}{v(u^2+v^2)}, \binom{u(u^2+v^2)^2}{v(u^2+v^2)^2}, \ldots, \binom{u(u^2+v^2)^D}{v(u^2+v^2)^D}\right), \quad (4.90)$$

$$\delta_{\text{tan}} \in V_{\text{tan}} := \text{span}\left(\binom{3u^2+v^2}{2uv}, \binom{2uv}{u^2+3v^2}\right), \quad (4.91)$$

and
$$\delta_{\text{thp}} \in V_{\text{thp}} := \text{span}\left(\begin{pmatrix} u^2+v^2 \\ 0 \end{pmatrix}, \begin{pmatrix} 0 \\ u^2+v^2 \end{pmatrix}\right). \tag{4.92}$$

Furthermore, we assume that there is a linear subspace $V_r \subset \mathcal{P}(\mathbb{R}^2, \mathbb{R}^2)$, which is disjoint to V_{rad}, V_{tan}, and V_{thp}, with $r \in V_r$. For a simpler notation we abbreviate $\hat{p} = \begin{pmatrix} u \\ v \end{pmatrix}$ with $(u, v, 1)^t = \Pi_z(p)$ for a point $p = (x, y, z) \in \mathbb{R}^2 \times \mathbb{R} \setminus \{0\}$. Thus, we are looking for a polynomial $q \in V := V_{\text{rad}} \oplus V_{\text{tan}} \oplus V_{\text{thp}} \oplus V_r \subset \mathcal{P}(\mathbb{R}^2, \mathbb{R}^2)$ such that

$$\sum_{p \in \mathbf{P}} \left\| P \circ \begin{pmatrix} (\text{id} + q)(\hat{p}) \\ 1 \end{pmatrix} - i_p \right\|^2 \tag{4.93}$$

$$= \sum_{p \in \mathbf{P}} \left\| P \begin{pmatrix} \hat{p} + q(\hat{p}) \\ 1 \end{pmatrix} - i_p \right\|^2 \tag{4.94}$$

$$= \sum_{p \in \mathbf{P}} \left\| A(\hat{p}) + A(q(\hat{p})) + \begin{pmatrix} u_0 \\ v_0 \end{pmatrix} - i_p \right\|^2 \tag{4.95}$$

$$= \sum_{p \in \mathbf{P}} \| \underbrace{A(\hat{p}) + \begin{pmatrix} u_0 \\ v_0 \end{pmatrix} - i_p}_{=:-y_p} + A(q(\hat{p})) \|^2 \tag{4.96}$$

$$= \sum_{p \in \mathbf{P}} \| A(q(\hat{p})) - y_p \|^2 \tag{4.97}$$

becomes minimal.

This is a linear least squares problem: Let $q_1, \ldots, q_m$ be a base of V and let $\mathbf{P} = \{p_1, \ldots, p_n\}$. Then we need to minimize the error

$$(c_1, \ldots, c_m) \mapsto \sum_{p \in \mathbf{P}} \left\| A \left(\sum_{i=1}^m c_i q_i(\hat{p}) \right) - y_p \right\|^2 \tag{4.98}$$

$$= \left\| M_{q_1, \ldots, q_m} \begin{pmatrix} c_1 \\ c_2 \\ \vdots \\ c_m \end{pmatrix} - y \right\|^2 \tag{4.99}$$

with

$$M_{q_1,\ldots,q_m} := \begin{pmatrix} Aq_1(\hat{p}_1) & Aq_2(\hat{p}_1) & \cdots & Aq_m(\hat{p}_1) \\ Aq_1(\hat{p}_2) & Aq_2(\hat{p}_2) & \cdots & Aq_m(\hat{p}_2) \\ \vdots & \vdots & \ddots & \vdots \\ Aq_1(\hat{p}_n) & Aq_2(\hat{p}_n) & \cdots & Aq_m(\hat{p}_n) \end{pmatrix} \in \mathbb{R}^{2n \times m} \quad (4.100)$$

and

$$y := \begin{pmatrix} y_{p_1} \\ \vdots \\ y_{p_n} \end{pmatrix} = \begin{pmatrix} i_{p_1} - \begin{pmatrix} u_0 \\ v_0 \end{pmatrix} - A\hat{p}_1 \\ \vdots \\ i_{p_n} - \begin{pmatrix} u_0 \\ v_0 \end{pmatrix} - A\hat{p}_n \end{pmatrix} \in \mathbb{R}^{2n}. \quad (4.101)$$

The determination of the coefficients $c_1, \ldots, c_m$ of the optimal solution $\delta_0 = \mathrm{id} + \sum_{i=1}^{m} c_i q_i$ can be performed by standard techniques such as the pseudo-inverse, Givens rotations, or Householder transformations (see e.g. [PTVF92]).

Remark 4.6.2
In definition 2.4.1 (page 17) we demanded that a distortion model can be adjusted over a compact subset $D \subset \mathbb{R}^k$ to ensure a global minimum of the calibration. It is obvious that a distortion model, which can be coded as $\Delta = \mathrm{id} + V$ for a linear function space V with dimension k, can be adjusted over $\mathbb{R}^k$ without loosing the existence of a global minimum.

4.7 Camera calibration with distortion as a semi-linear problem

4.7.1 Parameter reduction by semi-linear optimization

Usually the final non-linear optimization over all camera parameters including the distortion parameters determines the complete camera mapping. In [GH05] it is shown that in the case of a radial distortion all other camera parameters determine the distortion parameters. Therefore, a calibration algorithm with a reduced set of parameters is proposed. Although this method was formulated and proven for an arbitrary number of radial distortion parameters, in practical applications it turned out that the approach in [GH05] is not numerically stable for more than three radial distortion parameters. This is due to an inversion of a matrix with an unstable rank.

The main result of the preceding section is that camera calibration w.r.t. the pinhole camera with distortion contains a linear least squares part, if the distortion can be expressed by a linear space of functions. In this case the parameters of P and T define the distortion completely. We call such a non-linear problem which includes a linear (least squares) part a *semi-linear problem*. As camera calibration is a semi-linear problem, we are able to decouple the distortion from the pinhole camera parameters in the calibration routine. This yields a reduction of the search space of the non-linear optimization problem.

Let $M \in \mathbb{R}^{m \times n}$ with $m > n$ and $y \in \mathbb{R}^m$. Then a minimum $x_0 \in \mathbb{R}^n$ of the least squares problem $x \mapsto \|Mx - y\|^2$ for $b \in \mathbb{R}^m$ is well known to be found by the (Moore-Penrose) pseudo-inverse: It is $x_0 = (M^t M)^{-1} M^t y$ if $M^t M$ is invertible. For the residuum $r = \|Mx_0 - y\|$ the following holds:

$$
\begin{align}
r^2 &= \langle Mx_0 - y | Mx_0 - y \rangle \tag{4.102}\\
&= (Mx_0 - y)^t(Mx_0 - y) \tag{4.103}\\
&= x_0^t M^t M x_0 - 2x_0^t M^t y + y^t y \tag{4.104}\\
&= -\underbrace{y^t M}_{=:B} \underbrace{(M^t M)^{-1}}_{=:D^{-1}} \underbrace{M^t y}_{=:C} + \underbrace{y^t y}_{=:A} \tag{4.105}\\
&= A - BD^{-1}C \tag{4.106}\\
&= \det(A - BD^{-1}C) \tag{4.107}\\
&= \frac{1}{\det(D)} \det\begin{pmatrix} A & B \\ C & D \end{pmatrix} \tag{4.108}\\
&= \frac{1}{\det(M^t M)} \det\begin{pmatrix} y^t y & y^t M \\ M^t y & M^t M \end{pmatrix}. \tag{4.109}
\end{align}
$$

The second last equation follows by

$$
\det\begin{pmatrix} A & B \\ C & D \end{pmatrix} = \det(D)\det(A - BD^{-1}C) \tag{4.110}
$$

which holds for non-singular D (see e.g. Handbook of Matrices, [Lüt97], p. 50).

With (4.100) and (4.101) the matrix $M = M_{q_1,\ldots,q_m}$ and the vector y are functions in the parameters of the pinhole camera mapping without distortion. Therefore, the residuum r^2 itself is a function in the parameters of the image transformation and the extrinsic camera parameters. Since r^2 is the error function w.r.t. the projective error, it can be applied as an error function with a reduced set of parameters: the number of parameters of r^2 is independent from the distortion model as long as the distortion can be modeled by a vector space. Therefore, we call r^2 the *reduced parameters calibration function*.

4.7.2 Experimental results

For our experimental results we apply Zhang's initial solution to obtain a closed form estimate for the image transformation P and the extrinsic parameters T of each planar calibration pattern.

To show the benefit of decoupling the distortion part from the non-linear optimization we use three different setups: a CCD-camera with lens with a focal length of 8.5 mm and aperture 1:1.5, an off-the-shelf web-camera, and a CCD-camera with a focal length of 4.2 mm lens and aperture 1:1.6 , referred to as *normal*, *webcam*, and *wide angle lens* setup. For the normal setup we used 380 model points at 13 positions and for both other setups 380 model points at 4 positions. It should be noticed that in the case of the wide angle setup the distortion model is not sufficient (see *e.g.* [SA96]). All figures in this section show the number of iterations vs. the root mean square error of the objective function w.r.t. the projective error. We applied the projective camera calibration error function as defined in section 3.4.1 and the reduced parameters calibration function r^2. In the figures we refer to r^2 as "Reduced Parameters". For the projective camera calibration error function (to which we refer as standard objective function in the text and "Full Parameters" in the figures) we use the result of Zhang as presented in 4.6.2 as initial value for the radial distortion parameters. For any other distortion parameter we set zero as initial value.

For the tests we apply the several non-linear optimization algorithms: the BFGS algorithm, the method of Levenberg-Marquardt and the classic Gauss-Newton approach. In our tests we show the root mean square error for at most 100 iterations of the particular non-linear optimization algorithm. In some experiments - especially with the Levenberg-Marquardt routine - the nonlinear optimization stops before this number of iterations is reached. In the case of the pinhole camera model with a radial distortion with two parameters our implementation of the parameter reduction according to Graf ([GH05]) coincides with proposed parameter reduction in every case.

In all figures of the remaining section the first entry represents the result after the first iteration of the non-linear optimization routine. In every case the root mean square error of the reduced parameters calibration function r^2 is lower than for the standard objective function for the first step. This should be no surprise, since the semi-linear approach determines the optimal distortion in every step. This is not true for the standard objective function.

4.7.2.1 Results for the normal setup

For the normal setup we test three configurations: first a pinhole camera with two radial distortion parameters, second a pinhole camera with two radial distortion parameters and an additional tangential distortion, and third a pinhole camera with four radial distortion parameters and an additional tangential distortion is calibrated.

In all experiments the root mean square error of the reduced parameter function r^2 was lower than the root mean square error of the standard objective function.

In Figure 4.8, Figure 4.9, and Figure 4.10 we show the resulting progresses of the two objective functions w.r.t. to a pinhole camera with a radial distortion term with two parameters. In particular for the non-linear optimization with the Gauss-Newton algorithm, which performs best for this configuration, the gain of the parameter reduction is most significant.

It is remarkable that for the other remaining configurations (two radial parameters and tangential distortion or four tangential parameters and tangential distortion) neither the BFGS algorithm nor the Levenberg-Marquardt reach a comparable result (see Figure 4.11, Figure 4.12, Figure 4.14, and Figure 4.15). Only the non-linear optimization with the Gauss-Newton algorithm (Figure 4.13 and Figure 4.16) performs better for the configurations with more parameters. However, the improvement in the root means square error is insignificant compared to the first configuration.

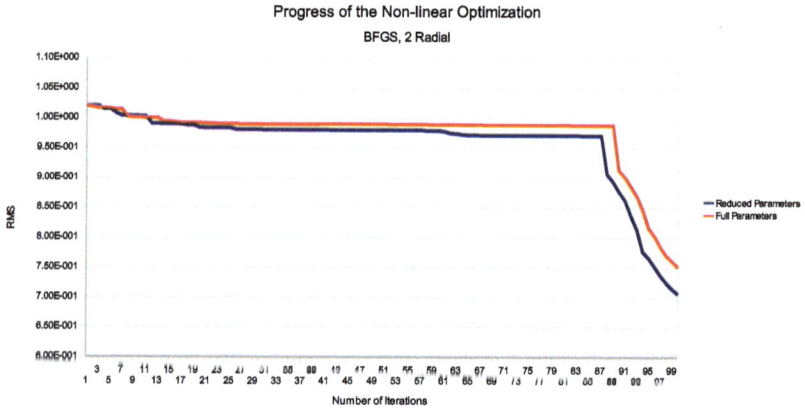

Figure 4.8: Root mean square error of the objective functions for the normal setup with two radial distortion parameters (non-linear optimization with BFGS).

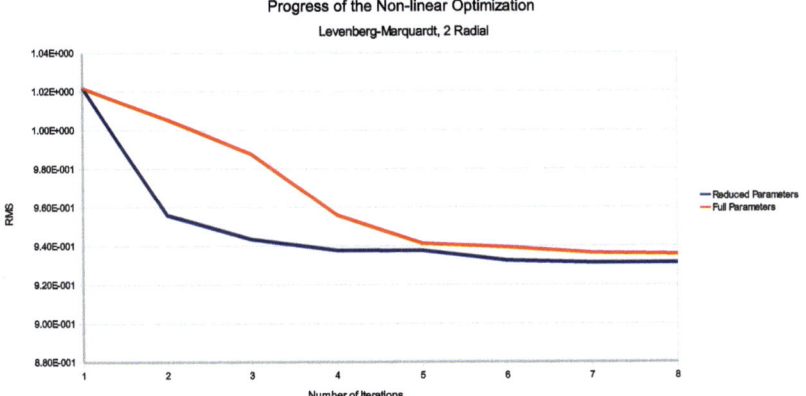

Figure 4.9: Root mean square error of the objective functions for the normal setup with two radial distortion parameters (non-linear optimization with Levenberg-Marquardt).

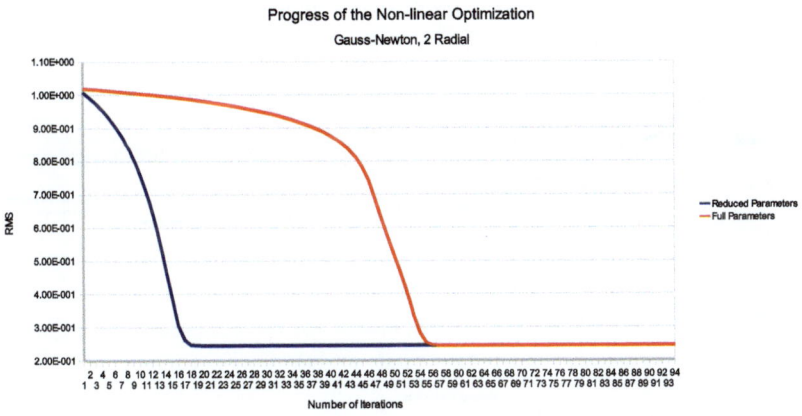

Figure 4.10: Root mean square error of the objective functions for the normal setup with two radial distortion parameters (non-linear optimization with Gauss-Newton).

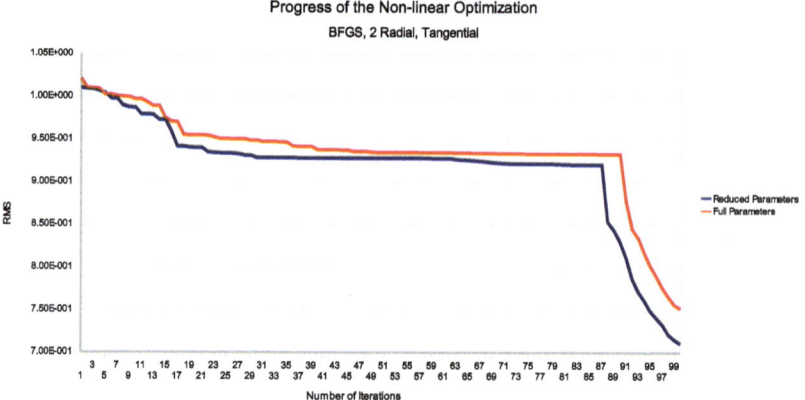

Figure 4.11: Root mean square error of the objective functions for the normal setup with two radial distortion parameters and a tangential distortion (non-linear optimization with BFGS).

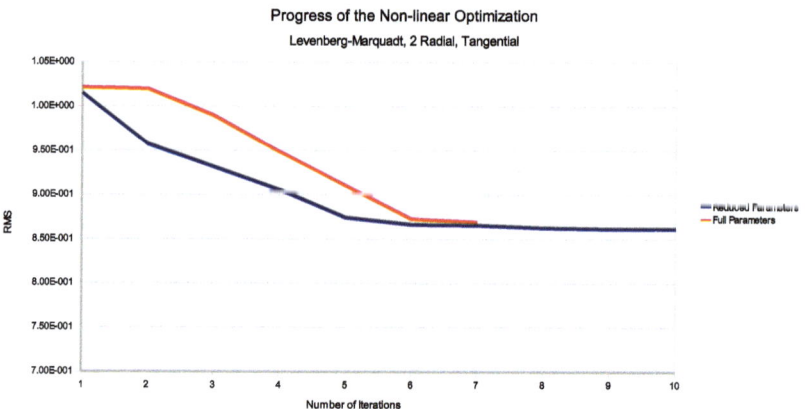

Figure 4.12: Root mean square error of the objective functions for the normal setup with two radial distortion parameters and a tangential distortion (non-linear optimization with Levenberg-Marquardt).

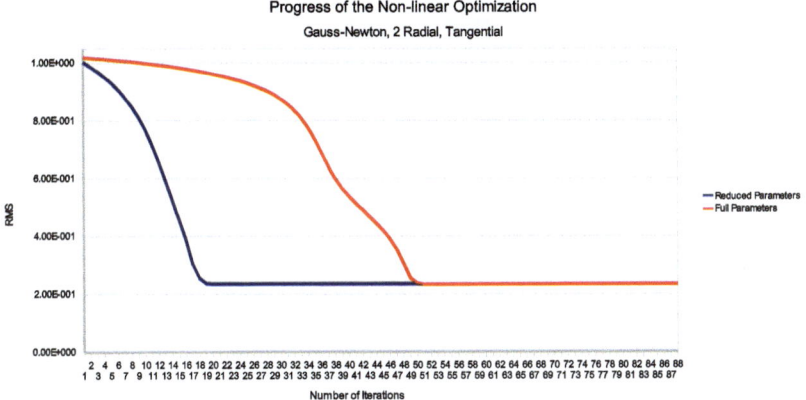

Figure 4.13: Root mean square error of the objective functions for the normal setup with two radial distortion parameters and a tangential distortion (non-linear optimization with Gauss-Newton).

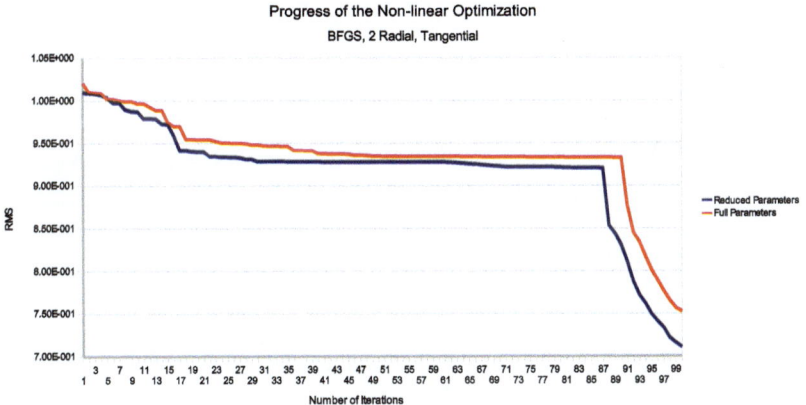

Figure 4.14: Root mean square error of the objective functions for the normal setup with four radial distortion parameters and a tangential distortion (non-linear optimization with BFGS).

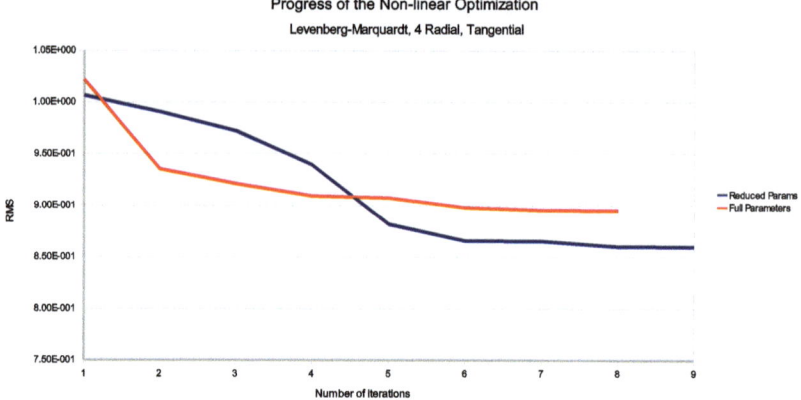

Figure 4.15: Root mean square error of the objective functions for the normal setup with four radial distortion parameters and a tangential distortion (non-linear optimization with Levenberg-Marquardt).

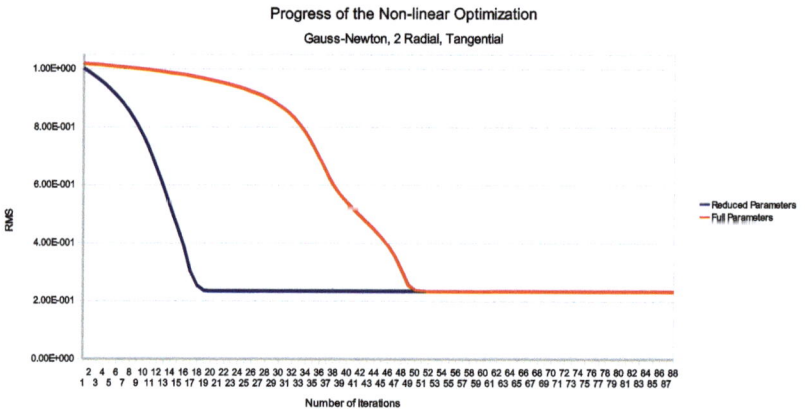

Figure 4.16: Root mean square error of the objective functions for the normal setup with four radial distortion parameters and a tangential distortion (non-linear optimization with Gauss-Newton).

4.7.2.2 Results for the webcam setup

For the test with the webcam setup we test two different camera models: first a pinhole camera with two radial distortion parameters, second a pinhole camera with four radial distortion parameters and an additional tangential distortion is calibrated.

In Figure 4.17, Figure 4.18, and Figure 4.19 we show the resulting progresses of the two objective functions w.r.t. to a pinhole camera with two radial distortion parameters. Except for the Levenberg-Marquardt experiment (Figure 4.18) the objective function for the reduced parameter set has a lower root mean square error in every iteration. Note that the Levenberg-Marquardt algorithm delivers the worst result for both objective functions.

If we apply a camera model with four radial distortion parameters and a tangential distortion the advantage of the reduced parameters calibration function r^2 becomes more visible (see Figure 4.20 and Figure 4.22). Since the Levenberg-Marquardt algorithm does not deliver a satisfactory result for both objective functions, Figure 4.21 does not contradict this observation.

In contrast to the normal setup the improvement of a camera model with more parameters is significant.

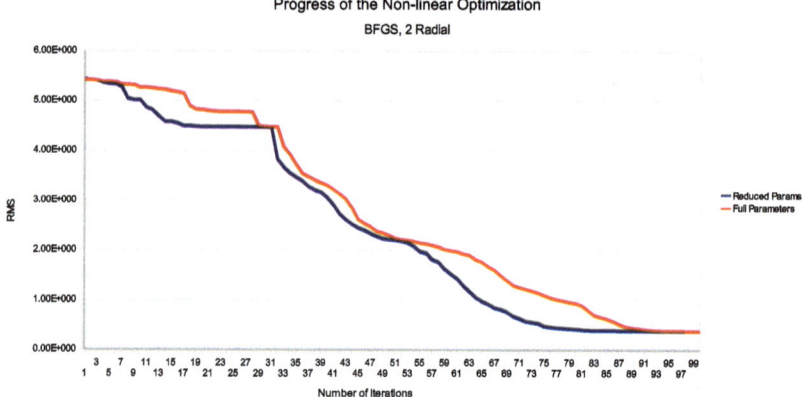

Figure 4.17: Root mean square error of the objective functions for the webcam setup with two radial distortion parameters (non-linear optimization with BFGS). The error curve following [GH05] coincides with the proposed reduced parameters approach.

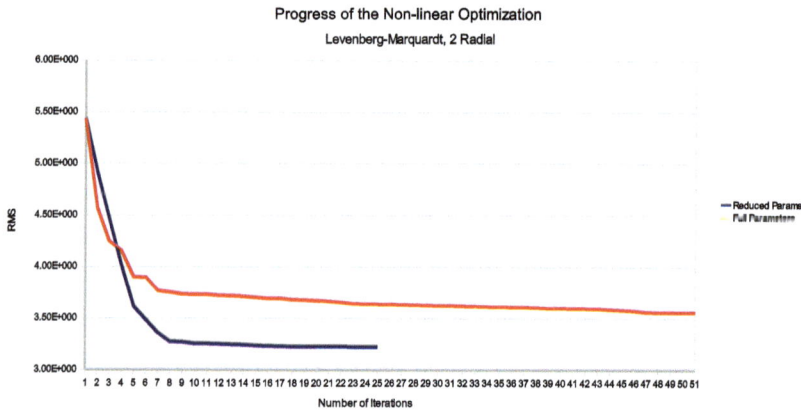

Figure 4.18: Root mean square error of the objective functions for the webcam setup with two radial distortion parameters (non-linear optimization with Levenberg-Marquardt). The error curve following [GH05] coincides with the proposed reduced parameters approach.

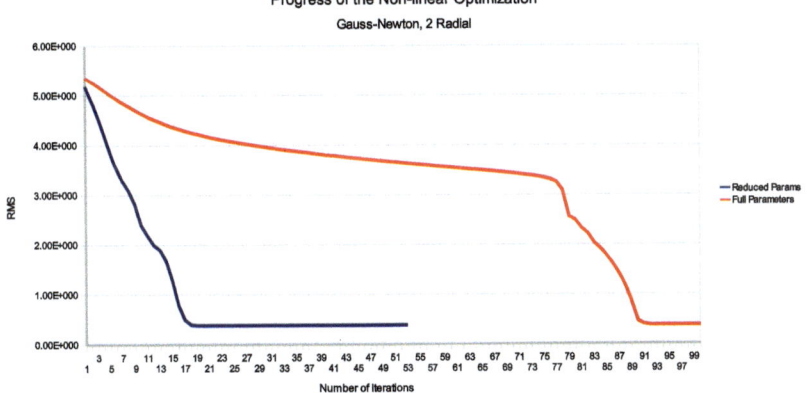

Figure 4.19: Root mean square error of the objective functions for the webcam setup with two radial distortion parameters (non-linear optimization with Gauss-Newton). The error curve following [GH05] coincides with the proposed reduced parameters approach.

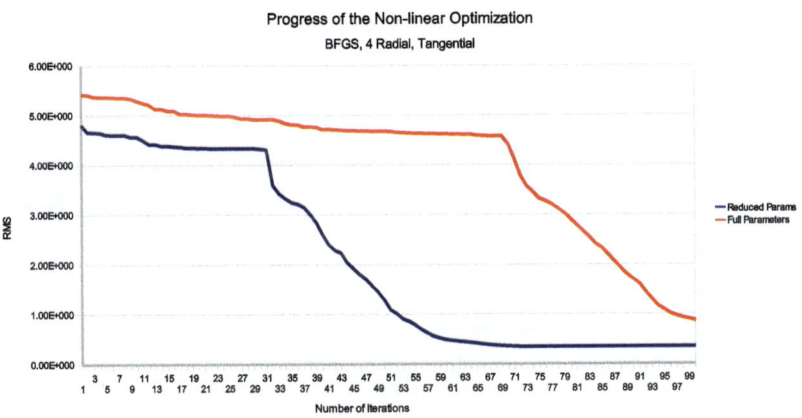

Figure 4.20: Root mean square error of the objective functions for the webcam setup with four radial distortion parameters and a tangential distortion (non-linear optimization with BFGS).

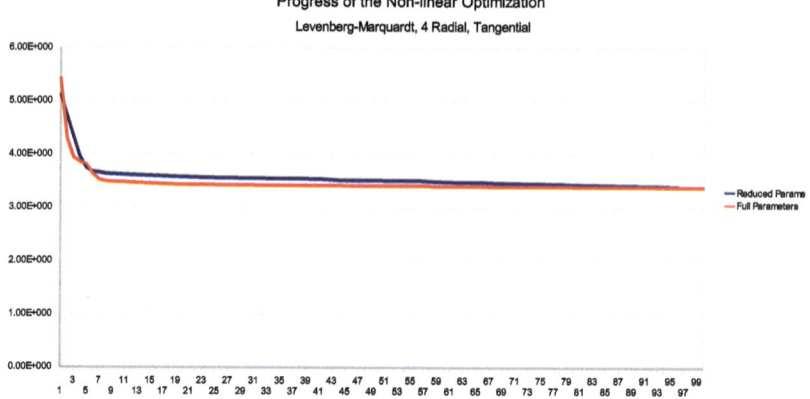

Figure 4.21: Root mean square error of the objective functions for the webcam setup with four radial distortion parameters and a tangential distortion (non-linear optimization with Levenberg-Marquardt).

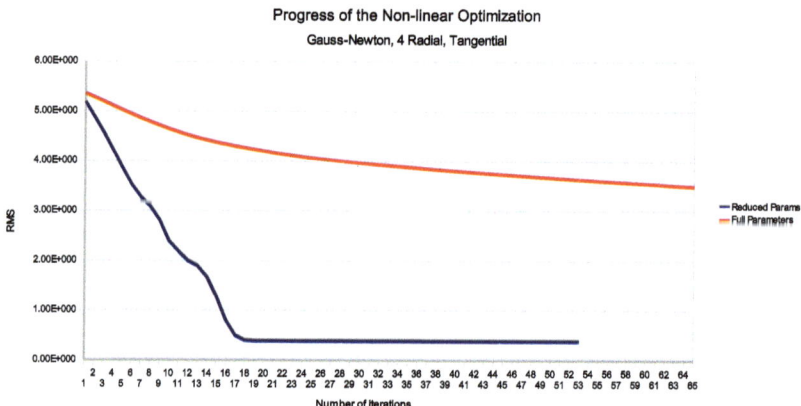

Figure 4.22: Root mean square error of the objective functions for the webcam setup with four radial distortion parameters and a tangential distortion (non-linear optimization with Gauss-Newton).

4.7.2.3 Results for the wide angle setup

For the wide angle setup we only apply the pinhole camera with four radial distortion parameters and an additional tangential distortion. For all non-linear optimization algorithms the parameter reduced objective function r^2 performs better than the standard objective function (see Figure 4.23, Figure 4.24, and Figure 4.25). It is remarkable that for the Gauss-Newton algorithm only the proposed reduced semi-linear optimization yields a significant improvement in the error function (see Figure 4.25).

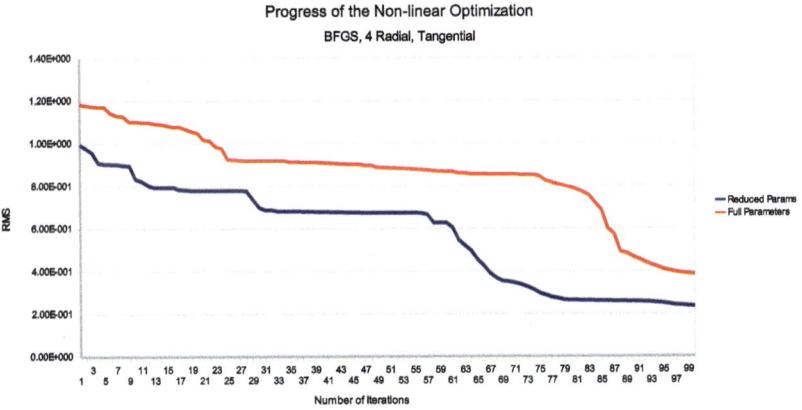

Figure 4.23: Root mean square error of the objective functions for the wide angle setup with four radial distortion parameters and a tangential distortion (non-linear optimization with BFGS).

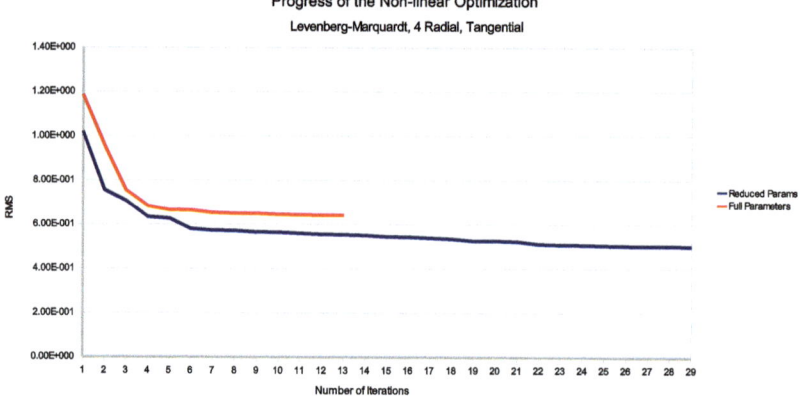

Figure 4.24: Root mean square error of the objective functions for the wide angle setup with four radial distortion parameters and a tangential distortion (non-linear optimization with Levenberg-Marquardt).

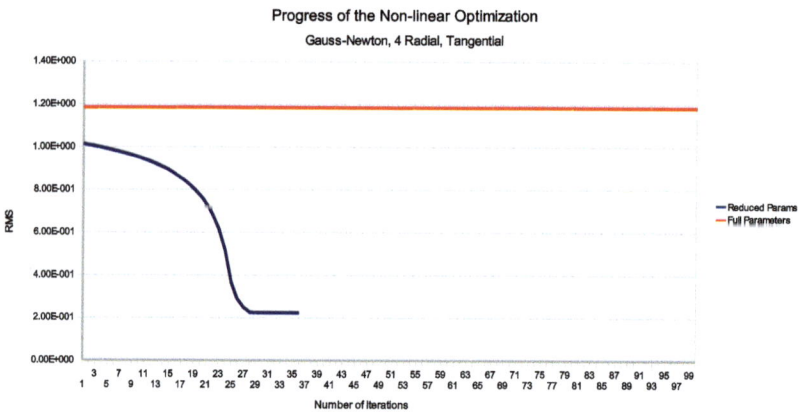

Figure 4.25: Root mean square error of the objective functions for the wide angle setup with four radial distortion parameters and a tangential distortion (non-linear optimization with Gauss-Newton).

Chapter 5

Calibration of a stereo camera system

5.1 Introduction

In the following we call a system of two cameras observing the same scene from different positions a *stereo camera system*. A simple way to calibrate such a stereo camera system is to calibrate each camera separately. However, the cameras of a stereo setup are not independent, since they look at the same scene from different positions. Usually this connection is utilized to solve the correspondence problem. Moreover, for pinhole cameras without distortion it can be described by a matrix called the *fundamental matrix*. In the next section we introduce the fundamental matrix and the constraint that a corresponding point can be determined up to a line. The theoretical background of this concept depends on the projective nature of the pinhole camera model. Any distortion of the camera is usually not mentioned in the theoretic framework. However, in optical measurement problems such distortions can not be neglected. Therefore, we define a generalized approach to the connection between two images and supply a way to calibrate a stereo camera setup which fulfills this generalized approach.

5.2 Epipolar geometry

The linear relationship between corresponding points in a stereo pinhole camera setup has been studied well (see *e.g.* [Fau93, Zha96a, LF96, CZZF97] or [HZ00]). Therefore, we sketch only some main results and introduce the basic terms in this section.

Throughout this section, we consider two pinhole cameras $\tilde{K}_l = \tilde{P}_l \begin{pmatrix} I_3 & 0 \end{pmatrix}$ and $\tilde{K}_r = \tilde{P}_r \begin{pmatrix} R & t \end{pmatrix}$ in a homogeneous frame of reference. Therefore, $\tilde{P}_l, \tilde{P}_r$ are upper triangular matrices with positive entries and $(\tilde{P}_l)_{3,3} = (\tilde{P}_r)_{3,3} = 1$ and $R \in SO_3, t \in \mathbb{R}^3$. In the following we refer to $\tilde{K}_l$ as the left camera and to $\tilde{K}_r$ as the right camera. Notice that the camera coordinate system of the left camera coincides with the reference coordinate system. The skew-symmetric matrix

$$Q_t := \begin{pmatrix} 0 & -t_3 & t_2 \\ t_3 & 0 & -t_1 \\ -t_2 & t_1 & 0 \end{pmatrix} \tag{5.1}$$

allows us to describe the cross product of a vector $x \in \mathbb{R}^3$ with $t = (t_1, t_2, t_3)^t \in \mathbb{R}^3$ as a matrix operation: It is $Q_t x = t \times x$ for all $x \in \mathbb{R}^3$. We need this to introduce the fundamental and the essential matrix.

Definition 5.2.1 (fundamental matrix, essential matrix)
Let $\tilde{K}_l = \tilde{P}_l \begin{pmatrix} I_3 & 0 \end{pmatrix}, \tilde{K}_r = \tilde{P}_r \begin{pmatrix} R & t \end{pmatrix}$ be two pure pinhole cameras in homogeneous representation (with $\tilde{P}_l, \tilde{P}_r, \begin{pmatrix} R & t \end{pmatrix}$ as defined above). Then the matrix

$$F = (\tilde{P}_r^{-1})^t Q_t R \tilde{P}_l^{-1} \in \mathbb{R}^{3 \times 3} \tag{5.2}$$

is called fundamental matrix. The matrix

$$E := Q_t R \tag{5.3}$$

is called essential matrix.

Let now $i_{p_l} = (u_l, v_l)^t$ be the observation of an object in the image of the left camera $\tilde{K}_l$ and $i_{p_r} = (u_r, v_r)^t$ the observation of the same object point in the image of the right camera $\tilde{K}_r$. In this case i_{p_l} and i_{p_r} are called *corresponding points*. For two corresponding points i_{p_l}, i_{p_r} in the image of the left and right camera

$$\tilde{i}_{p_r}^t F \tilde{i}_{p_l} = 0 \tag{5.4}$$

holds (see *e.g.* [HZ00]). Obviously, for a given observation in the image of $\tilde{K}_l$ any possible position of a corresponding point in the image of $\tilde{K}_l$ is constrained by (5.4) to a line called the *epipolar line*. This constraint is called *epipolar constraint*. It allows to narrow down the problem to detect corresponding points in images of a stereo camera system.

An epipolar line can be seen as a projection of the re-projected point in the image of the other camera. Therefore, the epipolar line can be obtained by the projection of any point along the re-projection. Thus, the projection of the camera center is on every epipolar line. (In the projective sense: *i.e.* for parallel image planes the projection of the camera center is a point at infinity on the epipolar line). Therefore, all epipolar lines intersect in one point called *epipole* (see Figure 5.1), which may be a point at infinity. The epipole is the projection of the camera center of the other camera.

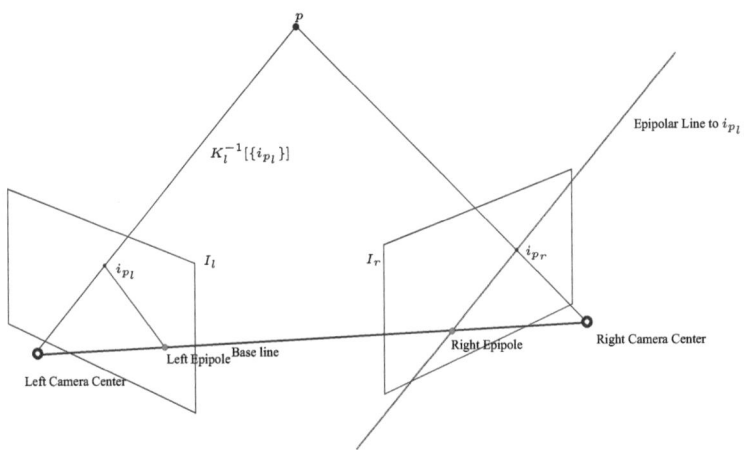

Figure 5.1: Sketch of the epipolar constraint.

The essential matrix E lifts this relation to the plane $\{z = 1\}$ w.r.t. the respective camera coordinate system: for $x_l = P_l^{-1}(i_{p_l})$ and $x_r = P_r^{-1}(i_{p_r})$

$$x_l^t E x_r = 0 \tag{5.5}$$

holds. Therefore, the description of the epipolar constraint by the essential matrix allows to handle a camera mapping with distortion:

Let $K_l = P_l \circ \delta_l \in \mathcal{I}_\Delta$ and $K_r = P_r \circ \delta_r \circ T \in \mathcal{K}_\Delta$ be two pinhole cameras with distortion. Then for $x_l = \tilde{\delta}_l^{-1} \circ P_l^{-1}(i_{p_l})$ and $x_r = \tilde{\delta}_r^{-1} \circ P_r^{-1}(i_{p_r})$ with $\delta_l, \delta_r \in \Delta$

$$x_l^t E x_r = 0 \tag{5.6}$$

must hold for corresponding points i_{p_l}, i_{p_r} (see section 2.5 for the problems concerning the correct definition of $\delta_l^{-1}, \delta_r^{-1}$). x_l and x_r are the un-distorted coordinates of the observed points w.r.t. the camera coordinate system. Some approaches can be found to formulate the un-distortion by a linear mapping in extended coordinates. In [CF05a] and [CF05b] Claus and Fitzgibbon introduce a simple but effective distortion model called *rational function lens distortion*. With respect to this distortion model they achieve a linear relation between corresponding points in extended coordinates (in a six dimensional space). Even though this relation is described w.r.t. the camera coordinate system (instead of the image coordinate system), they call the linear relation *lifted fundamental matrix*. With 36 corresponding points it is possible to determine the un-distortion mapping (within the rational function lens distortion) up to a projective mapping. It should be pointed out that this approach is based on a special distortion model which was generated to obtain a linear relation between corresponding points. Another special distortion model for this purpose is proposed by Barreto and Daniilidis in [BD05]. In [Gra08] Graf proposes the *radial essential matrix*, which allows to determine the un-distortion linear within the radial distortion model in extended coordinates using corresponding points.

5.3 Epipolar Curves

A natural way to determine the epipolar line in the image I_r of the right camera for a point $i_{p_l} \in I_l$, the image of the left camera, is to select points in $K_l^{-1}(\{i_{p_l}\})$ and project them by K_r on I_r. Assuming a pinhole camera model, the projected points must lie on the epipolar line belonging to i_{p_l} in I_r. Figure 5.1 sketches this situation for the pinhole camera model without distortion.

This approach to the epipolar line defines a constraint which a correct calibration of a stereo camera system should fulfill also for pinhole cameras with distortion. Figure 5.2 sketches this situation for the pinhole camera model with distortion.

Definition 5.3.1 (Generalized Epipolar Constraint)
Let $p \in \mathbb{R}^3$ be an object point in the reference coordinate system such that p can be observed by both cameras K_l and K_r. Let $i_{p_l} \in I_l$ and $i_{p_r} \in I_r$ be the observations of p in the images I_l and I_r of the left and right camera, then

$$\operatorname{dist}(i_{p_l}, \overline{K_l(K_r^{-1}[\{i_{p_r}\}] \setminus \{z = 0\})}) = 0 \quad \text{and} \tag{5.7}$$

$$\operatorname{dist}(i_{p_r}, \overline{K_r(K_l^{-1}[\{i_{p_l}\}] \setminus T_l^{-1}(\{z = 0\}))}) = 0 \tag{5.8}$$

should hold. We call these constraints the generalized epipolar constraints.

Remark 5.3.2 (K, K^{-1} as relations)
The careful reader may have noticed a discrepancy to the definition of the inverse camera mapping: in section 2.5 we constrained the domain of the camera mapping such that the distortion mapping becomes injective. In contrast, in this section the camera mapping is treated as a relation. Thus, we do not need such a restriction of the input data as defined in 2.5 to obtain an inverse mapping.

Note that $\overline{K_l\left[K_r^{-1}[\{i_{p_l}\}] \setminus \{z=0\}\right]}$ and $\overline{K_r\left[K_l^{-1}[\{i_{p_l}\}] \setminus T_l^{-1}[\{z=0\}]\right]}$ are not always straight lines in I_l and I_r. In fact, they are only straight lines if no distortion is modeled in the camera mappings.

In the case of a distorted camera projection $\overline{K_r\left[K_l^{-1}[\{i_{p_l}\}] \setminus T_l^{-1}[\{z=0\}]\right]}$ can be called *epipolar curve* for the image point i_{p_l} and (see Figure 5.2). Consequently, we call $\overline{K_l\left[K_r^{-1}[\{i_{p_l}\}] \setminus \{z=0\}\right]}$ the epipolar curve for i_{p_r}.

In [HGP04] we describe epipolar curves as sets in the image planes of the involved cameras by approximating the set by a graph of a quadratic function, although this does not be hold theoretically. In [Zha96b] Zhang claims that the set $K_r\left[K_l^{-1}[\{i_{p_r}\}]\right]$ is a cubic curve when merely considering a radial distortion with one coefficient ($\Delta_{r,1}$). In [Gra08] Graf shows that for a radial distortion with D coefficients ($\Delta_{r,D}$) the epipolar curve is the zero set of a bivariate polynomial with degree $2D+1$ in the plane $\{z=1\}$ w.r.t. to each respective camera coordinate system.

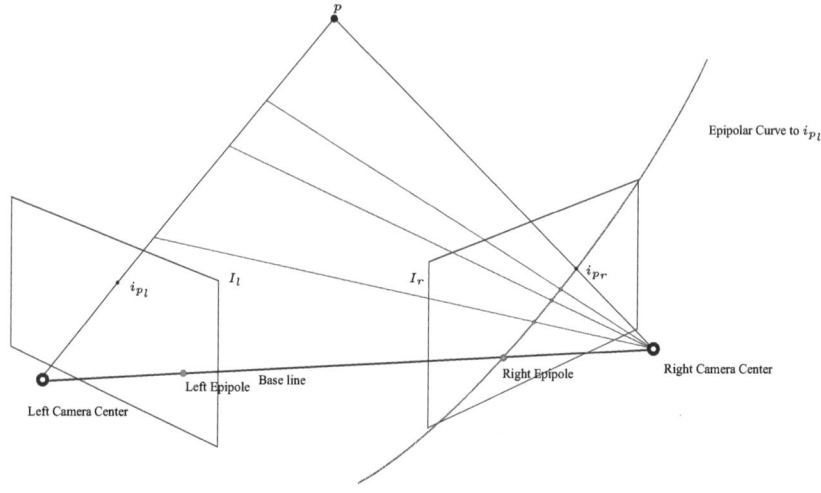

Figure 5.2: Sketch of an epipolar curve.

5.4 Stereo camera calibration with multiple targets

One way to calibrate the extrinsic parameters of a stereo setup with two cameras $K_l = B_l \circ T_l$ and $K_r = B_r \circ T_r$ with $B_l, B_r \in \mathcal{I}_\Delta, T_l, T_r \in \mathcal{T}(\mathbb{R}^3, \mathbb{R}^3)$ is to calculate the transformations T_l, T_r of each camera to the calibration pattern separately. In this case the reference coordinate system is defined by the calibration plate. For many applications (see *e.g.* [BKH07]) this procedure is satisfactory. To obtain a higher accuracy, multiple positions of the calibration target should be applied. Hence, a fixed reference coordinate system has to be chosen. A suitable choice is to put the reference coordinate system in one of the cameras. This is why we, without loss of generality, define the camera coordinate system of the left camera as the reference coordinate system. This leaves $K_l = B_l \circ \text{id} = B_l$ for the left camera.

Therefore, we only have to determine the transformation from the left to the right camera. Let $T_{l,C}$ be the transformation of the left camera to the calibration plate and $T_{r,C}$ the transformation of the right camera to the calibration plate. Then the transformation T_r from the reference coordinate system to the right camera coordinates system can be determined by $(T_{r,C})^{-1} \circ T_{l,C}$ (see Figure 5.3). This value can be determined independently of the position of the calibration plate, as long as the plate is visible for both cameras.

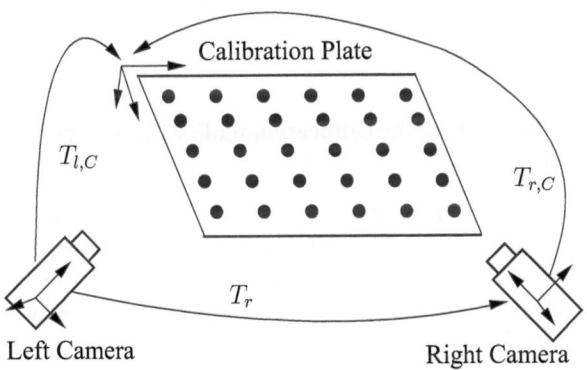

Figure 5.3: Stereo setup: Left and right camera, transformations to the calibration plate.

5.5 Extrinsic stereo camera calibration with generalized epipolar constraints

When we are only interested in the transformation T_r from the camera coordinate system of the left camera to the right camera coordinate system, we can treat the intrinsic camera parameters B_l, B_r of the left and the right camera as black boxes. Let $\mathbf{P} \subset \mathbb{R}^3$ be the model of our calibration pattern. Each observed position of the calibration pattern defines a set of points in the reference coordinate system that is related to the model $\mathbf{P}$ by a transformation which must only be known during the calibration process.

5.5.1 A two step algorithm

In [HGP04] we presented an algorithm which uses the Euclidean error to constrain the transformation between the two camera coordinate systems according to the generalized epipolar constraint.

The proposed algorithm uses two steps:

i. Determine the positions $C_1, \ldots, C_n$ of a set of observed calibration patterns w.r.t. the reference coordinate system defined by the left camera.

ii. Determine the position of the right camera w.r.t. all points calculated in step i.

i. Calculate the positions of the calibration plate with respect to the reference coordinate system

Let $C_1, \ldots, C_n$ be n positions of the calibration pattern with respect to the reference coordinate system which are observed by both cameras. We estimate the positions of $C_1, \ldots, C_n$ w.r.t. the left camera K_l. In fact, the first step is a pose determination for n positions of the calibration pattern. This can be done w.r.t. the projective error, but also w.r.t. the Euclidean error. Note that this step is a non-linear optimization. An initial value can be estimated according to section 4.5. Each $k \in \{1, \ldots, n\}$ and each point $p \in \mathbf{P}$ corresponds exactly to one point $c_p \in C_k$. And each $c_p \in C_k$ corresponds exactly to one image point $i_{p_l} \in I_l$ observed by the left camera, and exactly to one image point $i_{p_r} \in I_r$ observed by the right camera. For ideally calibrated cameras, $K_l(c_p) = i_{p_l}$

and $K_r(c_p) = i_{p_r}$ should hold. This means that the generalized epipolar constraint is fulfilled, because with $K_l(c_p) = i_{p_l}$ it is $c_p \in K_l^{-1}[\{i_{p_l}\}]$ and therefore $i_{p_r} = K_r(c_p) \in K_r\left[K_l^{-1}[\{i_{p_l}\}] \setminus T_r^{-1}[\{z=0\}]\right]$ (see definition 5.3.1).

Instead of measuring the error to the epipolar curve in the image ("$i_{p_r} \in K_r\left[K_l^{-1}[\{i_{p_l}\}] \setminus T_r^{-1}[\{z=0\}]\right]$") we can also penalize the distance in 3D ("$c_p \in K_l^{-1}[\{i_{p_l}\}]$"). This means that, instead of the standard projective error, we use the Euclidean error as defined in section 3.3. For a simpler notation we define the viewing line defined by each image point as $l_{i_{p_l}} := \overline{B_l^{-1}[\{i_{p_l}\}]}$ for the left camera and $l_{i_{p_r}} := \overline{B_r^{-1}[\{i_{p_r}\}]}$ for the right camera. Therefore, the first step is to determine the transformation T_k of the model $\mathbf{P}$ to C_k by minimizing

$$\begin{aligned}\mathcal{T}(\mathbb{R}^3, \mathbb{R}^3) &\to \mathbb{R}_+ \\ T &\mapsto \sum_{p \in \mathbf{P}} \text{dist}_3(T(p), l_{i_{p_l}})^2 \end{aligned} \quad (5.9)$$

The distance of a point p to a line $l_n = \{\lambda n \mid \lambda \in \mathbb{R}\}$ with direction $n \in \mathbb{R}^3$ with $\|n\| = 1$ containing the origin in Equation 5.9 can be calculated very easily by $\text{dist}_3(p, l_n)^2 = \|p\|^2 - \langle n|p\rangle^2$. Thus, the optimal movement T_k can be obtained efficiently by gradient based non-linear optimization algorithms like the algorithm of Levenberg and Marquardt or the BFGS-algorithm (see e.g. [PTVF92]).

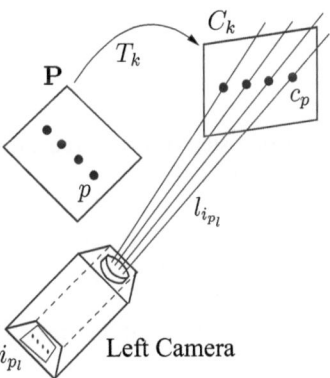

Figure 5.4: First step of the stereo calibration algorithm: calculate the k-th position of the observed model.

For $k \in \{1, \ldots, n\}$ we set $C_k := T_k(\mathbf{P})$. Figure 5.4 sketches the calculation of the position of the observed model w.r.t. the reference coordinate system.

ii. Calculate the position of the right camera

We obtained a set $C = C_1 \cup \cdots \cup C_n$ of 3D-points with respect to the reference coordinate system in the left camera. For each point $c_p \in C$ we know the corresponding observed point $i_{p_r} \in I_r$ in the image plane of the right camera. With $l_{p,r} = B_r^{-1}[\{i_{p_r}\}]$ we determine the position of the right camera by minimizing

$$\mathcal{T}(\mathbb{R}^3, \mathbb{R}^3) \to \mathbb{R}_+$$
$$T \mapsto \sum_{c_p \in C} \text{dist}_3(c_p, T(l_{p,r}))^2. \qquad (5.10)$$

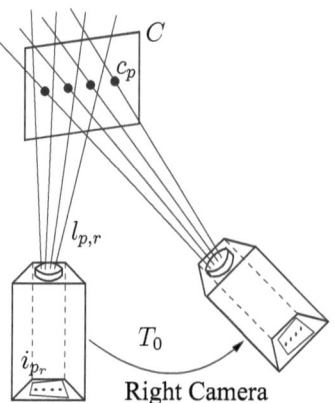

Figure 5.5: Sketch of the second step of the stereo calibration algorithm: determine the position of the right camera.

If T_0 is the result of minimizing (5.10) we set $T_r = T_0^{-1}$. Figure 5.5 sketches the calculation of the pose and orientation of the right camera with respect to the left camera.

Obviously, each step defines a non-linear optimization problem. Initial values can be obtained according to section 4.5.

5.5.2 A one step algorithm

As presented in [HGP04] we sketched an algorithm which consists of two steps in the previous section. Obviously, the error functions of the first step (5.9) and of the second step (5.10) can be combined in one error function.

For n observation of the model $\mathbf{P}$ by the left camera B_l and the right camera B_r the error function $\Psi_{ext} : \mathcal{T}(\mathbb{R}^3, \mathbb{R}^3)^{n+1} \to \mathbb{R}_+$ becomes

$$\Psi_{ext}(T_r, T_{C_1}, \ldots, T_{C_n}) = \qquad (5.11)$$

$$\sum_{k=1}^{n} \sum_{p \in \mathbf{P}} \text{dist}_3 \left(\overline{B_l^{-1}[\{i_{p_l}^{(k)}\}]}, T_{C_k}(p) \right)^2$$

$$+ \text{dist}_3 \left(\overline{(B_r \circ T_r)^{-1}[\{i_{p_r}^{(k)}\}]}, T_{C_k}(p) \right)^2$$

where $i_{p_l}^{(k)}$ and $i_{p_r}^{(k)}$ denotes the observation of point p in C_k in the image plane of the left camera and the right camera. As in the previous section, the positions $T_{C_1}, \ldots, T_{C_n}$ are only needed as intermediate results.

In most cases, both cameras of a stereo setup apply the same lens and imaging device. Thus, weighting both terms equally seems to be the best choice. In the case of two different optical systems, an individual weight for each term may be taken into account. Obviously, the minimization of Ψ_{ext} in (5.11) is a non-linear optimization problem. Initial values for $T_{C_1}, \ldots, T_{C_n}$ can be obtained according to section 4.5. An initial value for T_r can be determined following section 5.4.

5.5.3 Application and results

Epipolar lines - or in our case epipolar curves - can be used to overcome the correspondence problem for contours. For corresponding contours we can determine corresponding points by intersecting the contour with the epipolar curves determined by points on the other contour (see Figure 5.6).

In [HGP04] it is shown that for higher distorted cameras (*e.g.* common CCD cameras with cheap wide angle lenses) the extrinsic calibration of the stereo camera system with the proposed method reduces the reconstruction error by up to nearly 60 percent in comparison to the standard approach.

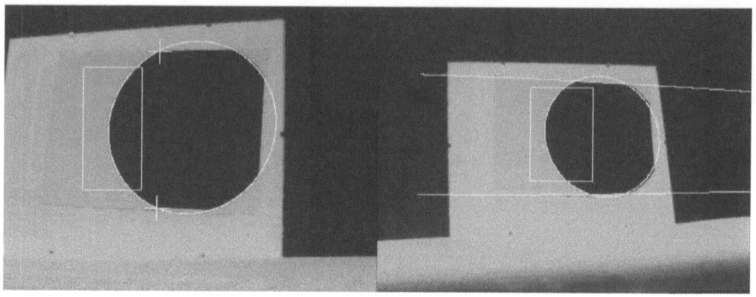

Figure 5.6: Epipolar curves: for two points marked by crosses in the left image, the epipolar curves are displayed in the image of the right camera. The intersection of curves with the extracted ellipse are taken as corresponding points to the marked right image points.

5.6 Extrinsic stereo camera calibration with respect to the projective error

The approach we proposed in section 5.5 avoids a complicated error function introduced by the generalized epipolar constraint by switching to the Euclidean error. However, we can also formulate an error function for the stereo camera calibration with generalized epipolar constraints w.r.t. the projective error.

Obviously, the projective approach to the generalized epipolar constraint itself defines not an appropriate error function to determine the transformation T_r of the right camera to the left camera.

Let us consider

$$\Psi_{\text{proj}}(T_r) = \sum_{p \in P} \text{dist}_2(i_{p_r}, \overline{(B_r \circ T_r) \left[B_l^{-1}[\{i_{p_l}\}] \setminus T_r^{-1}[\{z=0\}] \right]})^2$$
$$+ \text{dist}_2(i_{p_l}, \overline{B_l \left[(B_r \circ T_r)^{-1}[\{i_{p_r}\}] \setminus \{z=0\} \right]})^2 \quad (5.12)$$

for fixed inner camera parameters $B_l, B_r \in \mathcal{I}_\Delta$ of the left and right camera. Then, for a setup with parallel image planes and no distortion we obtain parallel epipolar lines (see Figure 5.7). In this case every transformation of the right camera along the baseline delivers the same value for Ψ_{Proj}.

Therefore, the determination of the optimal transformation minimizing (5.12) can only be applied to restricted transformations. For example, the translation part of the transformation could be fixed. Given a fixed transformation t_r and inner camera parameters B_l, B_r, a refinement of the rotation R_r of the right camera to the left camera should minimize the error function $\Psi_{\text{Rot}} : SO_3 \to \mathbb{R}_+$ defined by

$$\Psi_{\text{Rot}}(R) = \sum_{p \in P} \text{dist}_2(i_{p_r}, \overline{(B_r \circ T_{t_r}(R)) \left[B_l^{-1}[\{i_{p_l}\}] \setminus T_{t_r}^{-1}[\{z=0\}] \right]})^2$$
$$+ \text{dist}_2(i_{p_l}, \overline{B_l \left[(B_r \circ T_{t_r}(R))^{-1}[\{i_{p_r}\}] \setminus \{z=0\} \right]})^2 \quad (5.13)$$

where $T_{t_r}(R)$ denotes the transformation $x \mapsto Rx + t_r$.

A difficulty in applying the projective error is to calculate the distance of the observed image point to the epipolar curve. A simple way is to un-distort the observed image to achieve epipolar lines and then work on a pinhole stereo camera system. However, it is not fully understood how the un-distortion influences the reconstruction.

Another way is to approximate the set $\overline{K_r \left[K_l^{-1}[\{i_{p_l}\}] \setminus T_r^{-1}(\{z=0\}) \right]}$ by a function. As stated in section 5.3 the representation of the epipolar curve depends

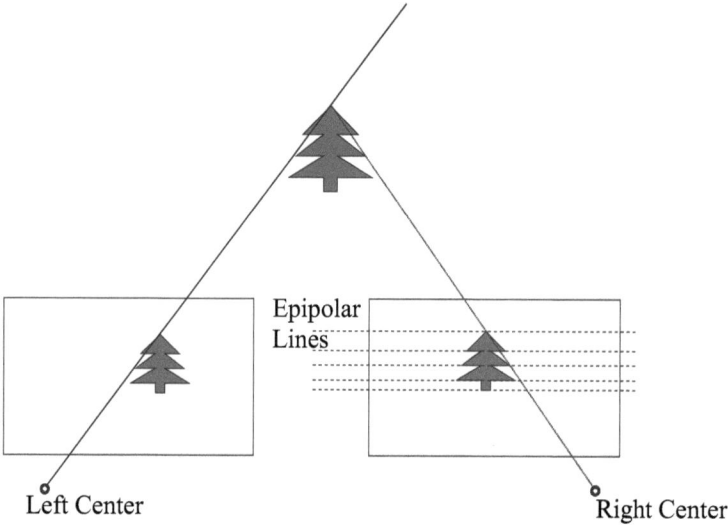

Figure 5.7: Sketch of a setup with parallel epipolar lines.

on the distortion model. However, for the treatment of the involved cameras as black boxes we assume that a local approximation of the observed projected data by a suitable function is sufficient for a further treatment. In Figure 5.6 we used parabolas to represent the curves. This was also done for the results in Figure 5.8 and in [HGP04]: we fitted a parabola to the projection of six points along the re-projection of the point of interest.

5.7 Extrinsic and intrinsic stereo camera calibration

In [Han06] we extended the methods of section 5.5 to the intrinsic camera parameters. The proceeding is very much the same, but instead of only optimizing the extrinsic parameters in each step the intrinsic parameters will also be optimized. For a given camera model $\mathcal{I}_\Delta$ we are looking for inner camera parameters $B_l, B_r \in \mathcal{I}_\Delta$ of the left and right camera, and a transformation $T_r \in \mathcal{T}(\mathbb{R}^3, \mathbb{R}^3)$ from the left to the right camera.

The error function Ψ_{ext} in (5.11) is extended to the error function Ψ_{stereo} : $\mathcal{I}_\Delta^2 \times \mathcal{T}(\mathbb{R}^3, \mathbb{R}^3)^{n+1}$ defined by

$$\Psi_{stereo}(B_l, B_r, T_{C_1}, \ldots, T_{C_n}, T_r) = \qquad (5.14)$$
$$\sum_{k=1}^{n} \sum_{p \in P} \text{dist}_3 \left(\overline{B_l^{-1}[\{i_{p_l}{}^{(k)}\}]}, T_{C_k}(p) \right)^2$$
$$+ \text{dist}_3 \left(\overline{(B_r \circ T_r)^{-1}[\{i_{p_r}{}^{(k)}\}]}, T_{C_k}(p) \right)^2$$

where $i_{p_l}{}^{(k)}$ and $i_{p_r}{}^{(k)}$ denotes the observation of point p in C_k in the image plane of the left camera and the right camera. For more details see [Han06]. Experiments in that article show that the reconstruction preserves well the distance of adjacent points on a calibration pattern (see Figure 5.8), whereas the planarity of the reconstructed points does not improve in comparison to the standard approach.

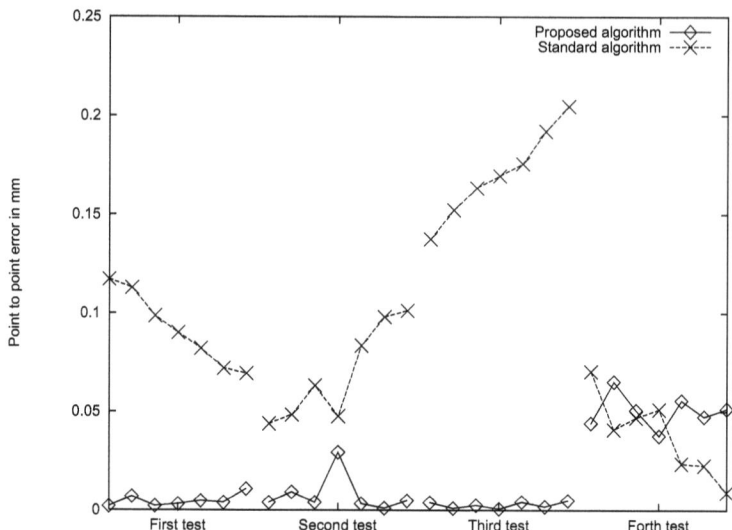

Figure 5.8: Result of a stereo reconstruction for an 8 mm stereo camera setup. We calibrated the stereo rig w.r.t. the standard algorithm (each camera on its own) and w.r.t. the proposed algorithm of section 5.7. We measured the average error to the distance of adjacent points on a reconstructed calibration pattern. The pattern with 9×5 points at distance of 5 cm to each other was located at 4 different positions: For the first, second and third test the calibration pattern was located at a distance of 1.6 m, 2 m and 2.4 m, nearly parallel to the stereo base. For the fourth test the pattern was held at an angle of about 45 deg to the stereo base at a distance of 1.6 m. The results for the classic calibration is very sensitive to the distance to the cameras. Although the proposed algorithm produces a stable result, both methods have difficulties with the position of the pattern diagonally to the image plane (fourth test).

Chapter 6
Non-standard camera models

6.1 Introduction

Like every model the pinhole camera is only an approximation to the real behavior of a camera. Even if we assume that the third order optics describe the observed camera mapping sufficiently, the first four monochromatic aberrations of a lens system (*i.e.* the first four of the five Seidel aberrations: spherical aberration, coma, astigmatism and field curvature) are not be modeled by the pinhole camera with distortion (see section 2.3).

Modelling the distortion as an in-plane mapping assumes that the observed distortion of a point does not depend on its distance to the lens plane. However, several experiments show that this assumption does not hold for real camera systems: In [Bro71, FS92, PWH97] or [HS07b] the authors noticed a change of camera parameters for calibrations performed at different distances. In photogrammetry it is well known that for the pinhole camera model the observed distortion varies not only with focusing the lens but also within the depth of field for a fixed focus (see *e.g.* [Atk96] or [Luh03]).

As already worked out in section 2.1, there is a determined object plane where the observation of an object appears sharp in the image. At any other position of the object the observation must appear blurred. In general, the image plane, *i.e.* the plane of the image sensor in the camera, does not coincide with the focal plane. This can be observed by a blurring of the image.

The problem of a focal plane out of the image plane is known in computer vision. In fact, there are many articles which propose to use the observed blurring to estimate the depth of an object (see section 2.1.2). Sometimes an extended approach to the calibration is proposed, where the camera parameters are a function of focus, iris and/or zoom (see [BAOM02]).

The problem of the observed depth dependent distortion was addressed more by the photogrammetrists than by the computer vision community. In [FB92], Fryer and Brown propose a linear combination of the focal length parameters determined at two different distances for images obtained at a distance in between. This leads to a camera model with a focal length depending on the depth of the observed object.

Fraser and Shortis suggest an analogous treatment of the distortion parameters in [FS92]. The parameters describing the linear combination of the distortion parameters have to be determined empirically. Dold ([Dol97]) presents a method to integrate parameters describing a linear relation between two sets of distortion parameters into the bundle adjustment. All these approaches include the depth-dependent treatment of the distortion into the calibration of all camera parameters.

One approach to explain a varying behavior of the camera mapping in depth is to analyze the feature point extraction. Apparently, the blurring is an effect which varies in depth and is not covered by the pinhole camera model. In the next section we present some standard routines to extract feature points for camera calibration. They all have in common that they assume a symmetric point spread function (PSF). However, as we explain in the third section, this assumption is not valid even within first order optics. In particular, it varies not only in depth but also in position.

To overcome the residual distortion which depends on the depth of the observed object, we present two approaches: a correction of the residual distortion by a correction spline which depends also on the depth of observed object, and a new distortion model in two-planes, which eases the pinhole assumption. In the fourth section we present the correction by a spline. We simply correct the error by an additional distortion mapping with a domain in $\mathbb{R}^3$. In contrast to the related work cited above, we separate the classic camera model with distortion from the depth-dependent correction of the feature point extraction. In the fifth section we present an approach which relaxes the pinhole assumption. We no longer demand that all re-projections meet in one point (the pinhole), but only lie near to a common point. We formulate such a camera model by introducing a two plane distortion model. To complete the representation of non-standard camera models we briefly sketch a common approach to a generic multi-plane camera in the sixth section.

Both approaches - the spline corrected camera and the two plane distortion model - do not determine the mapping of the object to a point spread function.

However, they correct the error of the feature point extraction caused by this phenomenon. Since the correction is coupled to the extraction, any reconstruction task will only improve if the same extraction method is used. Under this precondition both methods improve the stereo reconstruction, as we show in the seventh section of this chapter.

6.2 Feature point extraction

To achieve a high precision for reconstruction purposes it is not only the calibration target which must be well gauged, but also the extraction of the feature points in the acquired digital image must be performed accurately.

Typical calibration targets are checkerboards as used by Zhang in [Zha98] or in the Open Source Computer Vision library (see *e.g.* [Bra02]). In [HBK06] we used isolated black squares on a uniform background, which are arranged in a regular rectangular grid.

6.2.1 Standard feature point extraction

In a first approximation a calibration target can be anything whose behavior under a projective mapping is understood. This may vary from squares (see [HZ00]) or circles (see [KSH06]) to even table tennis balls (see [ZZW05]). If one can determine the projective mapping from the prototype of the target to the observed image, one can reconstruct the parameters of the underlying pure pinhole camera (see [Zha98, HZ00]). However, when we leave the pure pinhole camera model by adding a distortion mapping, the observed mapping from a model to the observed pattern is no longer a projective mapping.

A very simple approach to calibration targets are point grids. There are several methods to extract the center of an observed point with sub-pixel precision. For black points on a white background one can take the (gray-value weighted) barycenter of a (pixel-)connected component below a threshold. Another way to determine the sub-pixel position of a feature point (as proposed *e.g.* by Haas in [Haa00]) is to approximate the discrete gray-value image by a polynomial in a local window and to determine the minimum (in the case of black dots) of the polynomial (see Figure 6.2).

Another popular calibration pattern is defined by a regular grid of circles (see *e.g.* [LT88, Tsa87, WM93] or [Hei00]). A circle can be seen as a special case of a conic section. Conic sections remain conic sections under homographies (see *e.g.* [HZ00]). Thus, to extract feature points from images of circles, an algorithm to extract conic sections has to be applied, if we assume a pinhole camera without distortion. In practical applications the image of a circle will be an ellipse. Several algorithms can be found in the literature to extract ellipses with sub-pixel accuracy (see *e.g.* [Zho86], [Hei98] or [Pis05]).

Unfortunately, the estimation of the center of a projected circle by the center of the observed ellipse is biased, as shown by Heikkilä in [Hei97]. Since the bias

Figure 6.1: Calibration cube with a regular point grid pattern. Such a three-dimensional calibration pattern can be used for the direct linear transformation approach (see section 4.3).

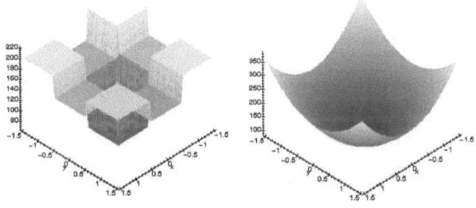

Figure 6.2: Approximation with polynomials of total degree 2 in a 3 × 3 pixel neighborhood.

depends on the camera parameters, Heikkilä proposes an iterative correction of the center of the observed ellipse during the camera calibration ([HS97]). However, the bias tends to zero when the radius of the circles is infinitesimal small. Hence, we obtain a very small bias when we extract tiny points as feature points (see above).

The Open Source Computer Vision Library [1] (short: OpenCV) uses a checkerboard as calibration target (see Figure 6.4). For a compact set $M \subset \mathbb{R}^2$ let the sensor input function $g \in \mathcal{L}^2(M, \mathbb{R}) \cap \mathcal{C}_\infty(\mathbb{R}^2, \mathbb{R})$ be the observed image of a checkerboard pattern. The OpenCV detects the vertices of the checkerboard pattern by the adjacent black-white transitions. Let p be an edge point (of a black-white-transition), i.e. a local gradient maximum, in a neighborhood of q. Then the

---

[1] http://opencvlibrary.sourceforge.net/, visited on Sep. 12th 2008

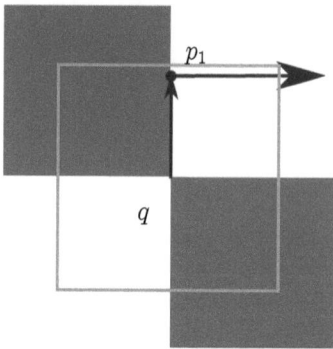

Figure 6.3: Draft of a calibration pattern showing a vertex q and an edge point p with $\langle \nabla g(p) | q - p \rangle = 0$.

algorithm assumes that the vector $q - p$ is perpendicular to the gradient ∇g of the image g in p. This means that

$$\langle \nabla g(p) | q - p \rangle = 0 \tag{6.1}$$

defines a necessary criterion for a vertex q (see Figure 6.3). For discrete gray-value images $g_d : \{1, \ldots, n\} \times \{1, \ldots, n\} \to \mathbb{N}$ the gradient ∇g has to be replaced by a discrete version which we denote by $\text{grad} g_d$. In most cases algorithms use simple filters like Prewitt or Sobel as discrete analogon to a gradient. From the criterion for a vertex in the continuous image we derive the following algorithm for discrete images:

i. Determine a set of edge pixel positions P

For a starting value $q_s \in \mathbb{R}^2$ of the vertex position a let $P \subset \mathbb{N}^2$ be a set of pixel positions in a local neighborhood of q_s such that

- P contains pixel positions near the edges of quadrangles adjacent to q_s (a typical local neighborhood of q_s is displayed red in Figure 6.3),
- the positions in P are on edges which are adjacent to the vertex which is to be determined,
- the gradient norm of all $p \in P$ exceeds a threshold, and
- points near the center q_s are in P.

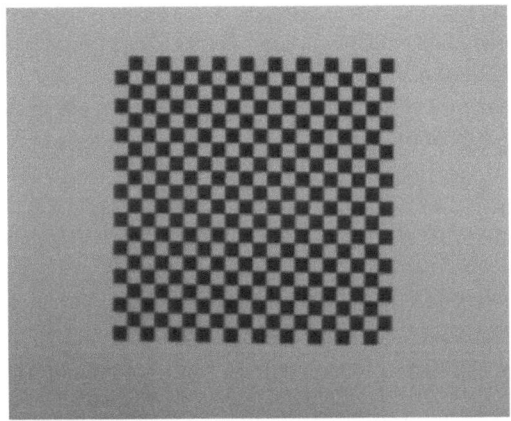

Figure 6.4: Checkerboard pattern which can be used in OpenCV.

ii. Determine the position of the vertex q satisfying the necessary condition

Based on the selection of P the term

$$\sum_{p \in P} \langle \text{grad} g_d(p) | q \rangle - \sum_{p \in P} \langle \text{grad} g_d(p) | p \rangle = 0 \quad (6.2)$$

introduces a system of linear equations in q. Due to the over-determination an approximation of the vertex q has to be obtained by a linear least squares optimization. Note that the solution of the linear least squares problem is a position with sub-pixel accuracy.

iii. Optional: Iterate the algorithm with the result of ii. as starting point.

Since the set P is determined w.r.t. the start solution q_s, the choice of the position belonging to P can be iterated w.r.t. the solution obtained in ii.

6.2.2 Model based extraction of isolated squares

In [HBK06] we presented an algorithm which extracts the desired feature points invariantly under a large family of mollifiers. We used isolated black squares on a uniform background so that we assumed that the ideal image g_{ideal} (see section 2.1.2) is (locally) a piecewise continuous function $g_{\text{ideal}} = \alpha \mathbf{1}_Q + \beta \mathbf{1}_{M \setminus Q}$ where Q determines the dark quadrangle and $M \setminus Q$ the white background. The sensor input function $g = g_{\text{ideal}} * k$, which is observed by the sensor array behind the lens, is obtained as a convolution of g_{ideal} with a point spread function k for which we assume $\int k \mathrm{d}\lambda = 1$ (see also section 2.1.2).

For our approach we also neglected the gaps between the sensors in the sensor array, as treated for example in [PST97]. For $n, m \in \mathbb{N}$ and a $M = [0, n] \times [0, m]$ let $\mathbb{P} := \{[i, i+1[\times [j, j+1[\,|\, 0 \le i < n, 0 \le j < m\}$ be the set of pixels of M. The discretization $D : \mathcal{L}^2(M, \mathbb{R}) \to \mathcal{L}^2(M, \mathbb{R})$ with $D(g) := \sum_{p \in \mathbb{P}} 1_p \frac{1}{\lambda(p)} \int_p g \mathrm{d}\lambda$ of the sensor input function g results in a function which is constant on pixels.

Let now $\mathfrak{A}$ denote the set of all quadrangles in $\mathbb{R}^2$. Then we additionally demand that for every $Q \in \mathfrak{A}$ and every pixel $p \in \mathbb{P}$

$$\int_{p \cap Q} g \mathrm{d}\lambda = \lambda(p \cap Q) D(g)(p) \text{ and } \int_{p \setminus Q} g \mathrm{d}\lambda = \lambda(p \setminus Q) D(g)(p) \qquad (6.3)$$

holds for the discretization $D(g)$ of the observed image g.

With all these presumptions we are looking for an $A \in \mathfrak{A}$ and $\alpha, \beta \in \mathbb{R}$ minimizing

$$\Psi(A, \alpha, \beta) = \int \| D \left(g_{\text{ideal}} * k - (\alpha 1_A + \beta 1_{M \setminus A}) * k \right) \|^2 \mathrm{d}\lambda. \qquad (6.4)$$

The corners of the optimal $A \in \mathfrak{A}$ define the feature points.

Popular approaches to this problem are the edge detector proposed by Canny ([Can86]) for 1D-signals or the 2D model based approach of Deriche and Blaszka ([BD95]). These works assume the knowledge of the kernel k. In particular, they model k as a Gaussian filter, which can be replaced by an exponential filter for computational purposes.

For images of step functions on a one dimensional domain we only need to know the mass of the image to obtain the original edge. Let $g_{\text{ideal}} = \alpha 1_{[-s, t[} + \beta 1_{[t, m+s]}$, a function on $[-s, m+s]$ with a step in $t \in]0, m[$, be the ideal image. Let $[-s, s]$ be the support of the point spread function k.

For $\int k \mathrm{d}\lambda = 1$ it is easy to see that $\int g_{\text{ideal}} * k \mathrm{d}\lambda = \int g_{\text{ideal}} \mathrm{d}\lambda =: I$ holds. Thus, we can determine the edge t, provided we know α, β, simply by

$$I = \alpha \int_{[0,t]} 1 \mathrm{d}\lambda + \beta \int_{[t,m]} 1 \mathrm{d}\lambda \qquad (6.5)$$
$$= t\alpha + (m-t)\beta \qquad (6.6)$$
$$\Rightarrow t = \frac{I - m\beta}{\alpha - \beta}. \qquad (6.7)$$

The problem to determine α, β minimizing (6.4) can be solved by the moment preservation method ([TM84]). In [HBK06] we demanded that for an $s \in \mathbb{R}_+$ with $\text{supp}(k) \subseteq [-s, s]$ the relation $s < \min\{\frac{t}{2}, \frac{m-t}{2}\}$ holds. Therefore, it is $(g_{\text{ideal}} * k)(x) = \alpha$ for $x \in [0, t-s]$ and $(g_{\text{ideal}} * k)(x) = \beta$ for $x \in [t+s, m]$ (see Figure 6.5).

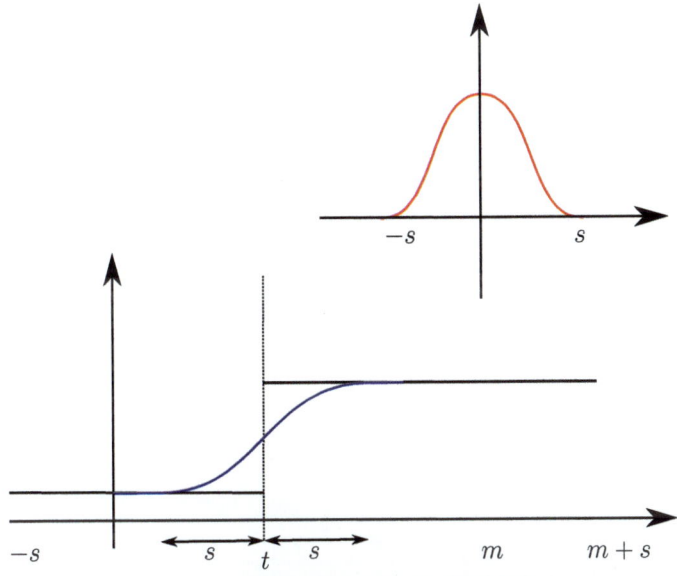

Figure 6.5: Sketch of the ideal function $g_{\text{ideal}} : [-s, m+s] \to \mathbb{R}$ (black), the point spread function $k : [-s, s] \to \mathbb{R}$ (red), and the sensor input function g (blue and black).

The transformation of the one dimensional problem to a two dimensional problem complicates its parametrization. In 1D we can describe an edge by three parameters α, β, t. In the two dimensional domain we have to choose a suitable representation of the term "edge" or "contour". Since we are only interested in the precise extraction of a quadrangle, we may represent $A \in \mathfrak{A}$ by the four vertices, which can be obtained as intersection of the border lines. Thus, the simplest approach to the two dimensional problem is to downsize it to the one dimensional problem. This is a common approach in computer vision, in particular for the extraction of ellipses for calibration purposes (see e.g. [Zho86], [Hei98] or

[PKH05]): We simply take each pixel line intersecting the quadrangle and determine the edges of the obtained discretized one dimensional function (see Figure 6.6). We now have to detect two edges in an one dimensional function. Therefore, we can either use one value β for the background or two values β, γ for the background. The borders of the quadrangle can be obtained by line fitting and the corners are the intersections of the fitted lines (see Figure 6.7). This multiple 1D approach defines a very fast way to estimate the edges of Q in f

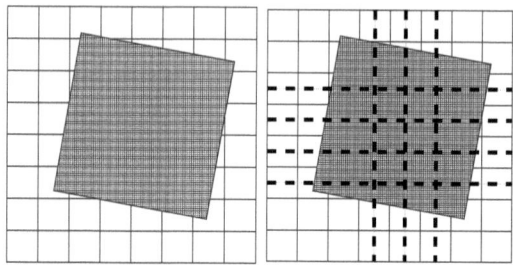

Figure 6.6: Ideal image function g and the one-dimensional cuts.

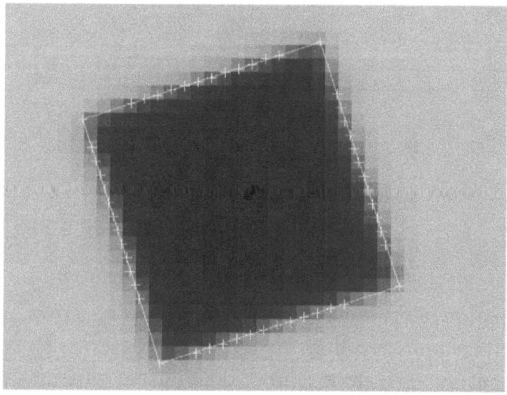

Figure 6.7: Estimated quadrangle by line fitting of 1D-edges.

For the 2D problem Lauren adds the determination of the kernel as another parameter to the problem ([Lau06]): The set of Gauss functions $\{G_{\sigma,0} \mid \sigma > 0\}$ with $G_{\sigma,0}(x) = \frac{1}{\sqrt{2\pi\sigma^2}} e^{-\frac{1}{2}\left(\frac{x}{\sigma}\right)^2}$ defines a sufficient set of kernels, which is easy to adjust, to minimize the problem

$$(A, \alpha, \beta, \sigma) \mapsto \int \|D\left(g_{\text{ideal}} * G_{\sigma,0} - (\alpha 1_A + \beta 1_{M \setminus A}) * G_{\sigma,0}\right)\|^2 d\lambda. \quad (6.8)$$

Lauren shows that the choice of A and σ determines α and β as in the unconvoluted case. Note that this approach is computationally expensive.

In [HBK06] we presented stationary values for the problem (6.4) assuming that k is rotationally invariant, has a limited support, and $\int k d\lambda = 1$ holds.

6.2.3 Appropriability of the feature point extraction methods

6.2.3.1 Appropriability with respect to the sensor model

All presented approaches to feature point extraction use a simplified model of the image acquisition process. In computer vision, the relation between the ideal image g_{ideal} and the observed image g (before discretization) is often described as $g = (g_{\text{ideal}} * h) + \nu$ where ν denotes an additive noise term (see e.g. [Jai89, BLM90, FS98]).

The OpenCV approach in 6.2.1 does not consider convolution or noise. Considering the regularity of the checkerboard pattern, this simplification can be made for a rotationally symmetric point spread function and normal, independent, and identical distributed noise. If ν is normal, independent, and identical distributed for every pixel the central limit theorem applies for the problems in (6.4) or (6.8).

None of the presented approaches deals with asymmetric point spread functions. Of course, there are approaches to reconstruct the point spread function from observed images. However, these methods either assume some simplifications of the point spread function (like symmetry, see e.g. [Jän93]) and/or face a boot strap problem: To determine the point spread function, some feature points have to be extracted with high accuracy. For example, in [Pis06] the feature point extraction of the OpenCV is used to obtain such input data for a subsequent non-linear optimization which calculates the point spread functions.

6.2.3.2 Appropriability with respect to the camera model

The extraction of feature points should be consistent in connection with the model of the camera mapping. Therefore, all approaches which depend on extracting lines, circles, or ellipses must be seen critically when a distortion mapping is modeled in the camera mapping. Even if the assumption "straight lines have to be straight", which can be derived from the pinhole camera assumption (see *e.g.* [HZ00]), can be made in a first approximation for a small area of interest: due to noise, the point extraction will be erroneous. Obviously, this effect decreases with the size of the area of interest. On the other hand, for a decreasing size of the area of interest the stability of the line or ellipse fit will also decrease. Thus, there is a trade-off between the pinhole constraint and the compensation of noise by least squares fitting.

6.3 The residual distortion

6.3.1 The point spread function by first order optics

The point spread function (PSF) can be seen as the pulse response of the imaging system. All rays emitted from an infinitesimal small object point which pass the lens will hit the image plane parallel to the lens plane in a circle, the circle of confusion (see section 2.1.2). For any plane except the focal plane, this circle has a positive diameter. The circle of confusion is also the support of the PSF. A simple derivation of the fact that the PSF is not symmetric can be found in [Hor86], where it is shown that the irradiance of an observed point depends on the angle of the object to the lens. We extend this approach to determine the PSF on the circle of confusion for an image obtained off the focal plane. In our approach it is a function of the position of the object.

For our considerations we represent every point in a cylindrical coordinate system defined by the optical center O: Every point in this coordinate system can be represented by its distance z to the lens plane, its distance to the optical axis r and an angle ϕ to a fixed axis in the lens plane. In first order optics any way of a light ray can be determined by three points: given the object point in the object plane and its image point in the focal plane, we obtain the complete way of any emitted light ray through the lens if we know the point where the light ray hits the lens. However, we can also use a point in the image plane to determine the complete way of a light ray, if the image plane is not the focal plane.

Let the object be a point $p = (\phi_p, r_p, z_p)$ emitting light in every direction isotropically. Furthermore, let $i_p = (\phi_{i_p}, r_{i_p}, z_{i_p})$ be the position of the ideal projection of the object point in the focal plane and $c = (\phi_c, r_c, z_c)$ the center of the circle of confusion for the point object in the image plane. We assume that the image plane is located at a distance d to the focal plane. (See Figure 6.8 for a sketch of the identifiers).

If the focal length f is known, the the coordinates $(\phi_{i_p}, r_{i_p}, z_{i_p})$ of the image point on the focal plane can be expressed w.r.t. the object point p by

$$\phi_{i_p} = \phi_p + \pi, r_{i_p} = \frac{r_p f}{z_p - f} \text{ and } z_{i_p} = -\frac{z_p f}{z_p - f}. \tag{6.9}$$

This result follows by simple considerations (and applying the lens maker's equation (2.2)) w.r.t. to first order optics and a thin lens with focal length f.

Since the center ray is determined by p and i_p only, the coordinates (ϕ_c, r_c, z_c)

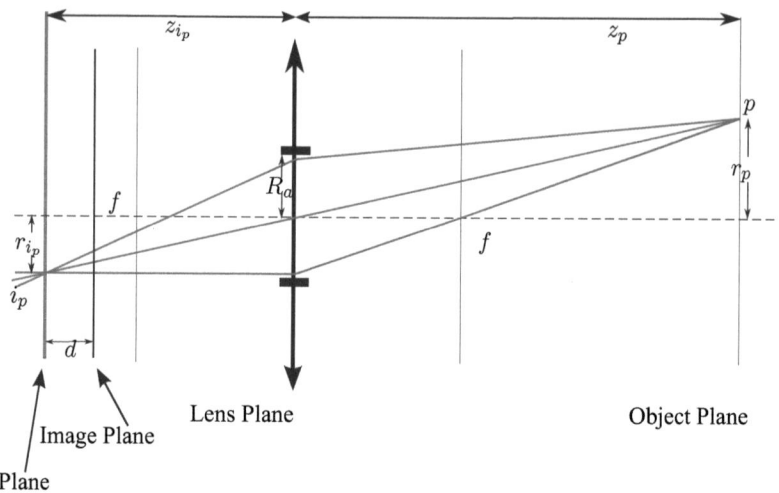

Figure 6.8: Identifiers for the object point p, ideal point projection i_p lens, focal plane and image plane in cylindrical coordinates.

of the center of the observed spot in the image plane are related to i_p by

$$\phi_c = \phi_{i_p}, r_c = r_{i_p} + \frac{r_{i_p} d}{z_{i_p}} \text{ (it is } z_{i_p} < 0\text{) and } z_c = z_{i_p} + d. \qquad (6.10)$$

Let now R_a be the radius of the aperture, which in our model is the radius of the translucent circle of the lens. Then the radius R_s of the circle of confusion is $R_s = \left|\frac{R_a d}{z_{i_p}}\right|$.

Let $ds = r_s dr_s d\phi$ be an infinitesimal area of the spot and dl be the corresponding area on the lens plane. Then $dl = \left(\frac{z_{i_p}}{d}\right)^2 ds$ and $r_l = \left|\frac{z_{i_p}}{d}\right| r_s$ and $\phi_l = \phi_s$ holds (see Figure 6.9).

The distance h from the infinitesimal area on the lens dl to object p is

$$h^2 = (r_p \cos(\phi_p) - r_l \cos(\phi_l))^2 + (r_p \sin(\phi_p) - r_l \sin(\phi_l))^2 + z_p^2. \qquad (6.11)$$

The angle between the normal of the lens and the ray from the object is $\alpha = \arccos(\frac{z_p}{h})$. Let dl' be the infinitesimal area perpendicular to this ray: $dl' = dl \cos(\alpha) = dl \frac{z_p}{h}$. The (infinitesimal) solid angle dw in p, which spans

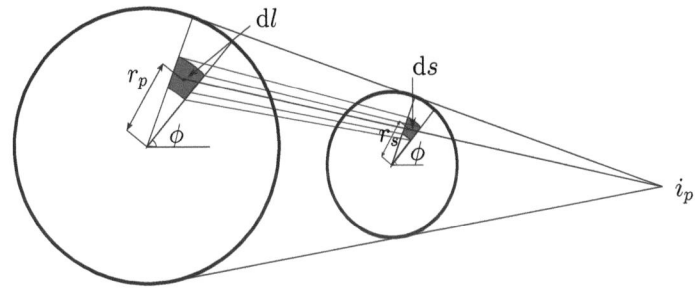

Figure 6.9: Identifiers for the infinitesimal areas dl on the lens and ds on the image plane.

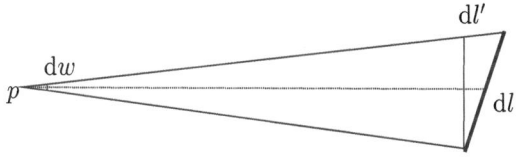

Figure 6.10: The object p, the area dl, and the area dl' perpendicular to the light ray.

this area, is given by

$$dw = \frac{dr'_l}{h^2} = dr_l \frac{z_p}{h^3} = \frac{z_p z_{i_p} r_s}{h^3 d^2} dr_s d\phi \qquad (6.12)$$

(see Figure 6.10).

Now, we are considering an isotropic light source in the object point p with an intensity of emitted light I. Let dI be the intensity emitted over dw, then it is

$$dI = I dw = I \frac{z_p z_{i_p}^2}{h^3 d^2} ds \qquad (6.13)$$

and therefore the intensity N of the light in ds becomes

$$N = \frac{dI}{ds} = I \frac{z_p z_{i_p}^2}{h^3 d^2}. \qquad (6.14)$$

In Figure 6.11, 6.12, 6.13, and 6.14 we show some examples of the point spread function (up to a scale factor) obtained from the light intensity N. In all figures we displayed the results in Cartesian coordinates, where origin is determined by the particular center (Φ_s, r_s, z_s) of the spot. Figure 6.11 shows a lens with unrealistic parameters: the distance of the object to the lens is smaller than twice the focal length. The purpose of this exaggeration is to point out the asymmetry of the point spread function. The resulting PSF for a more realistic setup is displayed in Figure 6.12. In this case, there is only a slight asymmetry. In contrast to the common assumption, the PSF is not a Gaussian at all. All lengths are displayed without a unit. If we assume a focal length of 4 mm the displacement of the image plane would be 0.5 mm and the distance of the light source to the lens plane would be 5 cm. The PSFs in Figure 6.13 and 6.14 are obtained from a light source at 5 m. In Figure 6.13 the light source is placed on the optical axis. Thus, the resulting PSF is a step function. In Figure 6.14 the light source was moved to a distance of 1 m to the optical axis. In this case the PSF becomes clearly asymmetric, but the effect is not as dramatic as for light sources nearer to the lens.

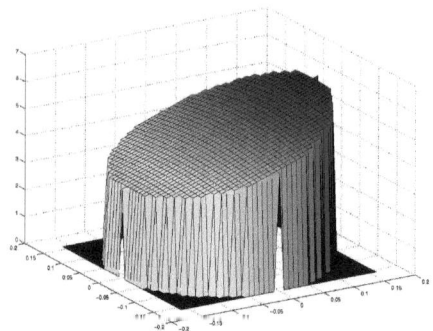

Figure 6.11: Intensity N of a spot in the image plane for an object at $(\phi_p, r_p, z_p) = (0, 4, 7)$ for a lens with focal length 4 and radius of aperture 3. The displacement d of the image plane to the focal plane is 0.5.

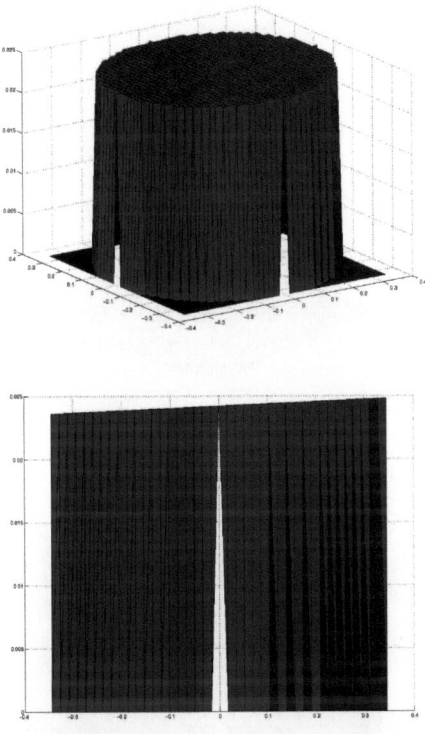

Figure 6.12: Intensity N of a spot in the image plane for an object at $(\phi_p, r_p, z_p) = (0, 20, 50)$ for a lens with focal length 4 and radius of aperture 3. The displacement d of the image plane to the focal plane is 0.5.

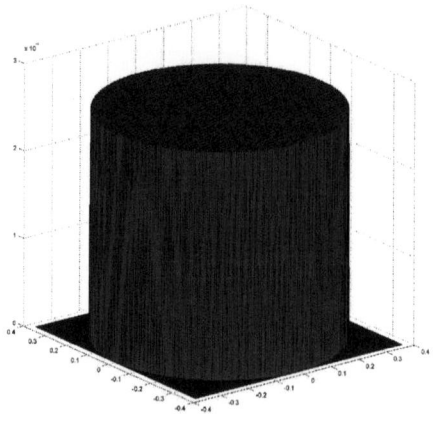

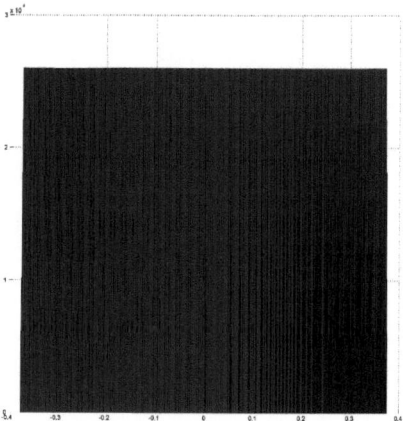

Figure 6.13: Intensity N of a spot in the sensor plane for an object at $(\phi_p, r_p, z_p) = (0, 0, 500)$ for a lens with focal length 4 and radius of aperture 3. The displacement d of the image plane to the focal plane is 0.5.

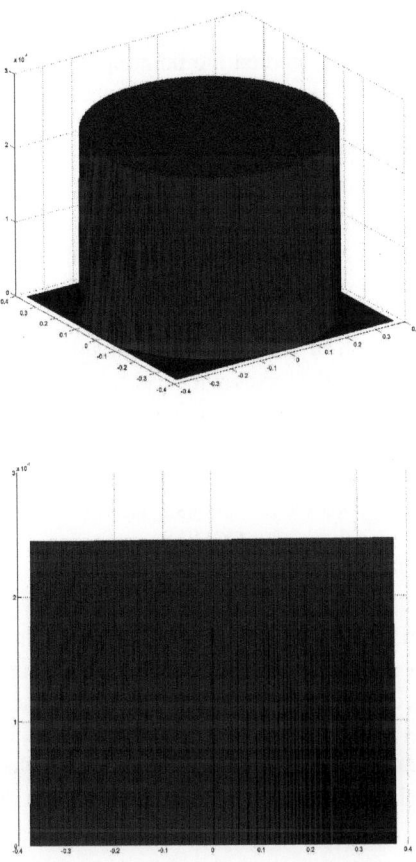

Figure 6.14: Intensity N of a spot in the image plane for an object at $(\phi_p, r_p, z_p) = (0, 100, 500)$ for a lens with focal length 4 and radius of aperture 3. The displacement d of the image plane to the focal plane is 0.5.

6.3.2 Other sources of residual distortion

In the preceding sections we studied the point spread function obtained by one spherical lens. In real cameras the expression "spherical lens" needs to be questioned: First, a cheap lens is not made of glass by the classic optic manufacturing process (rough shaping, blocking, grinding, polishing and centering), instead it is made of plastic and produced by molding (see *e.g.* [Smi08]). Therefore, an irregularity in the rotational symmetry is very likely. Second, modern cameras apply lens systems consisting of a set of lenses to obtain an appropriate image. The point spread function of such a complex system can only be simulated. If the parameters of all lenses are known, Software tools like Code V, OSLO, or Zemax can be used to obtain a simulation of the expected point spread function. Furthermore, any misalignment of the optical axes will lead to an observed distortion, which can not be modeled in the radial distortion model.

In all our consideration we assumed that the imaging areas of CCD and CMOS image sensors are flat. In [FSG95] Fraser and Shortis report an unflatness tolerance of up to 10μm for two CCD sensors. This is a typical value that can be looked up in several data sheets for CCD image sensors (*e.g.* Fairchild CCD485 (4K×4K), Phillips FFT 1010-M or Kodak KAF-4320). However, a systematic (linear) unevenness should be covered by the parameter γ of the image transformation P (see section 2.2). In [TL00], Tecklenburg and Luhmann consider a finite element approach on the image plane to model a non-linear deviation in flatness. It should be mentioned that in this case the image sensor itself has to be calibrated. If an optical system (lens) is placed before the sensor array, it will be very difficult to obtain untainted data for a sensor calibration. Nonetheless, unevenness in the sensor in the image plane will lead to a systematic error in reconstruction.

6.3.3 Experimental results

The preceding sections show two things:

i. For the pinhole camera model with distortion there will be a change of behavior depending on the depth of the observed objects. Not least, since feature extraction methods assume at most a symmetrical point spread function.

ii. Depending on the planarity of the sensor array, the quality of the lens manufacturing process, and the alignment of the lenses in the lens system there may be a residual distortion which can not be modeled by a radial function.

We confirm these observations by two experiments: In the first experiment we determine radial distortion parameters at varying depths. In the second experiment we investigate the residual distortion, which is present after a radial distortion model is applied.

In both experiments the observation of a planar calibration pattern covers the whole image. We choose the radial distortion model with four coefficients (*i.e.* ($\Delta_{r,4}$, see section 2.4.2). The calibration pattern is moved at different positions located equidistantly and nearly parallel to the image plane. The observed planes have a distance of 5cm to each other covering a distance from 60 to 130 cm to the camera. The calibration target itself is a 51×49 point grid with a point distance of 20 mm to each other. The diameter of the points is 2 mm and we use the gray value weighted barycenter of the points as feature extraction. The camera has a common 2/3" CCD sensor and a Pentax 6 mm lens.

In the first experiment, we determine the parameters of the radial distortion mapping for each position of planar calibration pattern. In Fig. 6.16 - 6.19 we show each distortion parameter $k_1, \ldots, k_4$ w.r.t. to the plane position. The first plane is nearest to the camera (*i.e.* the plane a at distance of 60 cm to the camera). One can see that there is an observable systematic change of the value of all distortion parameters obtained by this setup. This systematic change may result in a similar distortion mapping. Therefore, in Figure 6.20 we exemplary plot the distortion mapping obtained for the planes at a distance of 60 cm, 95 cm, and 130 cm. One can see that the distortion mapping varies in depth.

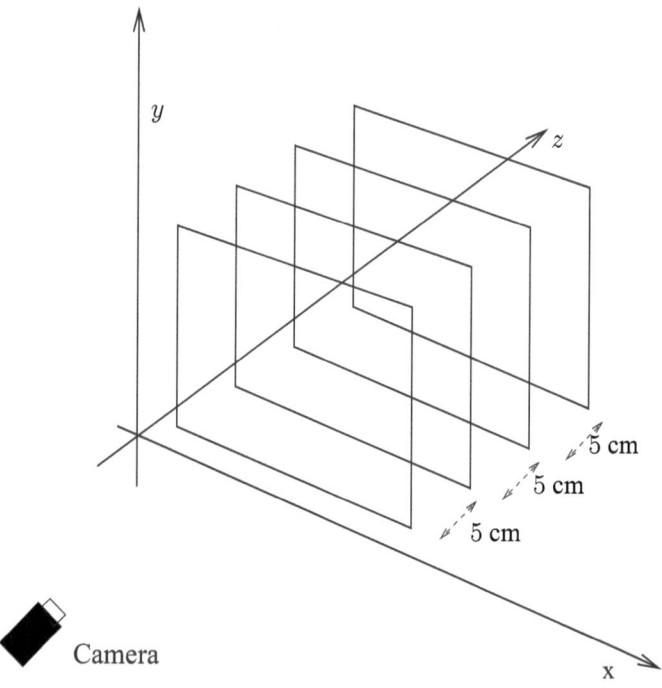

Figure 6.15: Experimental setup for both distortion experiments.

We use the same setup for the second experiment: since the standard pinhole camera with distortion already applies a radial distortion mapping in the image plane, it is not very likely that the residual distortion can be expressed by a function in the radius to a center of distortion.

In Figure 6.21 we determine the center of distortion for each observed calibration pattern. We define the point of least Euclidean distance to all lines containing $\Pi_z(p)$ and $P^{-1}(i_p)$ for all $p \in \mathbf{P}$ as the center of distortion. The blue diamonds show the center of distortion for the pinhole camera w.r.t. the image coordinate system. The result supports the presumption that for common cameras the distortion is dominated by the radial distortion: The center of distortion remains more or less in the center of the observed image for all examined distances of the calibration pattern. However, observing the residual distortion (green squares), *i.e.*

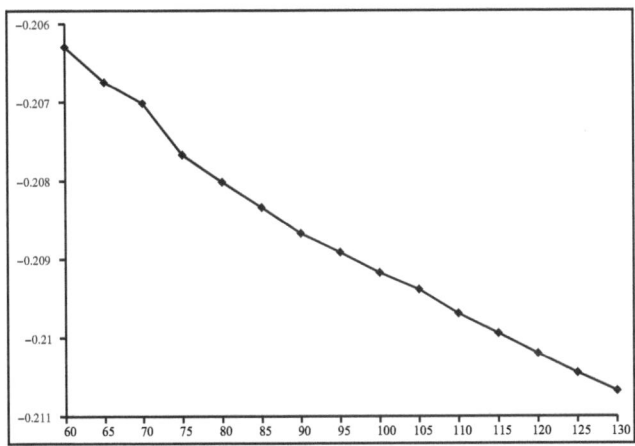

Figure 6.16: Value of the parameter k_1 (ordinate) w.r.t. the depth of the observed plate (abscissa).

the distortion which is left after applying radial distortion correction with 4 coefficients, this is not true.

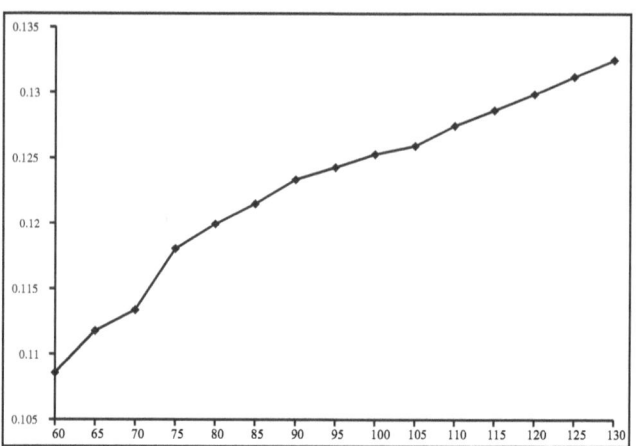

Figure 6.17: Value of the parameter k_2 (ordinate) w.r.t. the depth of the observed plate (abscissa).

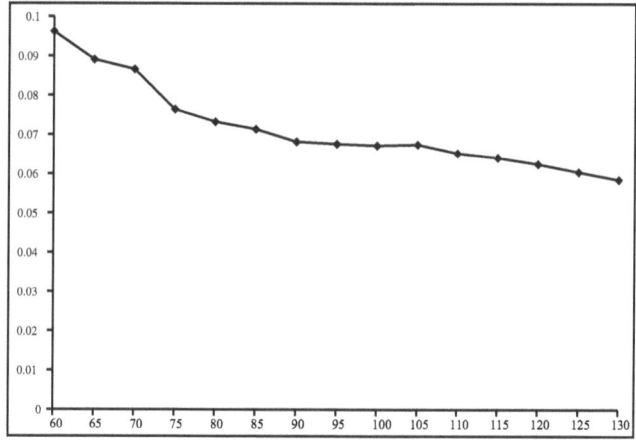

Figure 6.18: Value of the parameter k_3 (ordinate) w.r.t. the depth of the observed plate (abscissa).

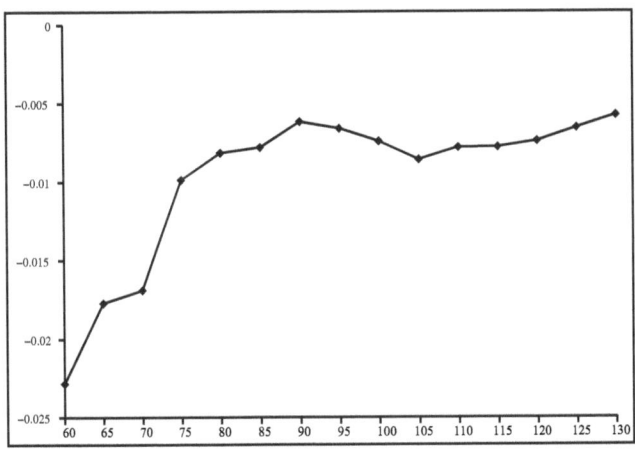

Figure 6.19: Value of the parameter k_4 (ordinate) w.r.t. the depth of the observed plate (abscissa).

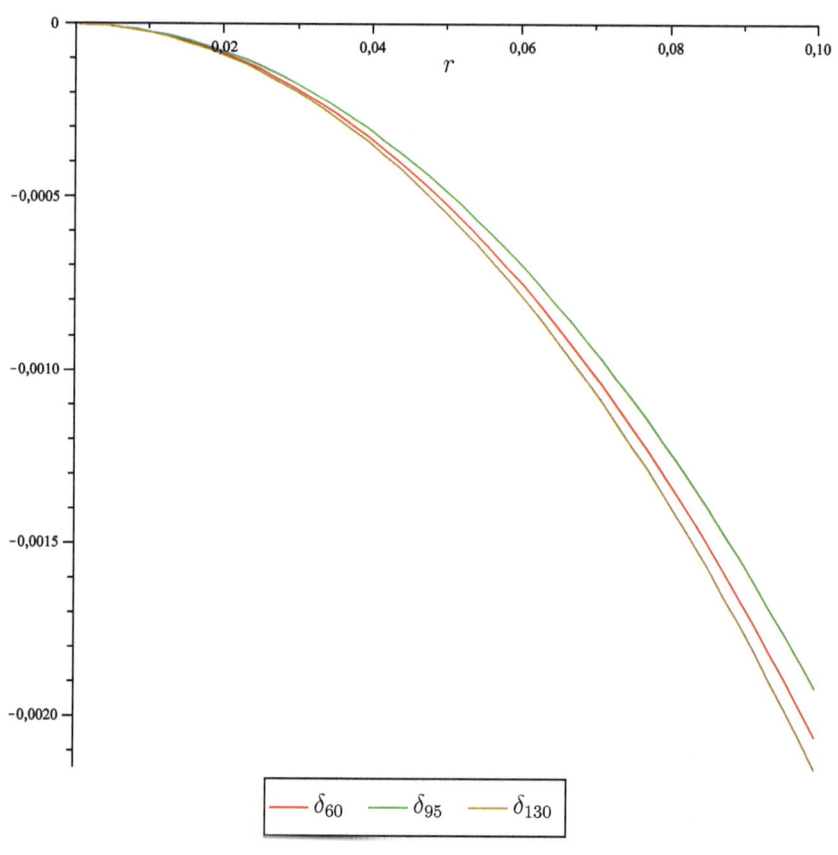

Figure 6.20: Distortion mapping $\delta_{60}, \delta_{90}, \delta_{130}$ defined by the parameters obtained at a distance of 60 mm, 90 mm, and 130 mm to the camera.

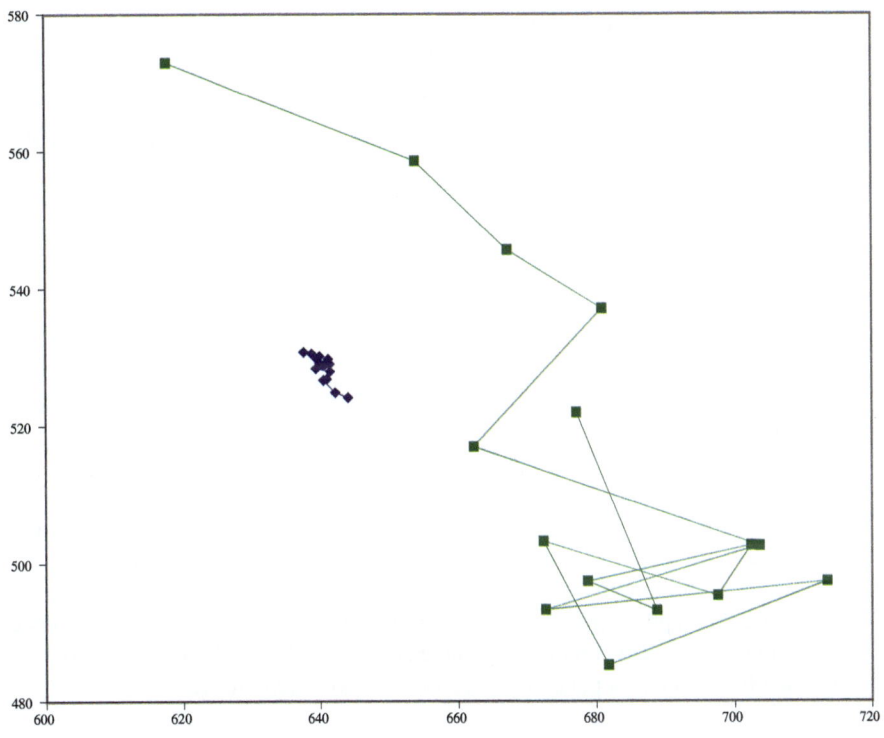

Figure 6.21: Location of the center of radial distortion (blue) and the residual distortion (green) w.r.t. the ICS for calibration planes at different distances.

6.4 Spline correction

6.4.1 Motivation and related work

The previous section shows that there is a depth-dependent component in the residual distortion. Our first approach to deal with the observed phenomenon is simply to add a depth-dependent term to the distortion mapping.

In [BBHM+06], Brauer-Burchardt *et al.* presented a calibration with a distance dependent distortion model for measurement systems with fringe projection. They determine a distortion matrix, *i.e.* a matrix of correction vectors, at five different distances to the camera and the projectors respectively. The distortion matrices are stacked into a distortion cube and the actual correction vector will be determined by a bi-cubic spline interpolation based on the nearest neighbors of the input data in the distortion cube.

In contrast to [BBHM+06], we propose a distortion model which combines standard in-plane distortion (like radial distortion) and a depth-dependent residual distortion. In particular, we separate the calibration w.r.t. the standard camera model from the determination of the depth-dependent correction. In a first run we determine the optimal pinhole camera with an in-plane distortion. Then we determine the depth-dependent correction term for the residual distortion. Since the residual distortion can not be parametrized radially (as shown section 6.3.3), we encode the depth-dependent correction as a non-radial function.

6.4.2 A depth-dependent distortion term

For a fixed camera mapping $P \circ \tilde{\delta} \circ \Pi_z$ with distortion δ we are looking for a smooth correction mapping $c : \mathbb{R}^3 \to \{z = 0\}$ which corrects the effect of the residual distortion caused by the point extraction.

Definition 6.4.1 (δ_c)
Let Δ be set of distortion mappings and $C \subset \mathcal{C}(\mathbb{R}^3, \{z = 0\})$ be a finite dimensional linear space of smooth mappings. For $\delta \in \Delta$ and $c \in C$ we define

$$\delta_c : \begin{array}{l} \mathbb{R}^3 \to \{z = 1\} \\ p \mapsto \tilde{\delta}(\Pi_z(p)) - c(p) \end{array} \quad (6.15)$$

as the depth-dependent correction mapping.

In real applications it is not necessary to define the correction on $\mathbb{R}^3$, since all observed points will have positive z-coordinates w.r.t. the camera coordinate system. Moreover, in section 6.4.4 we define a spline space as correction mapping with a bounded domain $D \subset \mathbb{R}^2 \times \mathbb{R}_+$. We set $\delta_c|_{\mathbb{R}^3 \setminus D} = 0$.

6.4.3 Depth-dependent distortion correction for the projective and re-projective error function

With respect to the projective camera calibration error as defined in section 3.4.1 we are looking for a minimum of

$$\Psi_P : \begin{array}{l} \mathcal{C} \to \mathbb{R}_+ \\ c \mapsto \sum_{p \in \mathbf{P}} \| (P \circ \delta_c)(p) - i_p \|^2 \end{array}. \qquad (6.16)$$

Instead of minimizing an error w.r.t. the ICS which is corrected w.r.t. the CCS, we switch to the CCS by applying P^{-1} on minuend and subtrahend. Actually, this means to switch to the plane $\{z = 1\}$: we obtain

$$\| \underbrace{\delta_c(p)}_{\in \{z=1\}} - \underbrace{P^{-1}(i_p)}_{\in \{z=1\}} \|, \qquad (6.17)$$

which remains a 2D distance, as stated in section 3.2.

Setting $q_p := \tilde{\delta}(\Pi_z(p)) - P^{-1}(i_p) \in \{z = 0\}$ for $p \in \mathbf{P}$ we are looking for a $c \in \mathcal{C}$ which minimizes

$$\Psi_R : \begin{array}{l} \mathcal{C} \to \mathbb{R}_+ \\ c \mapsto \sum_{p \in \mathbf{P}} \| q_p - c(p) \|^2 \end{array}. \qquad (6.18)$$

This is a linear least squares problem, since we demanded that $\mathcal{C}$ is a finite dimensional vector space.

Since Ψ_R is measures an error in the plane $\{z = 1\}$, we call a $c_o \in \mathcal{C}$ minimizing Ψ_R a *depth-dependent correction w.r.t. the re-projective error*.

6.4.4 The tensor spline space

A very useful finite dimensional vector space of functions is defined by tensor splines. To define this function space we introduce the tensor product of finite dimensional vector spaces:

Definition 6.4.2 (Tensor product)
Let $V, W \subset \mathcal{C}(\mathbb{R}, \mathbb{R}^d)$ be two finite dimensional vector spaces. For vectors $v = (v_1, \ldots, v_d)^t \in V, w = (w_1, \ldots, w_d)^t \in W$ we define $v \otimes w : \mathbb{R} \times \mathbb{R} \to \mathbb{R}^d$ by

$$\forall x, y \in \mathbb{R} : (v \otimes w)(x, y) := \begin{pmatrix} v_1(x) w_1(y) \\ \vdots \\ v_d(x) w_d(y) \end{pmatrix}. \tag{6.19}$$

$v \otimes w$ is called the tensor product of v and w. The tensor product space $V \otimes W$ defined by

$$V \otimes W := \{ v \otimes w \mid v \in V, w \in W \} \tag{6.20}$$

is a finite dimensional vector space itself. The dimension of $V \otimes W$ is the product of the dimensions of V and W.

For l finite dimensional vector spaces $V_1, \ldots, V_l \subset \mathcal{C}(\mathbb{R}, \mathbb{R}^d)$ we set

$$\bigotimes_{i=1}^{l} V_i := (\ldots((V_1 \otimes V_2) \otimes V_3) \otimes \ldots V_l) \tag{6.21}$$

In the following we apply tensor spline spaces as finite dimensional vector spaces. There are many ways to define splines. We use the recurrence formula introduced by Boor and Cox (see e.g. [dB78]).

Definition 6.4.3 (B-spline base)
Let $U = (u_{-n+1}, \cdots, u_{g+n})$ be a strictly increasing sequence of $g + 2n$ real numbers. U is called knot sequence and the u_i with $-n + 1 \leq i \leq g + n$ are called knots. The i-th B-Spline basis function of p-degree, denoted by $N_{i,p}(u)$, is defined by

$$N_{i,0}(u) = \begin{cases} 1 & , \text{if } u_i \leq u < u_{i+1} \\ 0 & , \text{otherwise} \end{cases}, \tag{6.22}$$

$$N_{i,p}(u) = \frac{u - u_i}{u_{i+p} - u_i} N_{i,p-1}(u) + \frac{u_{i+p+1} - u}{u_{i+p+1} - u_{i+1}} N_{i+1,p-1}(u)$$

$N := (N_{-n+1,n+1}, \ldots, N_{g,n+1})$ is a set of $g+n$ linear independent functions called B-splines which span the vector space of spline functions with degree $n + 1 \in \mathbb{N}$. N is called B-spline base. The knots $u_1, \ldots, u_g$ are called inner knots.

A B-spline base of a spline space is determined by the degree and the knot sequence. For the inner knots the B-spline have the "partition of unity property": It is $\sum_{i=-n+1}^{g} N_{i,n+1}(x) = 1$ for all $x \in [u_1, \ldots, u_g]$.

Since we want to model the distortion, we apply functions with an image in $\mathbb{R}^d$. Therefore, we define:

Definition 6.4.4 ($\mathcal{S}_{n,U}^d$)
For $n \in \mathbb{N}$ with $n \geq 1$ let U be a knot sequence with $g + 2n$ knots and $N := (N_{-n+1,n+1}, \ldots, N_{g,n+1})$ the B-spline base of degree $n + 1$. Then we define

$$\mathcal{S}_{n,U}^d := \left\{ s : [u_0, u_g] \to \mathbb{R}^d \; \middle| \; s(x) = \begin{pmatrix} \langle a_1 | N(x) \rangle \\ \vdots \\ \langle a_d | N(x) \rangle \end{pmatrix} \text{ with } a_1, \ldots, a_d \in \mathbb{R}^{n+g} \right\}. \tag{6.23}$$

We now take the tensor product space of the finite dimensional vector spaces $\mathcal{S}_{n_i, U_i}^d$ to define mappings with a multi-dimensional domain.

Definition 6.4.5 ($\mathcal{S}_{n,U}^{k,d}$)
Let $N_1, \ldots, N_k$ be B-spline bases of splines of degree $n = (n_1, \ldots, n_k) \in \mathbb{N}^k$ with knot sequences $U = (U_1, \ldots, U_k)$ with $g_1 + 2(n_1 - 1), \ldots, g_k + 2(n_k - 1)$ knots. For $D := \times_{i=1}^{k} [u_{i,0}, u_{i,g_x}]$, i.e. the cuboid defined by the inner $g_1, \ldots, g_k$ knots of U, we set

$$\mathcal{S}_{n,U}^{k,d} := \bigotimes \mathcal{S}_{n_i, U_i}^d. \tag{6.24}$$

In the following we will use different values for k and d. To implement a depth-dependent distortion as defined in section 6.4.3 it is $k = 3, d = 2$. For a depth-dependent distortion mapping which is optimal w.r.t. the Euclidean error it will be $k = 3, d = 3$ (see section 6.4.6). Furthermore, we will show some experiments where we use a spline space to model the standard in plane distortion Δ (see section 6.7).

6.4.5 Tensor splines for the re-projective depth-dependent distortion

Let U_x, U_y, U_z be knot sequences with g_x, g_y, g_z inner knots. To implement the depth-dependent distortion term δ_c as defined in section 6.4.3 we apply the tensor space $\mathcal{S}_{n,U}^{3,2}$ with $n = (n_x, n_y, n_z) \in \mathbb{N}^3$:
For $s \in \mathcal{S}_{n,U}^{3,2} = \left(\mathcal{S}_{n_x,U_x}^2 \otimes \mathcal{S}_{n_y,U_y}^2 \right) \otimes \mathcal{S}_{n_z,U_z}^2$ exist coefficient vectors $a, b \in$

$\mathbb{R}^{n_x-1+g_x}, c, d \in \mathbb{R}^{n_y-1+g_y}, e, f \in \mathbb{R}^{n_z-1+g_z}$ such that it is $s = s_{(a,b,c,d,e,f)}$ with

$$s_{(a,b,c,d,e,f)}(x,y,z) = \begin{pmatrix} \langle a|\,N_x(x)\rangle\,\langle c|\,N_y(y)\rangle\,\langle e|\,N_z(z)\rangle \\ \langle b|\,N_x(x)\rangle\,\langle d|\,N_y(y)\rangle\,\langle f|\,N_z(z)\rangle \end{pmatrix} \qquad (6.25)$$

where N_x, N_y, N_z are the B-spline bases of $\mathcal{S}^2_{n_x,U_x}, \mathcal{S}^2_{n_y,U_y}, \mathcal{S}^2_{n_z,U_z}$. For input points $p_1, \ldots, p_n \in \mathbb{R}^3$ and observed points $y_1, \ldots, y_n \in \mathbb{R}^2$ the problem of minimizing

$$(a,b,c,d,e,f) \to \sum_{i=1}^n \|s_{(a,b,c,d,e,f)}(p_i) - y_i\|^2 \qquad (6.26)$$

defines a linear least squares problem (see *e.g.* [Die93] or [Zim01]). Therefore, we set

$$\mathcal{C} := \begin{pmatrix} \mathcal{S}^{3,2}_{n,U} \\ 0 \end{pmatrix} \qquad (6.27)$$

in (6.18). To avoid over-parametrization the number of (inner) breakpoints should be kept small. If c minimizes Ψ_R, we set $P \circ \tilde{\delta}_c \circ \Pi_z$ as the new camera mapping with a depth-dependent correction term. In section 6.7 we show some experimental results for different configurations of $\mathcal{S}^{3,2}_{n,U}$.

6.4.6 Spline correction for the Euclidean error

To formulate a spline correction term depending on the depth of the observed point, we apply

$$\mathrm{dist}_3(\overline{B^{-1}[\{i_p\}]}, p) = \|\mathrm{Proj}_{\overline{B^{-1}[\{i_p\}]}}(p) - p\|^2, \qquad (6.28)$$

whereas $\mathrm{Proj}_L(p)$ denotes the orthogonal projection of $p \in \mathbb{R}^3$ on the line L. Thus, for a spline space $\mathcal{S}^{3,3}_{n,U} \subset \mathcal{C}(\mathbb{R}^3, \mathbb{R}^3)$ we are looking for a $\delta_{\mathrm{Euclid}} \in \mathcal{S}^{3,3}_{n,U}$ minimizing

$$\delta \mapsto \sum_{p \in \mathbf{P}} \|\delta(\mathrm{Proj}_{\overline{B^{-1}[\{i_p\}]}}(p)) - p\|^2. \qquad (6.29)$$

It is worth noticing that, depending on δ_{Euclid}, the set $\delta_{\mathrm{Euclid}}[B^{-1}[\{i_p\}]]$ may not be on a line.

6.4.7 The viewing ray for spline corrected cameras

For all spline corrected camera mappings presented in this section, the viewing ray (*i.e.* the pre-image of an observation) may not be a subset of a straight line. Therefore, we investigate the pre-image of an image point under a spline corrected camera mapping for standard 6 mm lens and a camera with a 1280×1024 sensor array. In Figure 6.22 and 6.23 we plot samples of four viewing rays obtained at the pixel position of a camera which was calibrated with a correction spline as presented in the previous section. We set $\mathcal{S}_{n,U}^{3,3}$ with $n = (5,5,3)$ and $U = (U_1, U_2, U_3)$ as $(10, 10, 3)$ equidistant inner knots in $D := [-0.6, 0.6] \times [-0.6, 0.6] \times [0.5, 1.1]$ (the unit is meter).

In Figure 6.22 and 6.23 we plotted the x- and y-coordinate w.r.t. the z-coordinate (depth) for 25 points on each viewing ray. One can see that there are only slight deviations to a linear dependence to depth. Therefore, each re-projection is nearly a line. In particular, we analyzed the spline corrected re-projection for every pixel position. For each re-projection we fitted a line through 25 sample points along the viewing ray and measured the average distance of the point to this line.

In our experiments this error was below 0.02 mm for every experiment. However, the average distance of all fitted lines to the origin was greater than 0.14 mm for every experiment. These numbers were confirmed in several tests with a spline correction for the re-projective error functions as formulated in section 6.4.3.

These observations indicate that a non-standard camera model where the re-projected image points remain straight lines, which are not forced to intersect in one point, is feasible. In section 6.5 we introduce such a camera model.

6.4.8 Spline correction for stereo reconstruction

The aim of camera calibration should not be the minimization of the calibration error, but a minimal reconstruction error. Therefore, for the stereo reconstruction we may also correct the result of the stereo reconstruction instead of the camera mapping. This requires a stereo rig observing model points which cover the whole area in which measurements will take place.

If p' is the result of a stereo reconstruction, then we are looking for a $\delta_\text{stereo} \in \mathcal{S}_{n,U}^{3,3}$ which minimizes

$$\sum_{p \in \mathbf{P}} \|\delta(p') - p\|^2, \qquad (6.30)$$

where $U = (U_x, U_y, U_z)$ is a suitable knot sequence and $n = (n_x, n_y, n_z)$ a suitable degree. If such a δ_{stereo} is determined, we correct all following results of the stereo setup with this δ_{stereo}.

6.4.9 Disadvantages of the spline correction

The spline correction of the depth-dependent distortion has some disadvantages:

i. Narrow field of view

The correction is a function of the whole field of view to $\mathbb{R}^2$. A calibration setup has to provide data in the whole observable scene. The convex hull of data acquired uniformly in the whole observable scene will not define a cuboid. Thus, to obtain a suitable domain for a correction tensor spline, one has to restrict the area in which the camera mapping is corrected. In Figure 6.24, we show an exemplary sketch of this situation. Certainly, it is possible to define a spline space with the convex hull of all observed calibration points as domain, but such an approach can not be formulated as tensor product.

ii. Vast number of parameters

The tensor spline correction demands a huge number of parameters: Configurations like the one which we apply in the section 6.7 introduce spline spaces with a dimension of more than 100. It should be clear that this exceeds the number of parameters of the classic pinhole camera with distortion by far. This is the main reason why we apply the spline correction only for the residual distortion. In a non-linear optimization which include all parameters of the camera the spline parameter will dominate the optimization.

In the next section we propose a non-standard camera model with a distortion model that does depend on depth but has not the disadvantages listed above.

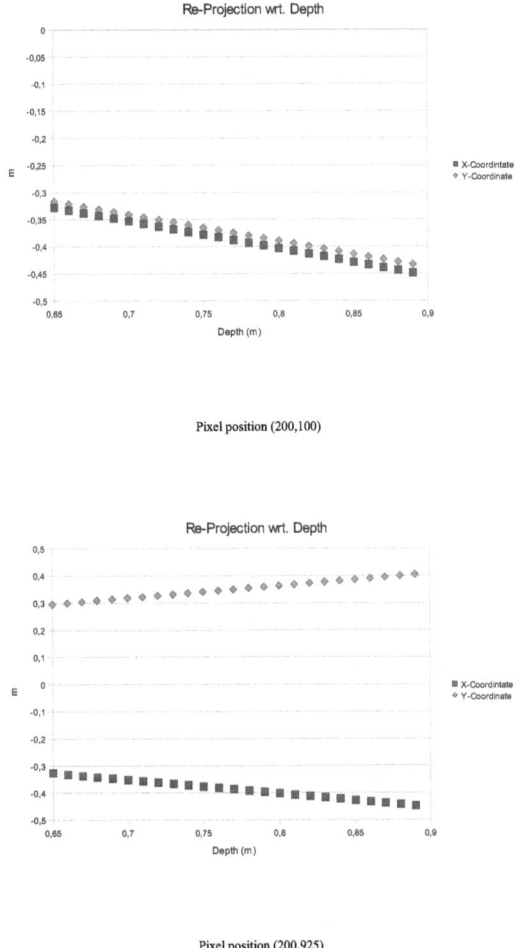

Figure 6.22: x- and y-coordinates of the re-projections at pixel position $(200, 100)$ and $(200, 925)$ w.r.t. the z-coordinate (sampled at distances of 1 cm).

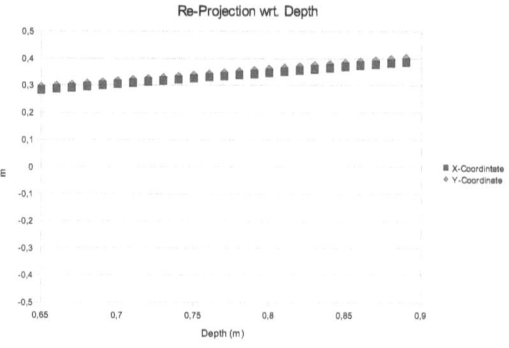

Pixel position (1025,100)

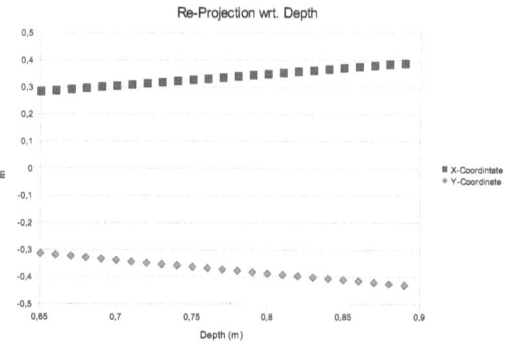

Pixel position (1025,925)

Figure 6.23: x- and y-coordinates of the re-projections at pixel position $(1025, 100)$ and $(1025, 925)$ w.r.t. the z-coordinate (sampled at distances of 1 cm).

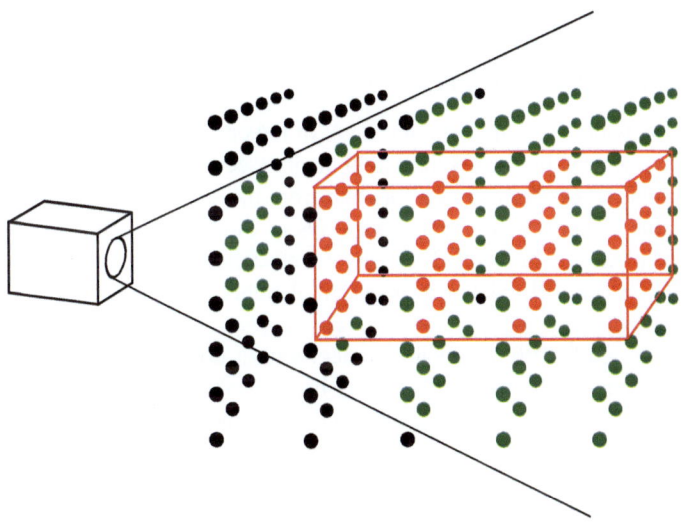

Figure 6.24: Sketch of calibration points uniformly distributed in the observable scene (black), the observed subset of these points (green) and the points in the cubic domain of a tensor spline correction (red).

6.5 A two-plane distortion model

6.5.1 Motivation and related work

One way to achieve a more complete sight of the optical behavior of an observed object is introduced by the 4D light field theory (see [AB91] for an introduction). The 4D light field is defined as a function from the set of all lines (light rays) to a light value. There are two principal ways to estimate this function, which is also called plenoptic function: Either by a well-defined movement of the camera (see *e.g.* [RB98] or [MP04]) or by a special plenoptic camera (see *e.g.* [AW92] or [NLB+05]).

Since we work with a standard camera with a non-well-defined movement, we can not recover the light field of an observed object. We apply the concept of describing the camera mapping completely by lines instead of a projection on $\{z = 1\}$. Therefore, we assume that the pre-image of each observed point is a line. In the following we describe this line by two points.

In [MBK81], Martins *et al.* made an early contribution to describe a camera by two planes. Given an image point they propose to determine the corresponding viewing ray by two points in two calibrated planes. These planes are parallel to the plane $\{z = 1\}$ w.r.t. the camera coordinate system. Positions on the calibrated planes are obtained by a linear interpolation, a quadratic interpolation or a linear spline extrapolation. Unfortunately, the authors compare their two-plane model with a pinhole camera model without distortion. Therefore, the model with the most parameters, *i.e.* the spline extrapolation, performs best in their test.

In [WM91] and [WM93] Wei and Ma extend the two-plane approach: They describe the mapping from each plane to the image as a projective mapping with an additional distortion term. Furthermore, they give an algorithm to obtain the parameters of a pinhole camera by the two-plane mapping. Also, they address the problem of epipolar curves within the two-plane model. Wei and Ma do not demand that the calibration planes are parallel to $\{z = 1\}$. However, in the experiments the calibration planes are parallel to each other.

In contrast to the approach of Wei and Ma we use no physical planes to describe the re-projection of observed image points. One point, which describes the re-projection, is located in $\{z = 1\}$ w.r.t. the camera coordinate system, a second point is located in $\{z = -1\}$ w.r.t. the camera coordinate system. A line which can not be described by points in these two planes can not be the pre-image of an observed point. Unlike the approaches described above, we formulate our two-plane model as an extension of the classic pinhole camera with distortion. We apply the two planes only to implement a depth-dependent distortion model for the pinhole camera.

6.5.2 The plane $\{z = -1\}$

We already introduced the plane $\{z = 1\}$ for the pinhole camera model as the domain of the distortion mapping. We now add the plane $\{z = -1\}$ w.r.t. the CCS as domain of a second distortion function.

Let $P_1 : \{z = 1\} \to \mathbb{R}^2$ be an image transformation. Then P_1 is a coordinate transformation from $\{z = 1\}$ w.r.t. the camera coordinate system to the image coordinate system with $P_1((x, y, 1)^t) = A \begin{pmatrix} x \\ y \end{pmatrix} + t$ where $A \in \mathbb{R}^{2 \times 2}$ is an upper triangular matrix with strictly positive diagonal entries and $t \in \mathbb{R}^2$. For this image transformation the inverse mapping is given by

$$P_1^{-1} : \begin{array}{c} \mathbb{R}^2 \to \{z = 1\} \\ \begin{pmatrix} u \\ v \end{pmatrix} \mapsto \begin{pmatrix} A^{-1}(\begin{pmatrix} u \\ v \end{pmatrix} - t) \\ 1 \end{pmatrix} \end{array} \qquad (6.31)$$

We now define a mapping from the plane $\{z = -1\}$ w.r.t. the CCS to the ICS: Let $P_2 : \{z = -1\} \to \mathbb{R}^2$ be defined as

$$P_2((x, y, -1)^t) = -A \begin{pmatrix} x \\ y \end{pmatrix} + t \qquad (6.32)$$

for the same $A \in \mathbb{R}^{2 \times 2}$ and t as in P_1. Then it is

$$P_1 \circ \Pi_z = P_2 \circ \Pi_{-z}, \qquad (6.33)$$

where

$$\Pi_{-z}((x, y, z)^t) := -\Pi_z((x, y, z)^t) = (-\frac{x}{z}, -\frac{y}{z}, -1)^t \qquad (6.34)$$

defines the projection on the plane $\{z = -1\}$.

Definition 6.5.1
Let $P_1 : \{z = 1\} \to \mathbb{R}^2$ be an image transformation. Then the mapping $P_2 : \{z = -1\} \to \mathbb{R}^2$ as defined in (6.32) is called the corresponding image transformation w.r.t. the plane $\{z = -1\}$.

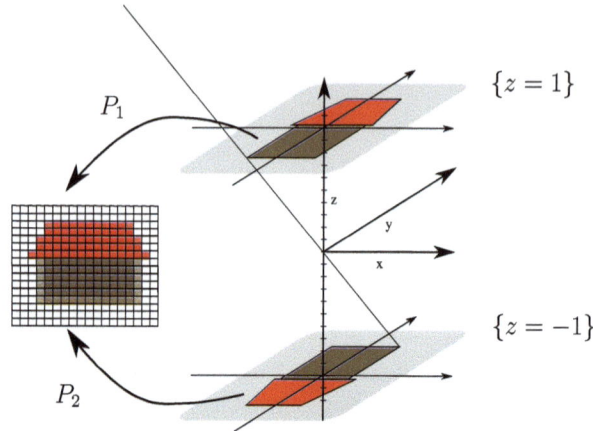

Figure 6.25: Sketch of the planes $\{z = 1\}$ and $\{z = -1\}$ and the mappings P_1 and P_2.

6.5.3 Distortion mappings in $\{z = 1\}$ and $\{z = -1\}$

We use the two planes $\{z = 1\}$ and $\{z = -1\}$ to implement different distortion mappings. Let $\Delta \subset \mathcal{C}_\infty(\mathbb{R}^2, \mathbb{R}^2)$ be a set of distortion mappings. To implement the distortion mapping in $\{z = -1\}$ we define

$$\tilde{\delta}^{-1} := \begin{pmatrix} \delta \\ -1 \end{pmatrix} \tag{6.35}$$

for $\delta \in \Delta$.

Furthermore, we want to treat both projection planes equivalently. This is necessary because it allows us to model common pinhole cameras with distortion model Δ as a subset of all cameras with the two-plane distortion model. Therefore, the set of distortion mappings Δ should be able to implement the same camera mapping with the aid of the plane $\{z = -1\}$ as for the plane $\{z = 1\}$. Thus, for $\delta_1 \in \Delta$ there should exist a $\delta_2 \in \Delta$ with $\left(P_1 \circ \tilde{\delta}_1 \circ \Pi_z\right)((x, y, z)^t) = \left(P_2 \circ \tilde{\delta}_2^{-1} \circ \Pi_{-z}\right)((x, y, z)^t)$ for all $(x, y, z)^t \in \mathbb{R}^3 \setminus \{z = 0\}$. Let $(u, v, 1)^t = \Pi_z((x, y, z)^t)$ and $\tilde{\delta}_1 = (\delta_1, 1)^t$ and $\tilde{\delta}_2^{-1} = (\delta_2, -1)$. Then it is $(-u, -v, -1)^t =$

$\Pi_{-z}((x,y,z)^t)$ and for $\delta_1 \in \Delta$ there should be a $\delta_2 \in \Delta$, such that

$$\left(P_1 \circ \tilde{\delta}_1 \circ \Pi_z\right)\begin{pmatrix}x\\y\\z\end{pmatrix} = P_2 \circ \tilde{\delta}_2 \circ \Pi_{-z}((x,y,z)^t) \quad (6.36)$$

$$\Leftrightarrow A\delta_1\left(\begin{pmatrix}u\\v\end{pmatrix}\right) = -A\delta_2\left(\begin{pmatrix}-u\\-v\end{pmatrix}\right) \quad (6.37)$$

$$\Leftrightarrow \delta_1\left(\begin{pmatrix}u\\v\end{pmatrix}\right) = -\delta_2\left(-\begin{pmatrix}u\\v\end{pmatrix}\right) \quad (6.38)$$

holds.

Therefore, we demand that

$$\forall \delta_1 \in \Delta : \exists \delta_2 \in \Delta : \forall p \in \mathbb{R}^2 : \delta_1(p) = -\delta_2(-p) \quad (6.39)$$

is true for Δ.

Note that this precondition holds for the radial, tangential and thin prism distortion. Furthermore, $\forall \delta_2 \in \Delta : \exists \delta_1 \in \Delta : \forall p \in \mathbb{R}^2 : -\delta_2(-p) = \delta_1(p)$ follows directly from (6.39).

Definition 6.5.2 (Distortion model w.r.t. the two-plane distortion)
We call a distortion model Δ satisfying (6.39) a distortion model w.r.t. the two-plane distortion.

6.5.4 The re-projection w.r.t. the two-plane distortion

To obtain the re-projection of a point observed in the image, we use the line defined by the distorted point in the plane $\{z = 1\}$ and in the plane $\{z = -1\}$. For the re-projection we need the inverse projections $(P_1 \circ \tilde{\delta}_1 \circ \Pi_z)^{-1}$ and $(P_2 \circ \tilde{\delta}_2 \circ \Pi_{-z})^{-1}$. This means that we actually need the un-distortion mapping $\delta^* \in \Delta$ instead of the distortion mapping $\delta \in \Delta$ (see section 2.5).

Definition 6.5.3 (T_{δ_1,δ_2})
Let $P_1 : \{z = 1\} \to \mathbb{R}^2$ be an image transformation and $P_2 : \{z = -1\} \to \mathbb{R}^2$ be the corresponding image transformation w.r.t. the plane $\{z = -1\}$. Furthermore, let $L(p_1, p_2) := \{p \in \mathbb{R}^3 \mid \exists \lambda \in \mathbb{R} : p = p_1 + \lambda(p_2 - p_1)\}$ be the line defined by p_1, p_2 and let $\mathcal{L}$ be the set of lines in $\mathbb{R}^3$. Let Δ be a distortion model w.r.t. the two-plane distortion and let $\delta_1, \delta_2 \in \Delta$ be two (un-)distortion functions. Then we set

$$T_{\delta_1,\delta_2} : \begin{array}{l} I \to \mathcal{L} \\ i_p \mapsto L(\tilde{\delta}_1(P_1^{-1}(i_p)), \tilde{\delta}_2^{-1}(P_2^{-1}(i_p))) \end{array} \quad (6.40)$$

to obtain the pre-image of an observed point i_p.

In analogy to the common pinhole camera model we call $T_{\delta_1,\delta_2}(i_p)$ the re-projection of the observed point i_p w.r.t. the two-plane distortion.

Furthermore, we set

$$\mathcal{T} := \left\{ T : \mathbb{R}^2 \to \mathcal{L} \,\middle|\, \exists \delta_1, \delta_2 \in \Delta : T = T_{\delta_1,\delta_2} \right\} \tag{6.41}$$

as the set of all adjustable two-plane re-projections w.r.t. the image transformation P_1 and the distortion model Δ.

Figure 6.25 sketches the re-projection of an observed point w.r.t. the two-plane distortion model. Note that depending on the choice of the (un-)distortion functions δ_1 and δ_2 there may be no point of intersection of all re-projected lines. This means that there is no optical center.

Remark 6.5.4 (One-plane distortion is a subset of the two-plane distortion)
For the pinhole camera model with distortion the distortion mapping is defined in the plane $\{z = 1\}$ only. Therefore, we call the standard distortion model as defined in section 2.4 one-plane distortion model. It is easy to see that definition 6.5.2 ensures that the one-plane distortion model is a subset of the two-plane distortion model:

Let P_1, P_2 be defined as definition 6.5.3. Let now $\delta_1, \delta_2 \in \Delta$ with $\forall p \in \mathbb{R}^2$: $\delta_1(p) = -\delta_2(-p)$ be the distortion mappings in T_{δ_1,δ_2}. Then $P_1 \circ \tilde{\delta}_1 \circ \Pi_z = P_2 \circ \tilde{\delta}_2^{-1} \circ \Pi_{-z}$ holds. Thus, it is

$$T_{\delta_1,\delta_2}(i_p) = \overline{\left(P_1 \circ \tilde{\delta}_1 \circ \Pi_z \right)^{-1} (\{i_p\})} \tag{6.42}$$

for every image point $i_p \in I$. Hence, the set of all adjustable two-plane re-projections is a superset of the one-plane re-projections. In this sense the one-plane distortion model is a subset of the two-plane distortion model.

6.5.5 Error functions for the two-plane distortion model

In this section we propose error functions for the two-plane distortion model. We follow the categorization of error functions for the pinhole camera model in section 3. All error functions depend on the depth of the observed point.

6.5.5.1 The projective error

In computer vision the projective error as defined in section 3.2 is the canonical way to measure the error of an observation to an projection. As stated in section 3.2 the error is measured in the image. For the two-plane distortion model this requires us to measure the error in two planes. Since each $T \in \mathcal{T}$ defines a projection $P_1 \circ \tilde{\delta}_1 \circ \Pi_z$ via $\{z = 1\}$ to the image plane and a projection $P_2 \circ \tilde{\delta}_2^{-1} \circ \Pi_{-z}$ via $\{z = -1\}$ to the image plane, one may minimize

$$\|i_p - P_1 \circ \delta_1 \circ \Pi_z(p)\|^2 + \|i_p - P_2 \circ \delta_2 \circ \Pi_{-z}(p)\|^2 \qquad (6.43)$$

to calibrate w.r.t. the two-plane distortion model. However, with $P_1 \circ \Pi_z = P_2 \circ \Pi_{-z}$, (6.43) actually defines the projective error function w.r.t. the standard one-plane distortion. This means that for this error function the two-plane distortion model would not be an improvement. Surprisingly, it is possible to implement a meaningful projective error in a slightly modified way (see remark 6.5.7).

6.5.5.2 The Euclidean error

Evidently, the Euclidean distance of a point to the re-projection of its observation defines an error for each model point. With this error the error function w.r.t. the two-plane camera model becomes

$$\Psi_E : \begin{array}{l} \mathcal{T} \to \mathbb{R}_+ \\ T \mapsto \sum_{p \in \mathbf{P}} \text{dist}_3(p, T(i_p))^2 \end{array}, \qquad (6.44)$$

where i_p denotes the observation of $p \in \mathbf{P}$. For the two-plane distortion model we define the Euclidean error as follows:

Definition 6.5.5 (Euclidean error)
Let for an image transformation P_1 and a distortion model Δ w.r.t. two-plane distortion $\mathcal{T} = \{T : \mathbb{R}^2 \to \mathcal{L} \mid \exists \delta_1, \delta_2 \in \Delta : T = T_{\delta_1, \delta_2}\}$ be the set of all adjustable two-plane re-projections Then for $T \in \mathcal{T}$, a point $p \in \mathbf{P}$, and its observation i_p in the image of the camera, the distance

$$\text{dist}_3(T(i_p), p)^2 \qquad (6.45)$$

is called Euclidean error w.r.t. the two-plane distortion model.

This error defines the same error as the Euclidean error in the case of the pinhole camera model (see section 3.3) but is no longer constrained to pinhole cameras. Therefore, the error function Ψ_E lacks the same weakness as the Euclidean error for pinhole cameras: Objects at a greater distance to the camera may contribute a greater error than objects near the camera plane, although their observation may be the same.

6.5.5.3 The projected Euclidean error

It is widely accepted in computer vision to measure the distance from the observed data to projected data of the model **P** in the image plane (see section 3.2). For an object point p and line L we set $\text{Proj}_L(p)$ as the orthogonal projection of p on L. Then we measure the Euclidean distance of $\Pi_z(p)$ to the projection of $\text{Proj}_{T_{\delta_1,\delta_2}(i_p)}(p)$ on $\{z = 1\}$ (see Fig. 6.26).

Definition 6.5.6 (projected Euclidean error)
Let for an image transformation P_1 and a distortion model Δ w.r.t. two-plane distortion $\mathcal{T} = \{T : \mathbb{R}^2 \to \mathcal{L} \mid \exists \delta_1, \delta_2 \in \Delta : T = T_{\delta_1,\delta_2}\}$ be the set of all adjustable two-plane re-projections. Then for $T \in \mathcal{T}$, a point $p \in \mathbf{P}$, and its observation i_p in the image of the camera, the distance

$$\text{dist}_3(\Pi_z(\text{Proj}_{T(i_p)}(p)), \Pi_z(p)) \qquad (6.46)$$

is called projected Euclidean error.

The projected Euclidean error is actually measured in $\{z = 1\}$ and is in fact a 2D error. Therefore, the projected Euclidean error is comparable to the re-projective error for the pinhole camera model.

The error function w.r.t. the projected Euclidean error is

$$\Psi_Z : \begin{array}{l} \mathcal{T} \to \mathbb{R}_+ \\ T \mapsto \sum_{p \in \mathbf{P}} \text{dist}_3(\Pi_z(\text{Proj}_{T(i_p)}(p)), \Pi_z(p))^2 \end{array}. \qquad (6.47)$$

Remark 6.5.7 (A projective error for the two-plane distortion model)
Obviously, the projections of p and $\text{Proj}_{T_{\delta_1,\delta_2}(i_p)}(p)$ can be transformed by P_1 into the image coordinate system and therefore may be used to formulate an projective error.

6.5.5.4 The normalized Euclidean error

The re-projective nature of the two-plane distortion model also enables us to transfer the normalized Euclidean error to the two-plane distortion model.

Definition 6.5.8 (normalized Euclidean error)
Let for an image transformation P_1 and a distortion model Δ w.r.t. the two-plane distortion $\mathcal{T} = \{T : \mathbb{R}^2 \to \mathcal{L} \mid \exists \delta_1, \delta_2 \in \Delta : T = T_{\delta_1, \delta_2}\}$ be the set of all adjustable two-plane re-projections. Then for $T \in \mathcal{T}$, a point $p \in \mathbf{P}$ with $p \notin \{z = 0\}$, and its observation i_p in the image of the camera, the distance

$$\text{dist}_3 \left(\frac{\text{Proj}_{T(i_p)}(p)}{\|\text{Proj}_{T(i_p)}(p)\|}, \frac{\Pi_z(p)}{\|\Pi_z(p)\|} \right) \quad (6.48)$$

is called normalized Euclidean error w.r.t. the two-plane distortion model.

In Figure 6.26 we sketch the normalized Euclidean error w.r.t. the two-plane distortion.

The error function w.r.t. the normalized Euclidean error becomes

$$\Psi_N : \begin{array}{l} \mathcal{T} \to \mathbb{R}_+ \\ T \mapsto \sum_{p \in \mathbf{P}} \text{dist}_3 \left(\frac{\text{Proj}_{T(i_p)}(p)}{\|\text{Proj}_{T(i_p)}(p)\|}, \frac{\Pi_z(p)}{\|\Pi_z(p)\|} \right)^2 \end{array}. \quad (6.49)$$

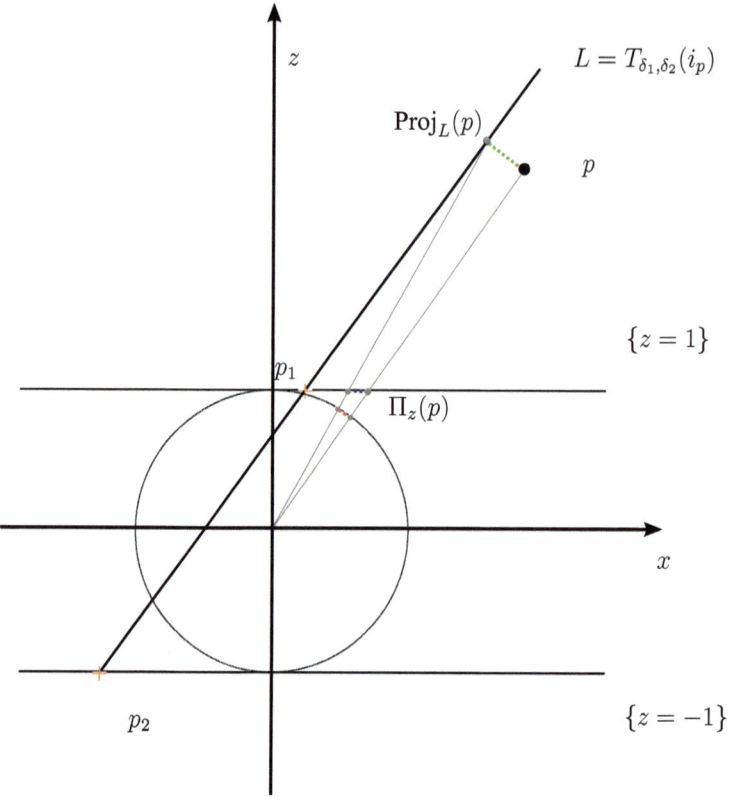

Figure 6.26: Sketch of the two error functions for the two-plane distortion model: For an image point i_p it is $p_1 = \delta_1(P_1^{-1}(i_p))$ and $p_2 = \delta_2(P_2^{-1}(i_p))$. The re-projected line $T_{\delta_1,\delta_2}(i_p)$ is defined by p_1 and p_2. The Euclidean error of the object point p to the re-projected line is displayed in green, the projected Euclidean error, *i.e.* the error of $\Pi_z(p)$ to $\mathrm{Proj}_{T_{\delta_1,\delta_2}(i_p)}(p)$ is displayed in blue, the normalized Euclidean error is displayed in red.

6.5.5.5 Depth-dependence of the two-plane distortion model

It should be emphasized that all errors w.r.t. to the two-plane distortion model depend on the depth of the observed point. An observed image point i_p defines a straight line $T_{\delta_1,\delta_2}(i_p)$, but all error functions use this line to derive a depth-dependency as one can observe in Figure 6.27: Although two points $p_1, p_2 \in \mathbb{R}^3$ may be projected on the same point $\Pi_z(p_1) = \Pi_z(p_2)$ in $\{z = 1\}$, the error caused by these points depends on the depth of p_1 and p_2. In Figure 6.27 the point p_2 causes a smaller error w.r.t. all proposed error functions than p_1.

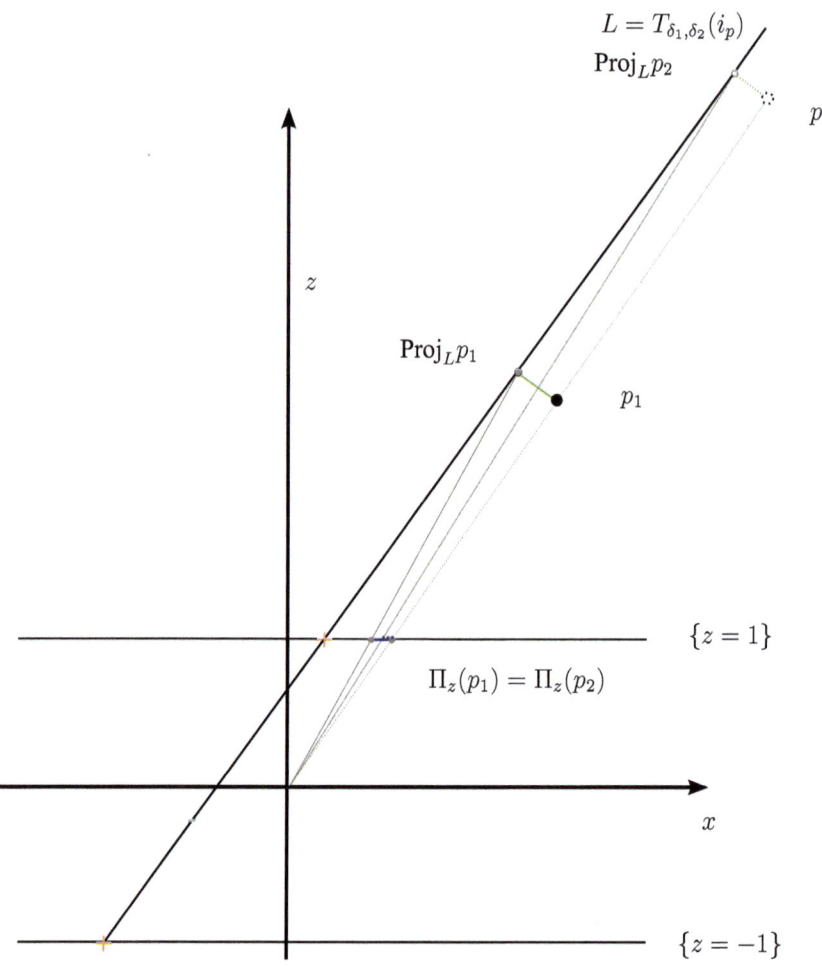

Figure 6.27: Influence of the depth on the measured error: Let i_p be the observation of p_1 and p_2 with $\Pi_z(p_1) = \Pi_z(p_2)$. In the situation of the sketch the error of p_1 is greater than the error of p_2. This holds for the Euclidean error (solid green line vs. dashed green line), the projected Euclidean error (solid blue line vs. dashed blue line) and the normalized Euclidean error (not displayed).

6.5.6 Calibration algorithm

Since we consider the two-plane distortion model as an extension of the standard pinhole camera model with distortion, the calibration w.r.t. the two-plane distortion model consists of two steps:

i. Calibration w.r.t. the standard one-plane distortion model

   The first step of our proposed calibration algorithm is a minimization of the projective error function Φ in (3.13) (see section 3.4.1). Since we want to perform a camera calibration with high precision, we propose to use the radial distortion $\Delta_{r,D}$ with at least four distortion parameters. This demands a sufficient number of model points $|\mathbf{P}|$. The results of this step are the image transformations P_1, P_2, which remain fixed in the second step, and a distortion δ_1, which provides an initial value for the two-plane distortion in step ii. (Notice that we need the inverse of δ_1 as an initial value for the two-plane distortion model!)

ii. Calibration w.r.t. the two-plane distortion model

   The second step of the calibration algorithm is to determine T_{δ_1,δ_2} which minimizes Ψ_Z in (6.47). In contrast to step i. we demand that there is one set of model points $\mathbf{P}$ defining a full 3D calibration cube, which we observe only at one position. For the non-linear optimization of Ψ_Z in (6.47) the algorithm of Broyden, Fletcher, Goldfarb, and Shanno (BFGS) with numerically computed gradients may be applied.

   Also, as we will show in our experiments in section 6.7, one should consider a distortion model, which is actually a superset of the distortion model chosen in step i.

6.6 A generic multi-plane camera

6.6.1 Introduction and related work

The two-plane distortion model defines a mapping for every image position $i \in I$ to a line $l_i \in \mathcal{L}$. We formulated this model as a refinement of the classic pinhole camera with distortion. The calibration w.r.t. the two-plane distortion model is carried out after an elaborate calibration w.r.t. the classic camera model. In particular, the image transformation P defines a crucial part of a camera with a two-plane distortion model which is not changed during the final refinement. Therefore, we are able to formulate a projective error for the two-plane distortion model.

As already stated in section 6.5.1, the two-plane camera model as introduced by Martins and propagated by Wei and Ma defines a camera model itself. Recent publications in the area of catadioptric cameras follow this more general approach to camera calibration. For catadioptric cameras, models without a focal point are considered. By definition a catadioptric camera contains mirrors (catoptrics) and lenses (dioptrics). Such systems are often used in surveillance or photography to obtain a panoramic view by looking at a curved mirror. The shape of the mirror determines whether all viewing rays (*i.e.* the pre-image of an image point) intersect in one point or not. Sturm and Ramalingam speak of "central" and "non central cameras" (see [SR04]). Methods to model and to calibrate a central catadioptric camera can be found *e.g.* in [GD02, Bar03, YH04]. For non-central catadioptric cameras calibration approaches are proposed in [Ali01, SGN01]. The non-central catadioptric cameras require a more general approach to the camera mapping. This general approach is characterized by mapping image positions to lines (see [GN01, SR04]).

6.6.2 From the image to a reference coordinate system

Each position of an observed planar calibration pattern **P** defines its own coordinate system. We call this coordinate system the *local plane coordinate system*. Let for the d-th observation of the pattern, C_d be the mapping from the image coordinate system to a d-th local plane coordinate system. For a pinhole camera without distortion C_d is a homography. In [WM91] Wei and Ma consider a homography with an additional distortion term to model C_d^{-1} (*i.e.* the mapping from the calibration plane to the image). However, they limit their approach to polynomials with degree two (in homogenous coordinates). The main reason for this is that they actually need to determine C_d.

For a general camera we only know for each observation i_p of a point $p \in \mathbf{P}$ the mapping C_d satisfies $C_d(i_p) = p$. This means that C_d is sampled at $|\mathbf{P}|$ points of the d-th planar pattern. Therefore, we may approximate C_d by a function $C'_d \in \mathcal{F}$ in the sense that C'_d minimizes

$$\sum_{p\in\mathbf{P}} \|(C'_d(i_p) - p\|^2 \qquad (6.50)$$

for functions in $\mathcal{F}$, where $\mathcal{F} \subset \mathcal{C}(\mathbb{R}^2, \mathbb{R}^2)$ is a finite dimensional vector space. Obviously, to diminish outliers $\dim(\mathcal{F})$ should be less than the number of observed points. As a result, we can extrapolate the coordinates of each observed position

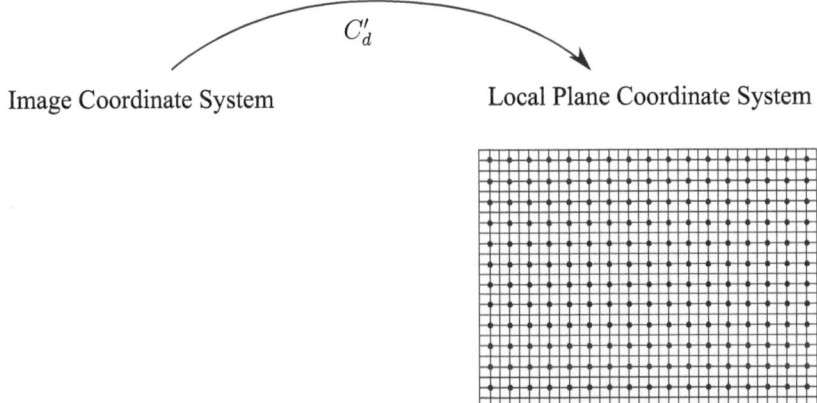

Figure 6.28: Sketch of the approximated mapping C'_d from the image coordinate system to the local plane coordinate system.

$i_p \in I$ with respect to the local plane coordinate system.

For k observations of the calibration pattern, we define C'_d with $d \in \{1, \ldots, k\}$ as the approximated coordinate transformation from the image coordinate system to the d-th observation of $\mathbf{P}$ (see Figure 6.28 for an exemplification). Furthermore, let $T_d \in \mathcal{T}(\mathbb{R}^3, \mathbb{R}^3)$ be the isometric coordinate transformation from d-th local plane coordinate system to a global reference coordinate system. Then we define

$$C : \begin{matrix} I \to \mathcal{L} \\ i \mapsto l(i) \end{matrix} \qquad (6.51)$$

where $l(i) \in \mathcal{L}(\mathbb{R}^3)$ is the line closest to the set

$$\mathcal{I}_i := \{T_1(C'_{d_1}(i), 0), \ldots T_k(C'_{d_n}(i), 0)\}. \tag{6.52}$$

Since we assume that $\mathcal{I}_i$ samples the pre-image of the image coordinate $i \in I$, $C(i)$ approximates the viewing ray for this pixel position (see Figure 6.29 for a sketch of sampled viewing rays obtained by extrapolated point positions).

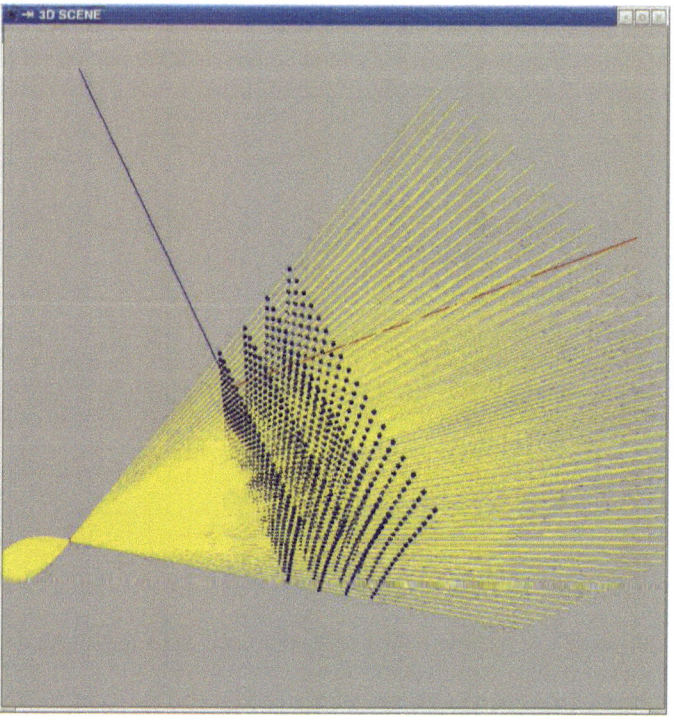

Figure 6.29: Determine viewing rays for every pixel position.

6.6.3 Tensor spline approximation of the coordinate transformation

In our implementation we use tensor product splines to approximate the mappings C_d for $d \in \{1, \ldots, k\}$. In the notation of section 6.4.4 let N_x, N_y be B-spline bases of splines of degree $n = (n_x, n_y)$ with knot sequences $U = (U_x, U_y)$ such that the inner knots cover the image equidistantly.

Then we set $D := [u_{x,0}, u_{x,g_x}] \times [u_{y,0}, u_{y,g_y}] = I$ as the rectangle defined by the inner g_x, g_y knots of U and set

$$\mathcal{S}_{n,U}^{2,2} := \left\{ s : D \to \mathbb{R}^2 \mid s(x,y) = s_{(a,b,c,d)}(x,y) \right.$$
$$\left. \text{for } a, b \in \mathbb{R}^{n_x + g_x}, c, d \in \mathbb{R}^{n_y + g_y} \right\} \quad (6.53)$$

with

$$s_{(a,b,c,d)}(x,y) = \begin{pmatrix} \langle a | N_x(x) \rangle & \langle c | N_y(y) \rangle \\ \langle b | N_x(x) \rangle & \langle d | N_y(y) \rangle \end{pmatrix}. \quad (6.54)$$

With $\mathcal{F} = \mathcal{S}_{n,U}^{2,2}$ the minimization problem in Equation 6.50 becomes a linear least squares problem.

6.6.4 A calibration setup for the generic multi-plane camera

Until now we have ignored a central problem of the general camera concept: The determination of the isometric coordinate transformations $T_1, \ldots, T_k$. In [SR04], Sturm and Ramalingam present an algorithm based on a collinearity constraint for the trifocal calibration tensor (see e.g. [HZ00]).

However, a simple approach is to use a calibration plane containing **P** which is moved along an axis perpendicular to the image plane with a very high precision. If the relative displacement ϑ for each position of the plane is known (see Figure 6.30), we take the coordinate system defined by the first position as reference coordinate system and set $T_1 = \text{id}, T_2 = (0, 0, \vartheta)^t, T_k = (0, 0, (k-1)\vartheta)^t$.

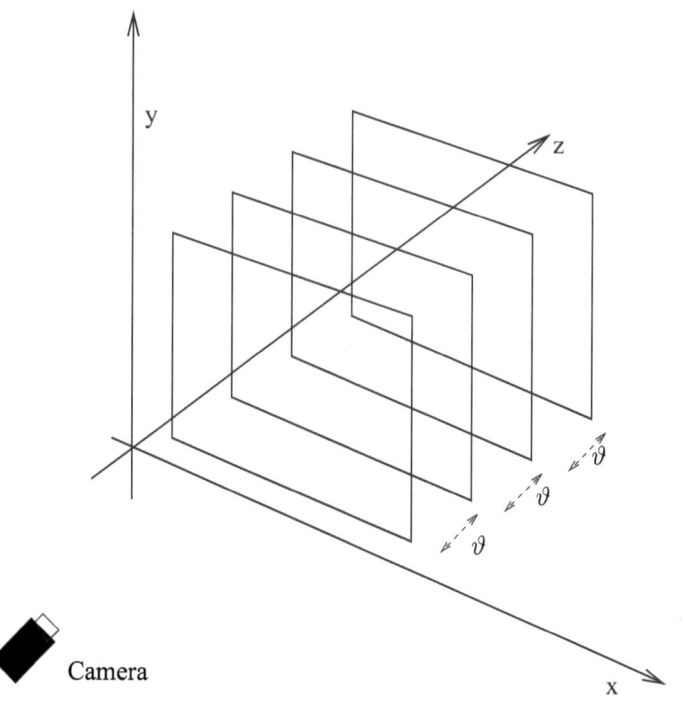

Figure 6.30: A simple setup where every local reference coordinate system is known w.r.t. to a global reference coordinate system.

6.7 Experimental results

6.7.1 Setup

In our experiments we use a planar calibration pattern with a grid of 51×49 points, where adjacent points have a distance of 2 cm to each other. Each point has a diameter of 2 mm. This calibration target can be used as flexible target. Furthermore, we are able to perform a defined linear movement of this target as illustrated in Figure 6.15 on page 128.

For all following experiments we used cameras with a 2/3" CCD imaging sensor (IBIS 5A[2]) with a pixel size of $6.7\mu m \times 6.7\mu m$ and a resolution of 1280×1024 pixels. The lens was a standard lens by Pentax with a focal length of 6 mm.

6.7.1.1 Calibration setup for the standard camera model

To calibrate the camera w.r.t. the standard pinhole camera model with distortion we observe the calibration target at 20 non coplanar positions and apply the algorithm described in [Zha98].

6.7.1.2 Calibration setup for the spline correction

To obtain the three-dimensional calibration data to determine the correction mapping as described in section 6.4 we moved the planar calibration target along the optical axis in 8 equidistant steps of 4 cm covering the distance of 60 to 90 cm to the camera.

6.7.1.3 Calibration setup for the two-plane distortion model

In our experiments we choose $\Delta := \Delta_{r,4} + \Delta_{P,n}$ with

$$\Delta_{P,n} := \mathcal{P}_n(\mathbb{R}^2, \mathbb{R}^2) \tag{6.55}$$

as distortion model w.r.t. the two-plane distortion, whereas $\mathcal{P}_n(\mathbb{R}^2, \mathbb{R}^2)$ is the set of all bivariate polynomials to $\mathbb{R}^2$ with total degree n. Note that $\Delta_{r,4} \cap \Delta_{P,n}$ is not empty. This must be considered in the parametrization of the distortion mapping.

To obtain the calibration cube as demanded in section 6.5.6 for the calibration algorithm w.r.t. to the two-plane distortion model, we observe the set of points

---

[2]http://www.ptgrey.com/support/kb/data/IBIS5A-1300.pdf, visited on July 16th 2008

in a defined movement along the $\vec{z}$-axis of the planar calibration pattern. Again, the distance between two subsequent positions of the calibration plane is 4 cm. However, the planes cover a distance of 98 cm to 50 cm to the camera plane.

6.7.2 Results for spline corrected cameras

6.7.2.1 Prototype reconstruction

In this section we apply one camera to reconstruct an observed planar calibration pattern. Depending on the applied error function we performed the prototype reconstruction (3.17) as defined in section 3.4.2.

In the following experiments we employ several spline corrections for a standard pinhole camera with a radial distortion term with four coefficients (*i.e.* $\Delta_{r,4}$ in definition 2.4.4).

For the evaluation of the spline correction we apply a data set, which is obtained as described in section 6.7.1.2, but is different to the calibration data. Thus, we are able to provide reference data within the coordinate system of the first calibration plate. The coordinate transformation from the camera coordinate system to this reference coordinate system can be obtained by minimizing the distance to all observed points. Thus, we assume that we reach such an accuracy in this coordinate transformation that the error to the real point w.r.t. camera coordinate system is negligible. This allows us to measure the distance of a reconstructed point the real point. We call this distance *point to point error*.

6.7.2.1.1 In-plane spline correction At first sight an improvement in reconstruction with a depth dependent spline correction seems obvious because it applies a model with more parameters. To refute this argument we first analyze a spline correction of the residual distortion without a depth component. We apply with different kinds of spline spaces in the plane $\{z = 1\}$ of the camera as distortion mapping. In the experiments we refer to the latter as *in-plane* correction spline or simply abbreviate **2d** in the following figures.

In Figure 6.31 the results for in-plane corrections with spline spaces $\mathcal{S}_{n,U}^{2,2}$ with different knot sequences U and degrees n are sketched. A test is performed with a knot sequence of 10 equidistant inner knots and degree 5 in each direction, with 10 equidistant inner knots and degree 7 in each direction, and with 20 equidistant inner knots and degree 10 in each direction.

The reconstruction w.r.t. a camera model which includes a spline correction introduces a non-linear problem. For the results in Figure 6.31 we applied the

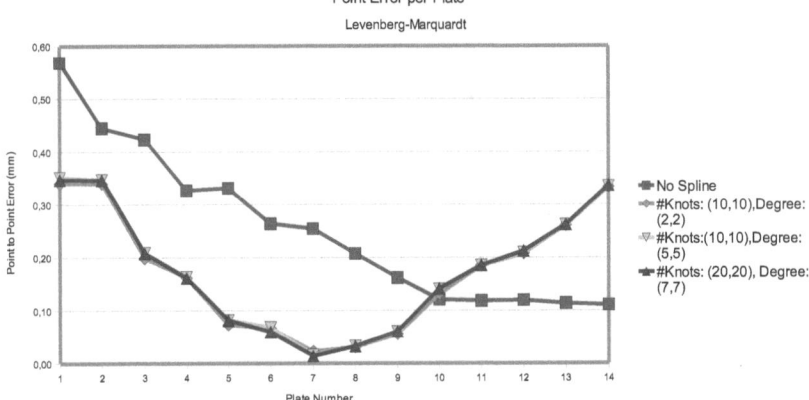

Figure 6.31: Average point to point error for the 14 parallel targets in increasing depth for the standard pinhole camera with four radial distortion parameters (standard) and several additional in-plane correction splines.

Levenberg-Marquardt algorithm. In the next section we also present some results for the BFGS algorithm.

One can see in Figure 6.31 that the spline space with the least number of parameters performs nearly as well as the spline space with the most number of parameters. The improvement is negligible. Moreover, it is very likely that splines with a higher number of parameters approximate not a systematic deviation but the observable noise.

6.7.2.1.2 3d spline correction
We now turn to spline corrections which depend on the depth of the observed points. In the following we denote **3d2d** for the spline correction w.r.t. the re-projective error as introduced in section 6.4.3. By **3d3d** we denote the spline correction w.r.t. the Euclidean error as proposed in section 6.4.6.

In our experimental setup only the last image of a sequence contains all points of the planar calibration pattern. Furthermore, we could not use the first position for a spline corrected reconstruction, since this position was not covered by the domain of the spline in the calibration phase (see 6.4.9).

To compare the results obtained by spline corrected reconstructions with a standard camera (with in-plane correction) we include the results of the previous paragraph.

Since the reconstruction w.r.t. a camera model which includes a spline correction introduces a non-linear problem, we apply two different non-linear optimization routines in our experiments: The BFGS-algorithm (Figure 6.32 and Figure 6.35) and the algorithm of Levenberg and Marquardt (Figure 6.33 and Figure 6.34) deliver very similar results. However, it seems that for spline spaces with a higher number of parameters the Levenberg-Marquardt method is more robust (at least for the **3d2d** approach, see Figure 6.35 and Figure 6.34).

The results in Figure 6.32, Figure 6.33, Figure 6.34, and Figure 6.35 show a relevant improvement in the point to point error for the depth-dependent spline correction.

For the results in Figure 6.32 and Figure 6.33 we apply a correction spline with degree $(5, 5, 3)$ for the **3d3d** correction spline and **3d2d** correction spline. We obtain a comparable result with splines of degree $(2, 2, 2)$ (Figure 6.34 and Figure 6.35). In all experiments we used a knot sequence with $(10, 10, 3)$ inner knots. The improvement for the **3d3d** spline correction is not significantly higher than for the **3d2d** spline correction, which needs less parameters.

Like in the case of the in-plane correction, the improvement of the depth-dependent correction with splines is limited: At some point an increasing number of parameters leads to numerical instabilities in reconstruction, since the prototype reconstruction problem becomes a complex non-linear problem. One can see in Figure 6.32 that the BFGS algorithms has already problems with a spline of degree $(5, 5, 3)$ and a knot sequence with $(10, 10, 2)$ inner knots. Any spline space with a higher number of parameters leads to incorrect results.

Figure 6.36 and Figure 6.37 show tests of several configurations to obtain an optimal adjustment of the number of inner knots and the order of the spline for the depth-dependent correction w.r.t. the re-projective error. One can see in Figure

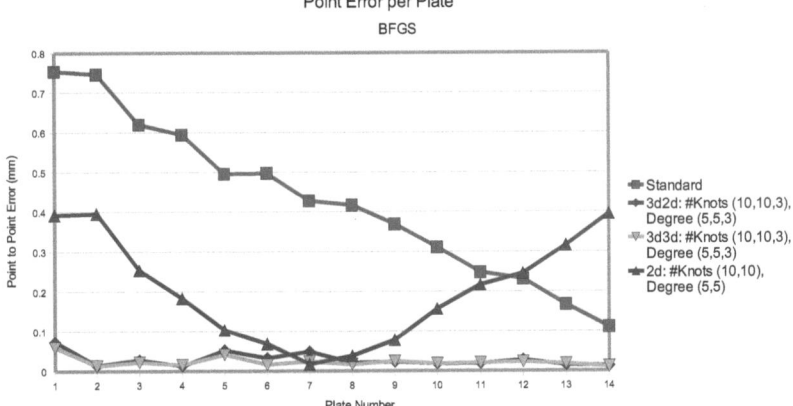

Figure 6.32: Average point to point error for the 14 parallel targets in increasing depth for the pinhole camera model with radial distortion (**Standard**), for correction w.r.t. re-projective error (**3d2d**), w.r.t. the Euclidean error (**3d3d**), and an in-plane correction spline (**2d**). Non-linear optimization with the BFGS algorithm.

6.36 that a degree lower than 2 in the plane z-direction w.r.t. the camera coordinate system yields an insignificant improvement, while the number of inner knots has only a minor influence. This motivates to use a polynomial space as distortion model w.r.t. the two-plane distortion model as introduced in section 6.7.1.3.

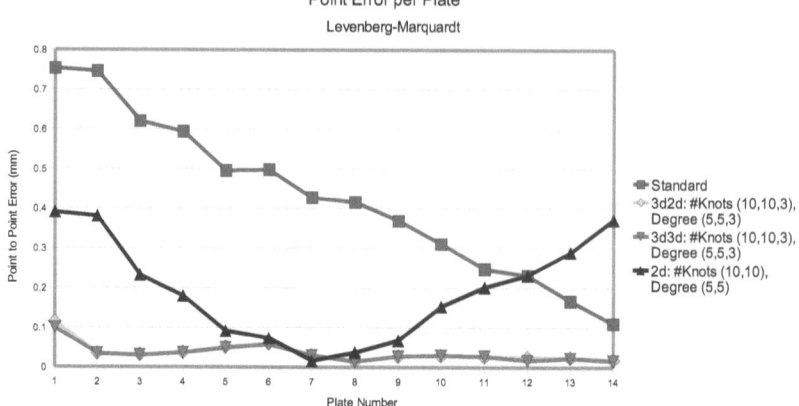

Figure 6.33: Average point to point error for the 14 parallel targets in increasing depth for the pinhole camera model with radial distortion (**Standard**), for correction w.r.t. re-projective error (**3d2d**), w.r.t. the Euclidean error (**3d3d**), and an in-plane correction spline (**2d**). Non-linear optimization with the Levenberg-Marquardt algorithm.

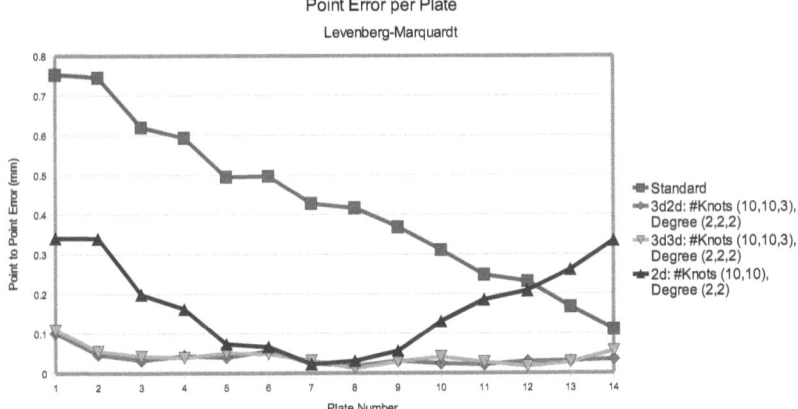

Figure 6.34: Average point to point error for the 14 parallel targets in increasing depth for the pinhole camera model with radial distortion (**Standard**), for correction w.r.t. re-projective error (**3d2d**), w.r.t. the Euclidean error (**3d3d**), and an in-plane correction spline (**2d**). Non-linear optimization with the Levenberg-Marquardt algorithm.

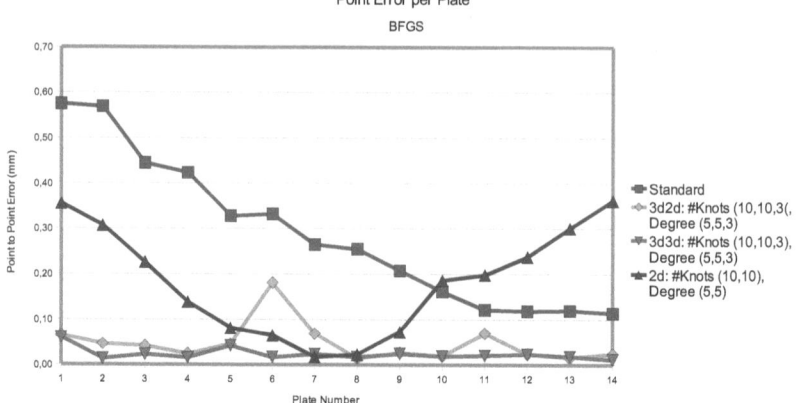

Figure 6.35: Average point to point error for the 14 parallel targets in increasing depth for the pinhole camera model with radial distortion (**Standard**), for correction w.r.t. re-projective error (**3d2d**), w.r.t. the Euclidean error (**3d3d**), and an in-plane correction spline (**2d**). Non-linear optimization with the BFGS algorithm.

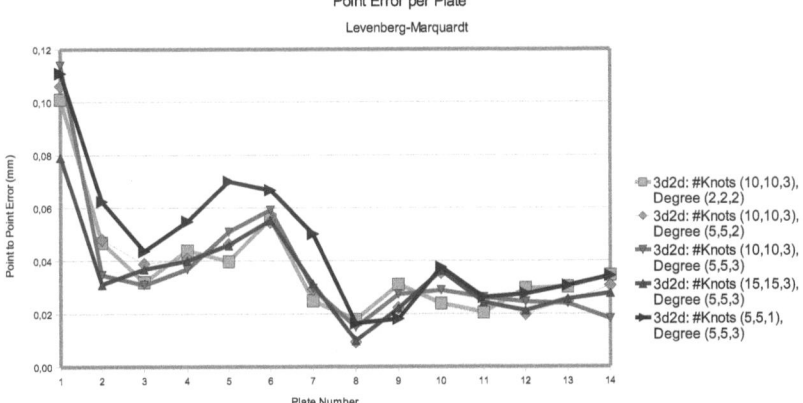

Figure 6.36: Average point to point error for the 14 parallel targets in increasing depth for the pinhole camera model with different spline corrections w.r.t. reprojective error (**3d2d**).

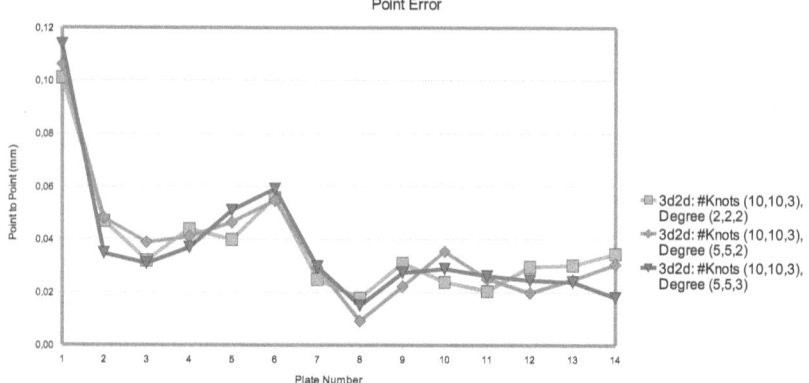

Figure 6.37: Average point to point error for the 14 parallel targets in increasing depth for the pinhole camera model with different spline corrections w.r.t. reprojective error (**3d2d**), subset of Figure 6.36.

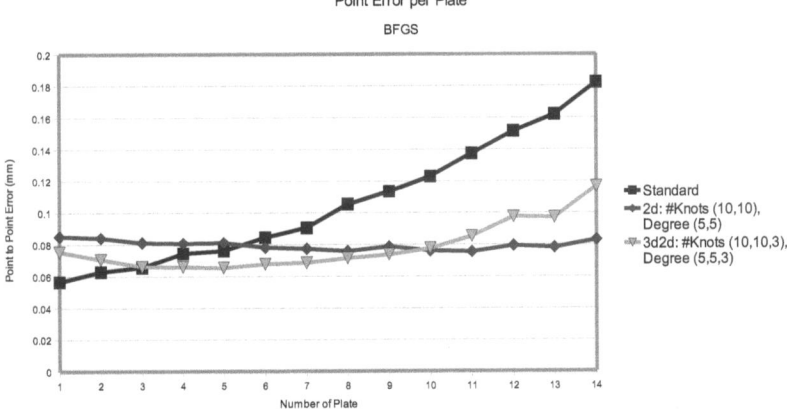

Figure 6.38: Result for a 3d2d spline correction with a small stereo base: the intersection of both domains is exhaustive.

6.7.2.2 Stereo reconstruction

We already stated in section 6.4.9 that a correction spline which depends on the depth of an observed object has a narrow field of view. In the case of a stereo reconstruction a spline correction can only be applied in the intersection of the domain of both correcting splines.

For two simple experiments we observe the a data set, which is obtained as described in section 6.7.1.2, but we look at it with two cameras. The two cameras are located with nearly parallel optical axes at a large and and a small stereo base.

Figure 6.38 and Figure 6.39 show that the depth dependent spline correction yields a negligible result in stereo reconstruction compared with the in-plane correction. However, a small stereo base, which results in a larger common range of depth in the spline domain, yields better results (see Figure 6.38).

However, we obtain a better result with less parameters for a stereo reconstruction if we apply a correcting spline on the stereo reconstruction as described in section 6.4.8. In Figure 6.40 we show the result for correction spline $s \in \mathcal{S}_{n,U}^{3,3}$ where the number of the equidistant inner knots is $(5, 5, 3)$ and the degree is $n = (5, 5, 2)$.

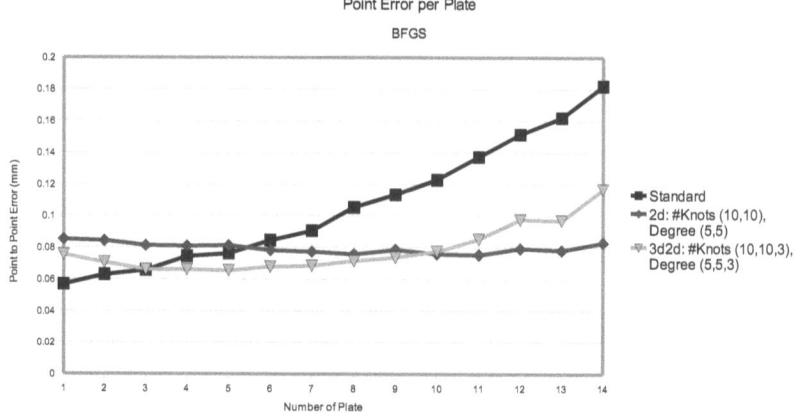

Figure 6.39: Result for 3d2d spline correction with a wide stereo base: the intersection of both domains does not cover all observed points.

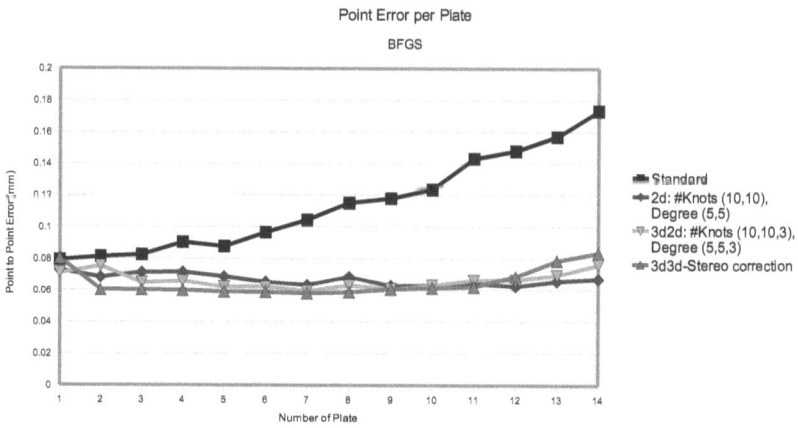

Figure 6.40: Result for 3d3d spline correction of the stereo reconstruction compared to other results.

6.7.3 Results for the two-plane distortion model

In contrast to the depth depending spline correction, we emphasize the stereo reconstruction as application for the two-plane distortion model.

6.7.3.1 Stereo reconstruction

For the evaluation of the two-plane distortion model we use a setup which is modified to a stereo setup: two calibrated cameras are placed at an angle of approximately 15° to the 24 parallel planes. To measure the performance of the stereo reconstruction we investigate two errors: we measure the 3D-distance of points reconstructed from our calibration pattern and the angle of the reconstructed plane.

For the first comparison we reconstruct each point of the calibration pattern by stereo reconstruction. We measure the distance to the actual point and plot the average distance of all points of an observed pattern as a result. This error is called *point to point error*.

For the another comparison we measure the angle of each reconstructed plane to the real plane, for which the coordinates are known by a coordinate-measuring machine. A smaller angle indicates a better reconstruction of the observed plane points. We call the distance between the reconstructed angle and the real angle *angle error*.

6.7.3.2 Point to point error

First we show the profit of the two-plane distortion model in comparison to the standard model by applying the same set of distortion mappings. In Figure 6.41 we choose $\Delta = \Delta_{r,4}$ as distortion model for the one-plane camera and for the two-plane camera. As one can see in Figure 6.41 the point to point error for the two-plane distortion model is up to 50% lower than for the one-plane distortion.

An improvement of the observed error seems natural, since the two-plane distortion introduces more parameters than the one-plane model. However, as Figure 6.42 shows, additional parameters for the one-plane distortion model will not lead to better reconstruction results automatically: Additional polynomials with a degree higher than six yield no visible improvement in reconstruction.

For the two-plane model an additional polynomial distortion mapping improves the observed error even for low order polynomials. Figure 6.43 shows that there is also a considerable improvement in the point to point error for $\Delta_{P,4}$ to $\Delta_{P,2}$. Polynomials with a degree 5 or higher yield only a slight improvement.

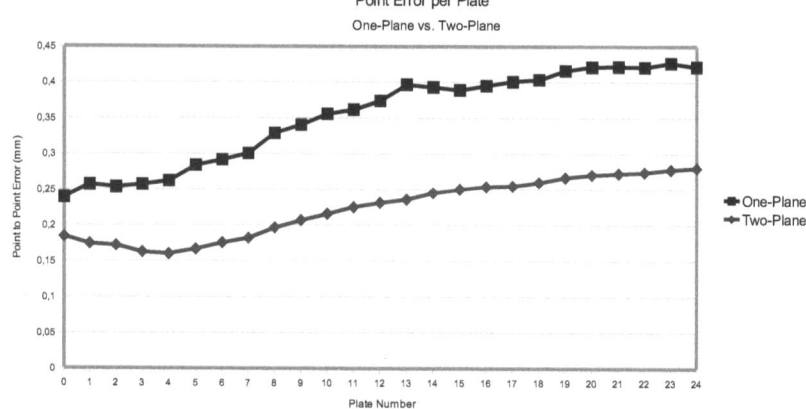

Figure 6.41: Point to point error (average point distance) for the standard one-plane distortion and for the two-plane distortion model with $\Delta = \Delta_{r,4}$.

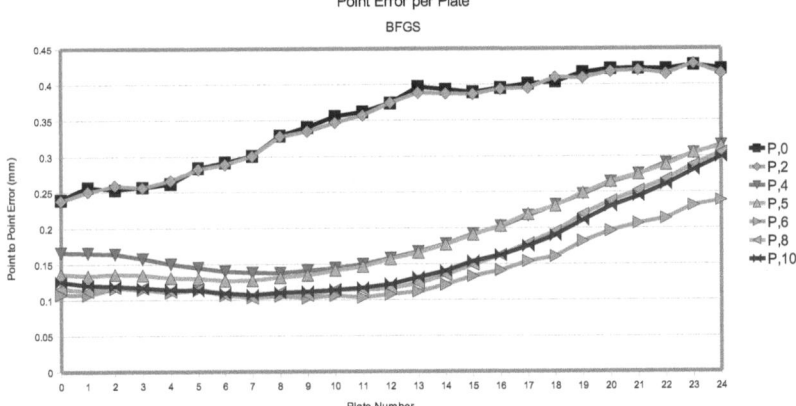

Figure 6.42: Point to point error (average point distance for the standard one-plane distortion with $\Delta = \Delta_{r,4} + \Delta_{P,i}$ with $i \in \{0, 2, 4, 5, 6, 8, 10\}$. One can see that there is no improvement for the point to point error for $i > 6$. In fact the error gets worse for higher degrees!

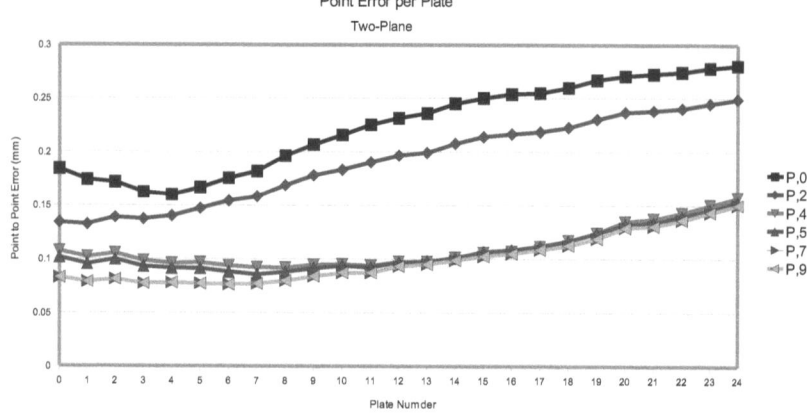

Figure 6.43: Point to point error (average point distance) for the proposed two-plane distortion with $\Delta = \Delta_{r,4} + \Delta_{P,i}$ with $i \in \{0, 2, 4, 5, 7, 9\}$.

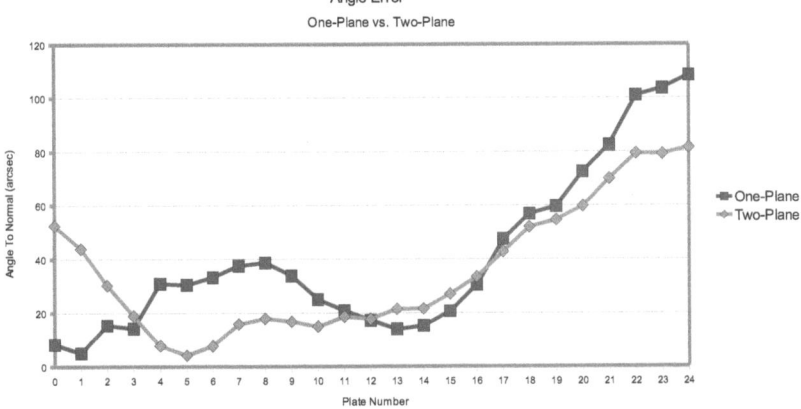

Figure 6.44: Angle error (arcseconds to real normal) for the standard one-plane distortion and for the two-plane distortion model with $\Delta = \Delta_{r,4}$.

6.7.3.3 Angles of reconstructed planes

Another reason to introduce an additional polynomial distortion mapping for the two-plane distortion model is its effect on the angle error. In our experiments we notice that the switch from the one-plane distortion model to the two-plane does not improve the angle error remarkably, as one can see in Figure 6.44. With the additional distortion space $\Delta_{P,5}$ we obtain an improvement of up to 80% as one can see in Figure 6.45.

In Figure 6.46 we show the difference between a calibration w.r.t. the Euclidean error as in Equation 6.44 and the proposed calibration w.r.t. the projected Euclidean error function as in Equation 6.49. One can see easily that a calibration w.r.t. the projected Euclidean error yields better stereo-reconstruction results, in particular for the nearer targets.

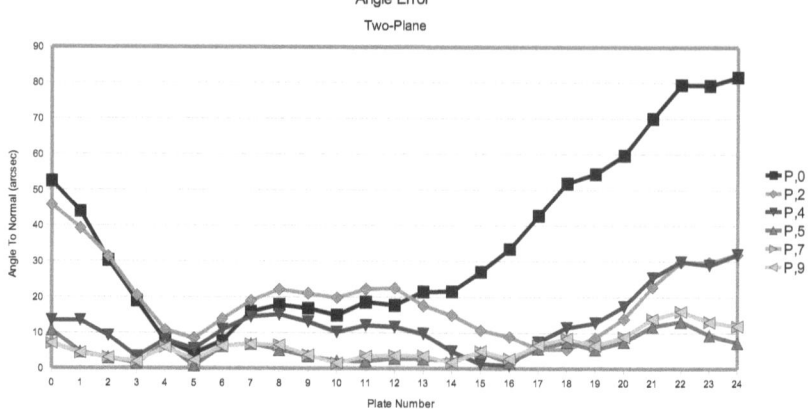

Figure 6.45: Angle to the real normal in arcseconds for the proposed two-plane distortion model with $\Delta = \Delta_{r,4} + \Delta_{P,i}$ with $i \in \{0, 2, 4, 5, 7, 9\}$.

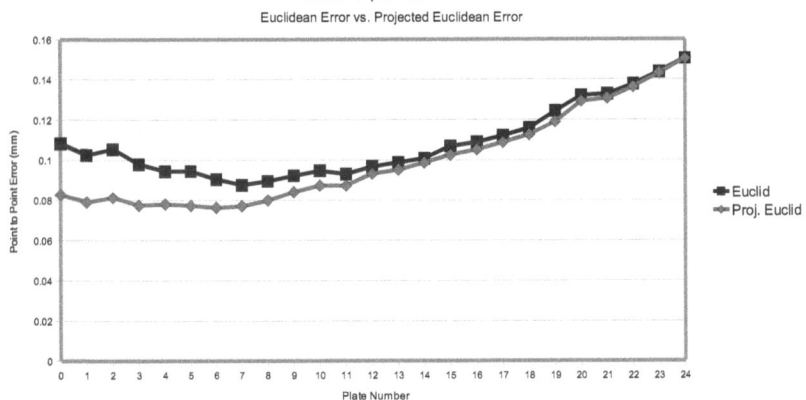

Figure 6.46: Point to point error (average point distance) for the proposed two-plane distortion with $\Delta = \Delta_{r,4} + \Delta_{P,7}$ calibrated w.r.t. the Euclidean error function Ψ_E in Equation 6.44) and w.r.t. the projected Euclidean error function Ψ_Z in Equation 6.47.

6.7.3.4 Other test series

To confirm the results for the point to point error and the angle error we performed seven other test sequences with the same setup. For the following tests we set $\Delta = \Delta_{r,4}$ as the standard approach (**Standard**), $\Delta = \Delta_{r,4} + \Delta_{P,5}$ for the two-plane distortion model (**Two-Plane**) and $\Delta = \Delta_{r,4} + \Delta_{P,6}$ for the one-plane distortion model with polynomial correction (**One-Plane**).

The figures 6.47 - 6.52 show that in all cases the two-plane distortion model yields the best results for the point to point error as well as for the angle error.

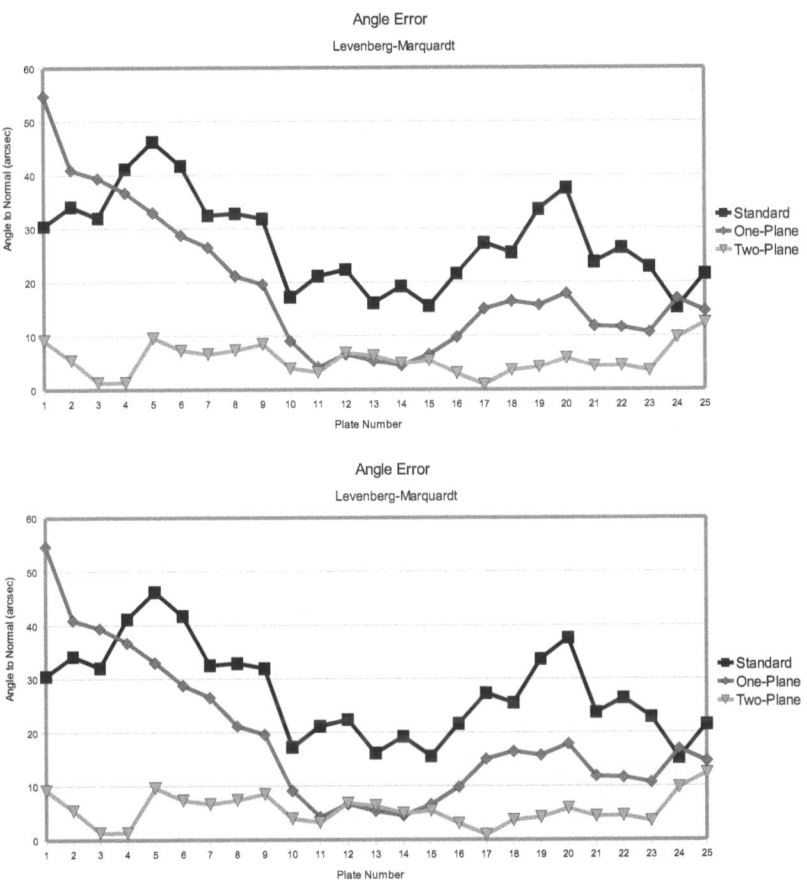

Figure 6.47: Point to point error and angle error for the one-plane and two-plane distortion model. (Test sequence 2).

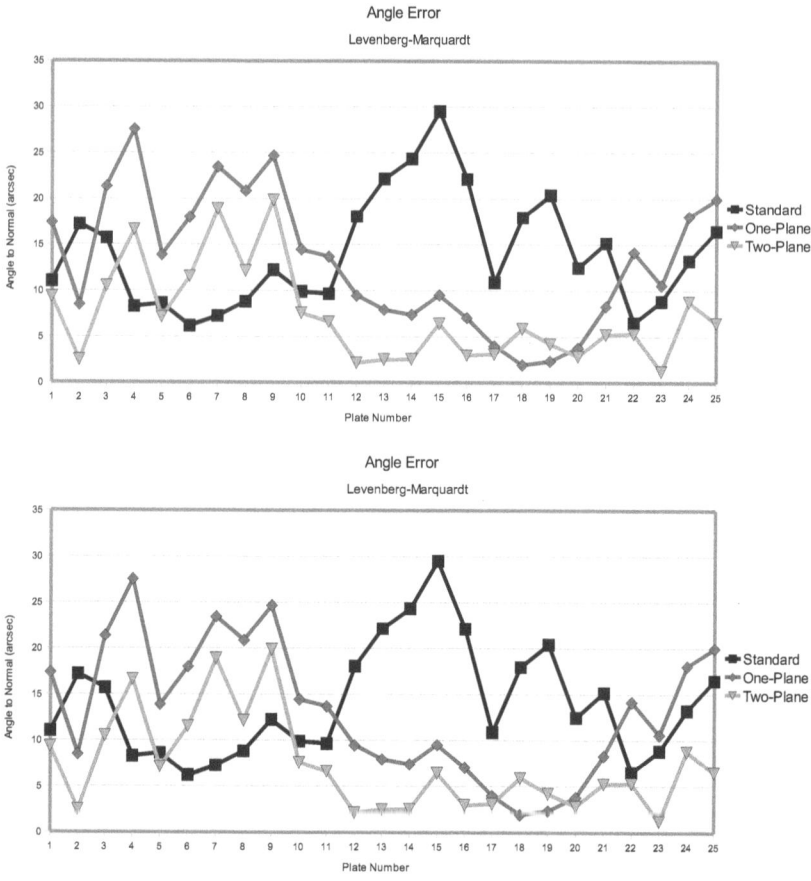

Figure 6.48: Point to point error and angle error for the one-plane and two-plane distortion model. (Test sequence 3).

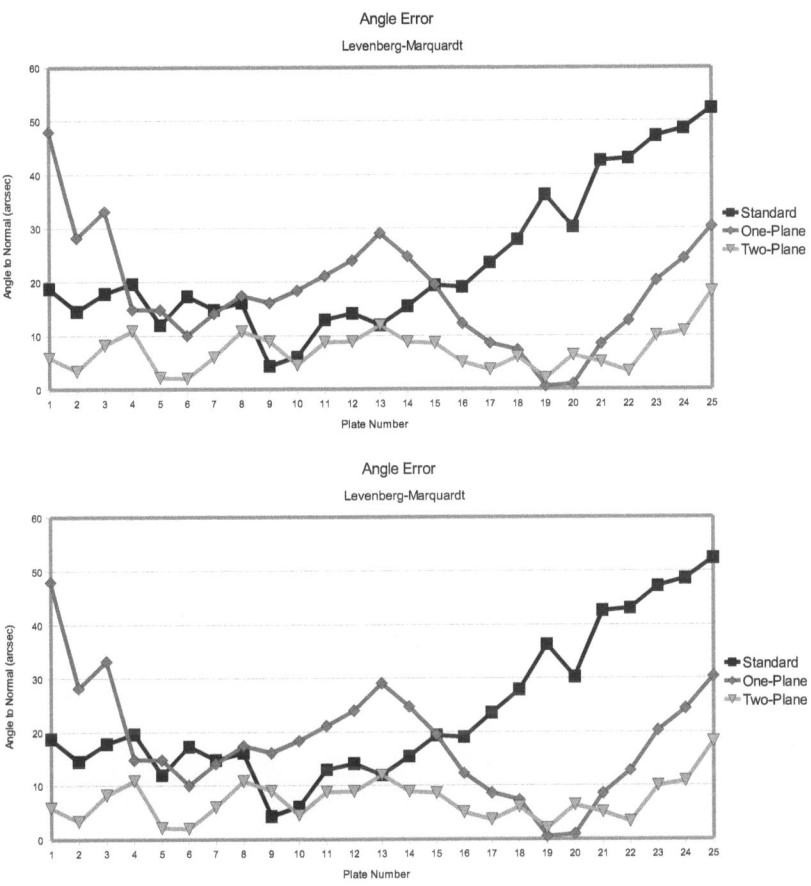

Figure 6.49: Point to point error and angle error for the one-plane and two-plane distortion model. (Test sequence 4).

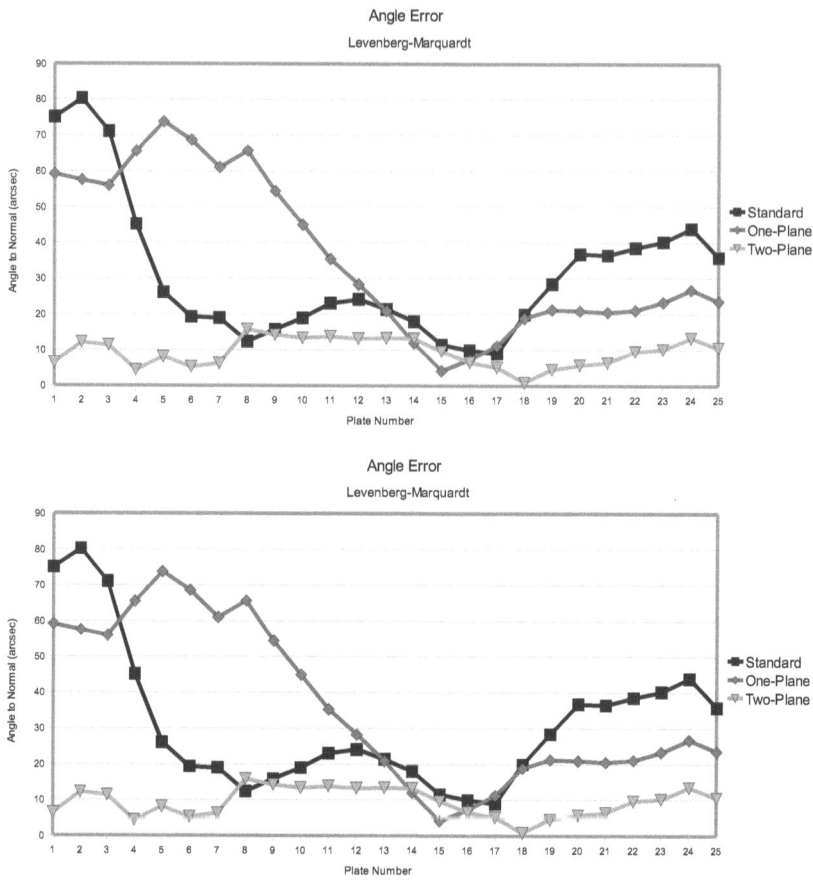

Figure 6.50: Point to point error and angle error for the one-plane and two-plane distortion model. (Test sequence 5).

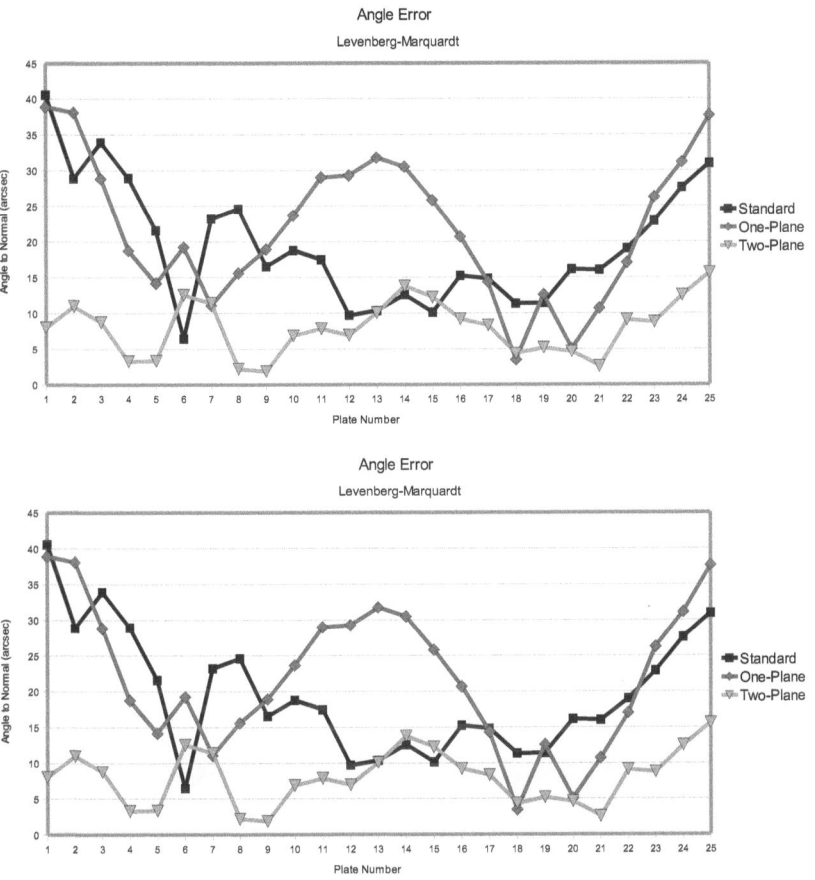

Figure 6.51: Point to point error and angle error for the one-plane and two-plane distortion model. (Test sequence 6).

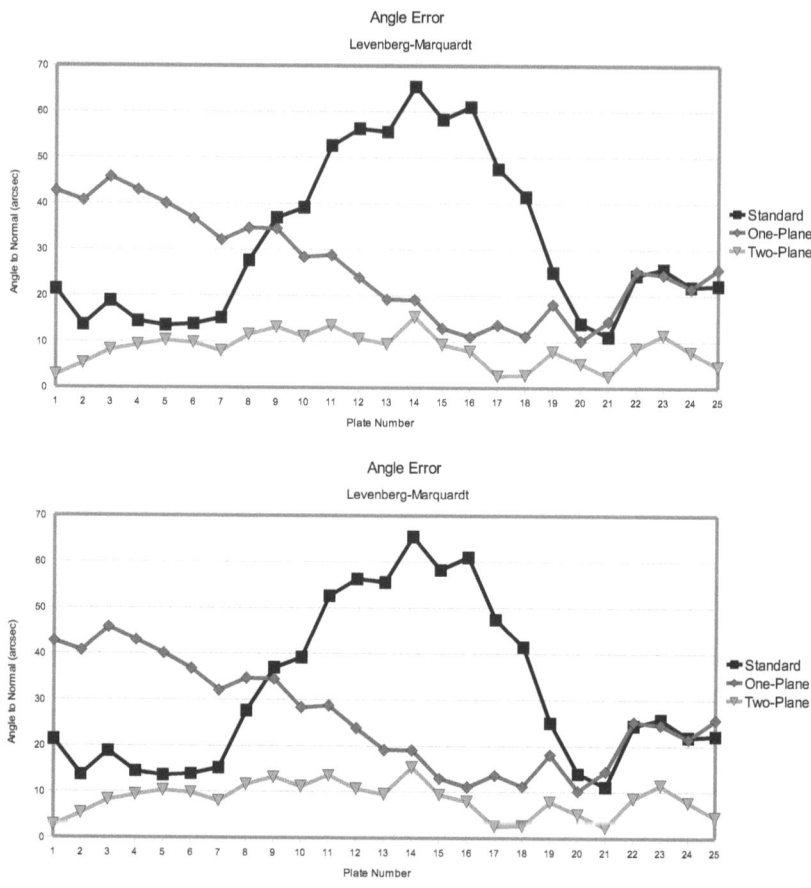

Figure 6.52: Point to point error and angle error for the one-plane and two-plane distortion model. (Test sequence 7).

6.7.3.5 Planarity test

A major drawback of the point to point error is that one needs exact 3D data w.r.t. a reference coordinate system. A planar calibration target provides only planar reference data. Therefore, one can not apply the point to point error outside this plane.

A test which can be performed without exact reference data is the test of planarity. For the planarity test we fit a plane through the reconstructed points and measure the distance of the points to the fitted plane. The planarity of a reconstructed plane can be seen as a necessary condition for a correct reconstruction. However, it is not a sufficient criterion for the correctness.

Figure 6.53, Figure 6.54, Figure 6.55, and Figure 6.56 show the results of the planarity test for the same test sequences we used for the point to point and angle error.

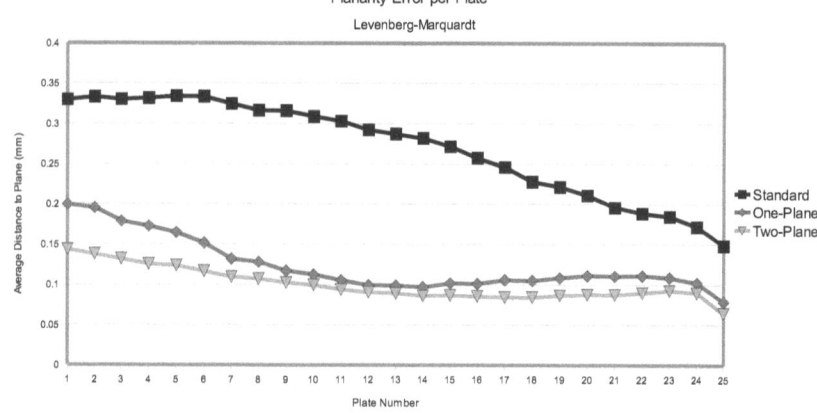

Test sequence 1

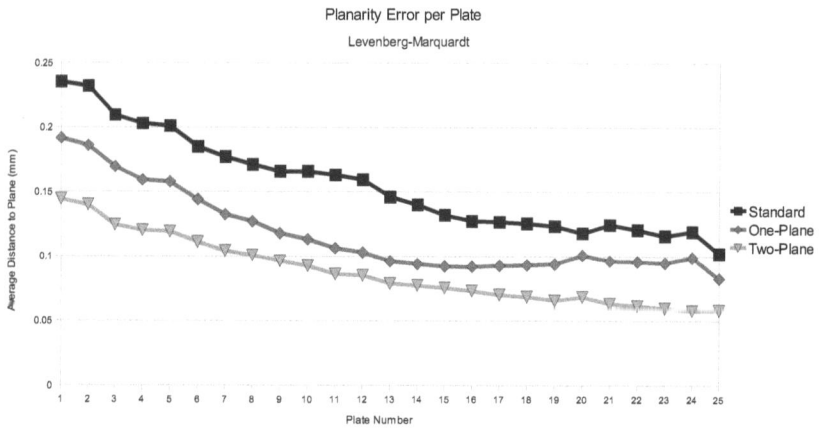

Test sequence 2

Figure 6.53: Planarity test for the first and second test sequence.

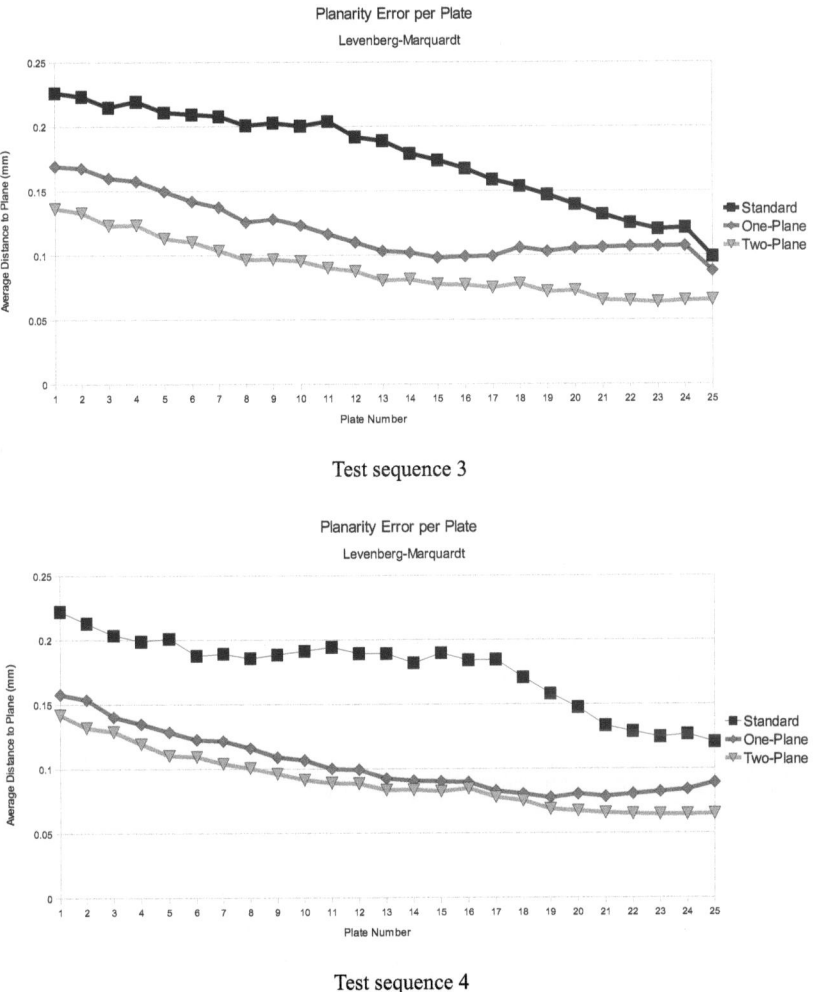

Figure 6.54: Planarity test for the third and fourth test sequence.

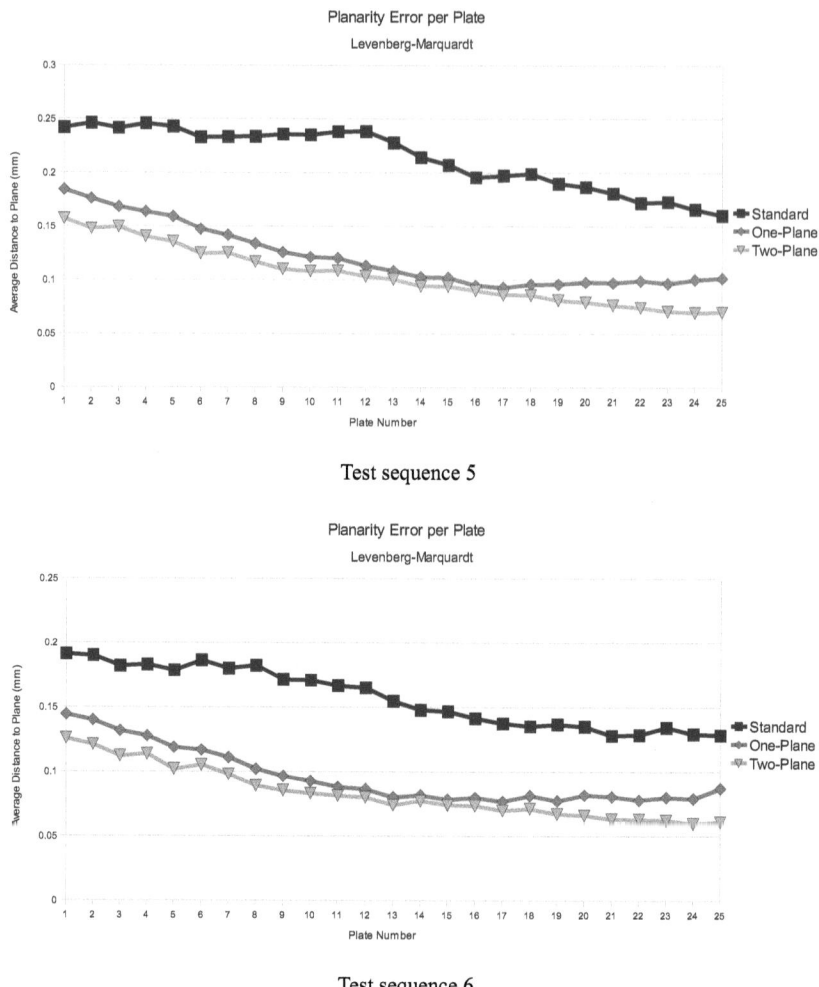

Test sequence 5

Test sequence 6

Figure 6.55: Planarity test for the fifth and sixth test sequence.

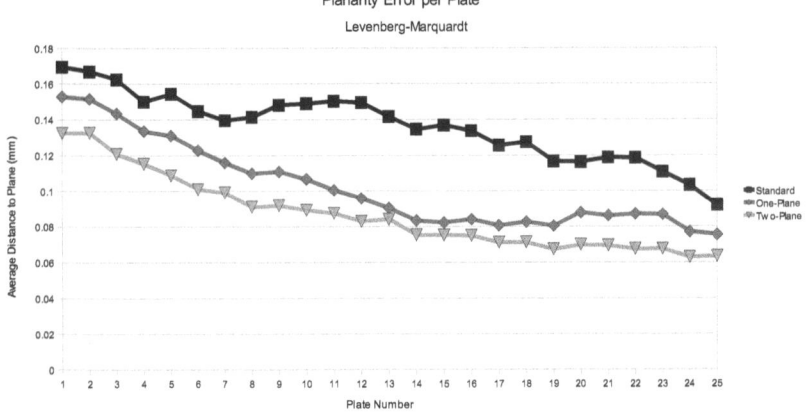

Test sequence 7

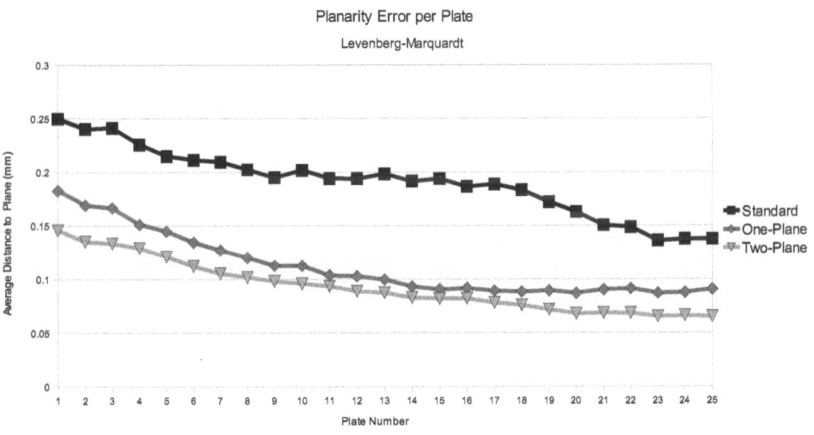

Test sequence 8

Figure 6.56: Planarity test for the seventh and eighth sequence.

6.7.3.6 Prototype reconstruction

For a comparison in prototype reconstruction we apply a comparative test: In Figure 6.57, Figure 6.58, Figure 6.59, and Figure 6.60 we present the results of a monocular prototype reconstruction by

- a standard pinhole camera with four radial distortion parameters (denoted by **Standard**),

- a standard pinhole camera with four radial distortion parameters and a one-plane polynomial distortion model with degree 6 (denoted by **One-Plane**),

- a 3d2d spline corrected camera w.r.t. the re-projective error as introduced in section 6.4.3 with degree (5,5,3) and inner knots (10,10) (denoted by **3d2d-Spline**, and

- a camera with a two-plane distortion model $\Delta = \Delta_{r,4} + \Delta_{P,6}$ (denoted by **Two-Plane**).

The test sequences in the following figures are obtained by the right camera of the stereo setup which we used for the stereo reconstruction test. Therefore, the observed calibration pattern is located at an angle to the camera. Furthermore, some points of the pattern may be located in an area which is not covered by the domain of the correction spline. This explains the behavior of the spline corrected camera in the sixth test sequence (see Figure 6.59; the result for the first position of the calibration pattern of the eighth test sequence in Figure 6.60 is not displayed!).

In summary the tests show that the depth dependent spline correction may deliver the best results for the prototype reconstruction if the pose of the observed object fits to the domain of the correction spline (see *e.g.* test sequence 1, Figure 6.57 or test sequence 5, Figure 6.59). However, in this case the two-plane distortion model is comparable to the best result. Moreover, the two-plane distortion model is much more stable than the 3d2d spline correction: in no case the result w.r.t. the two-plane distortion model is worse than the result of the standard camera model or the result of one-plane polynomial distortion model.

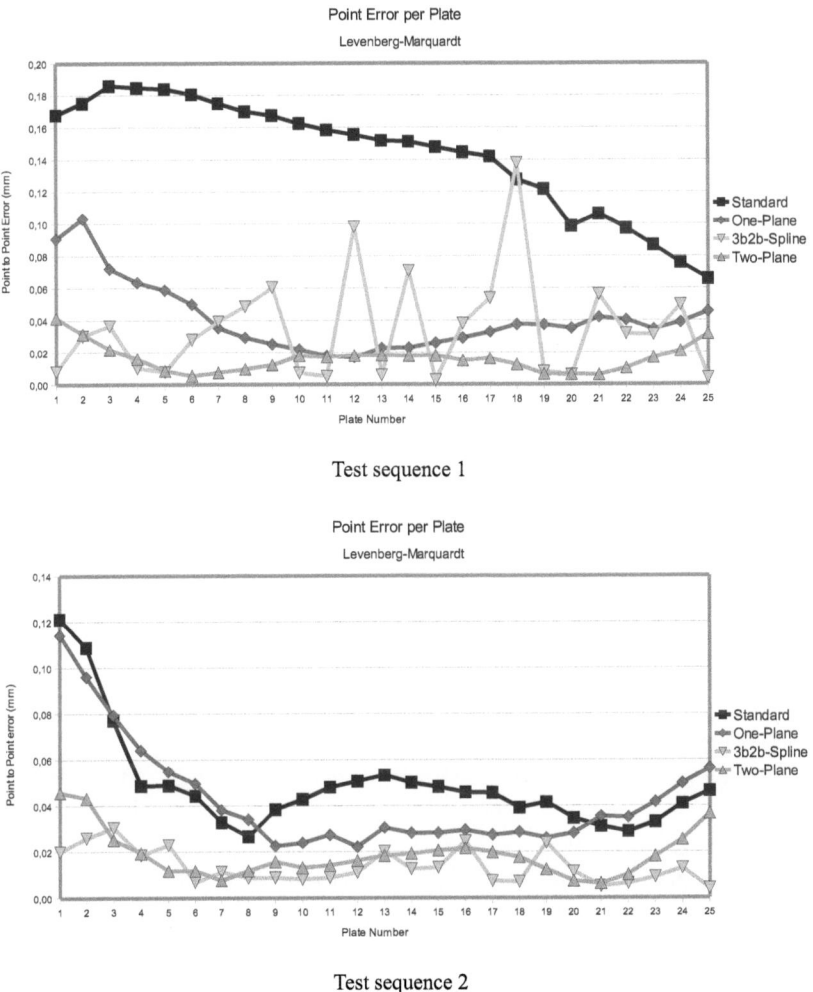

Figure 6.57: Point to point error for the prototype reconstruction by the right camera for the test sequences 1 and 2.

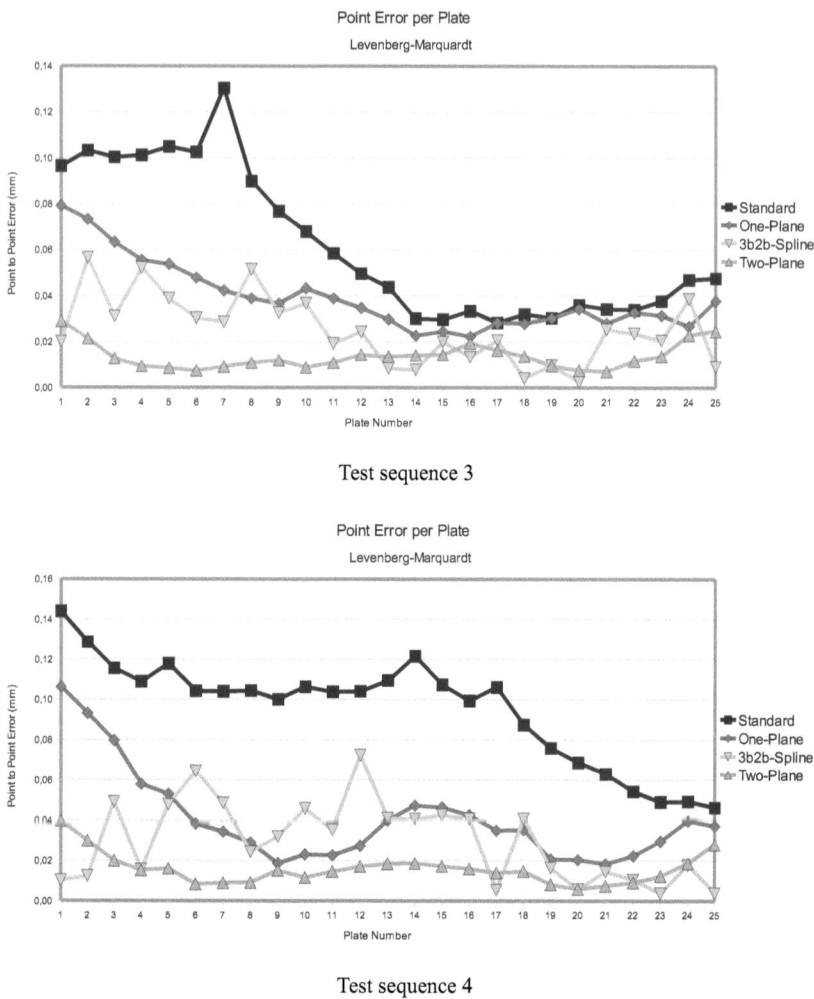

Figure 6.58: Point to point error for the prototype reconstruction by the right camera for the test sequences 3 and 4.

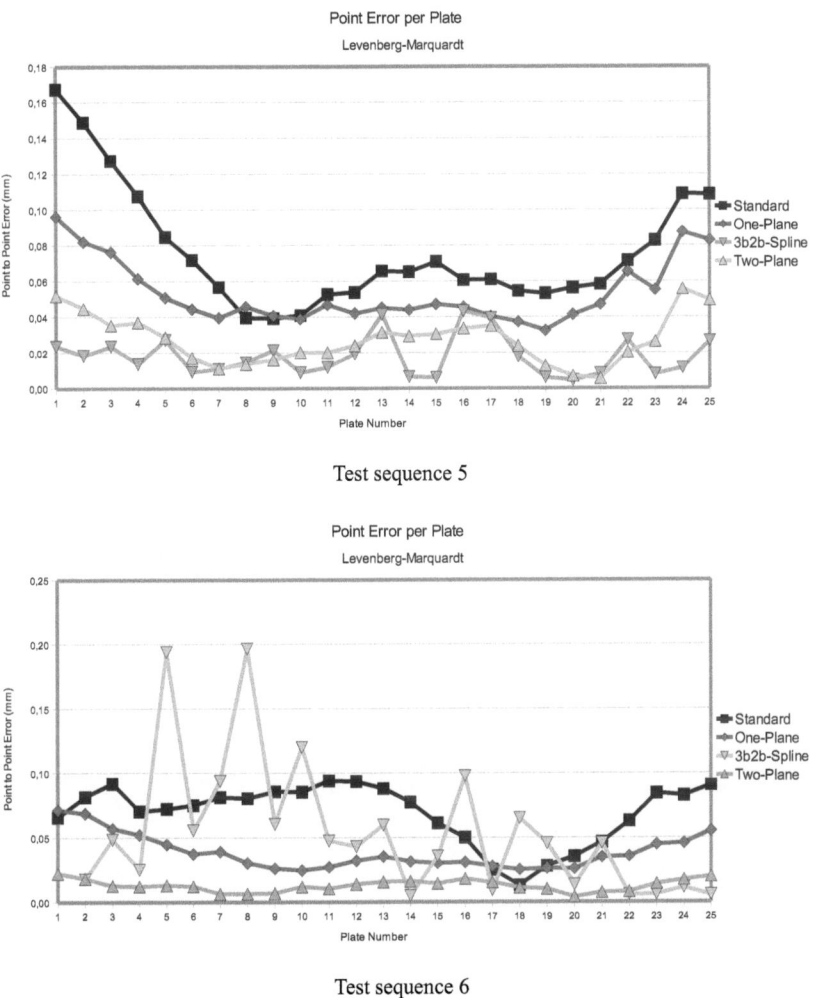

Figure 6.59: Point to point error for the prototype reconstruction by the right camera for the test sequences 5 and 6.

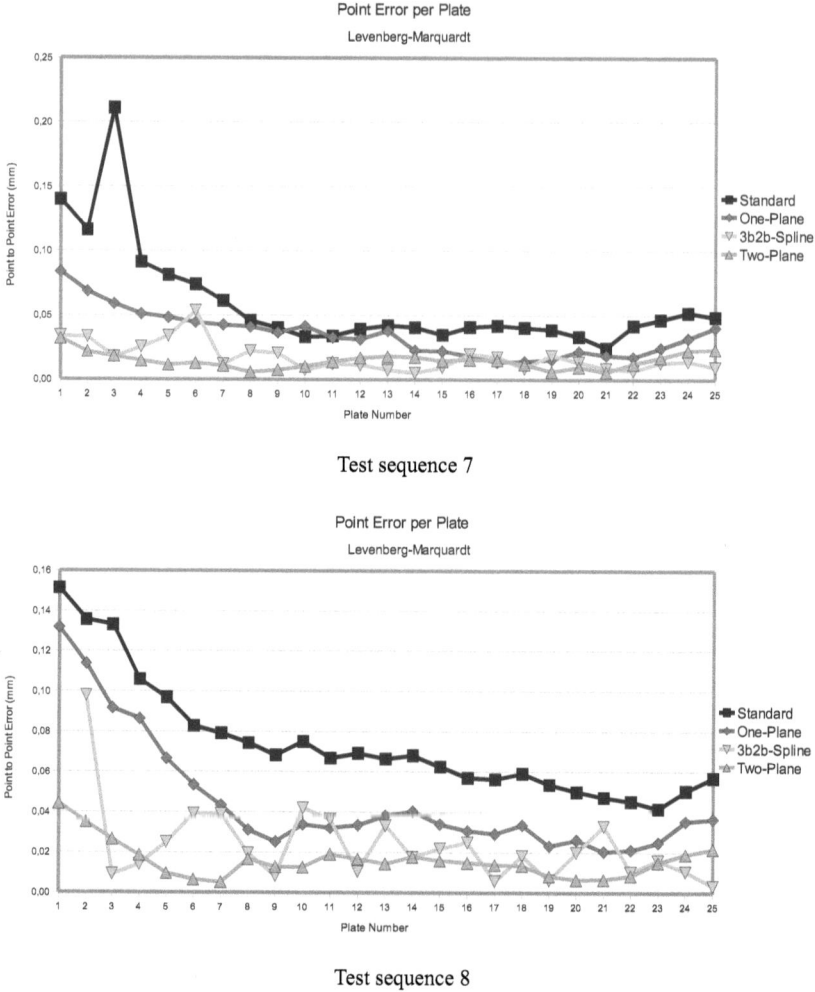

Test sequence 7

Test sequence 8

Figure 6.60: Point to point error for the prototype reconstruction by the right camera for the test sequences 7 and 8.

Chapter 7

Conclusions

Camera calibration consists of the formulation of a camera model and the determination of the best instance of the model w.r.t. the observation. A suitable camera model should be simple in its parameters and exhaustive in reconstruction. The standard way is to model the camera mapping as a pinhole camera with a distortion function in the image plane. In this work we presented two non-standard camera models which actually extend the standard model.

Thus, a correct determination of the best fitting camera w.r.t. the standard camera model is a crucial factor for a calibration w.r.t. the extended models. The calibration of the standard camera w.r.t. to one of the error functions presented in section 3.4 is a non-linear problem which needs an initial value. Therefore, we presented a stratified approach to obtain initial values: First, we determine initial values for the pure pinhole camera parameters, second, we compute the distortion parameters. For the determination of the intrinsic pinhole parameters we formulated some additional constraints for the closed form initial value proposed by Zhang under different restrictions of the camera mapping. Some of these restrictions (like a known principal point) are quite common or — as in the case of a known aspect ratio — are easy to obtain. However, even if the aspect ratio is unknown we are able to formulate a necessary quadratic side condition for a valid solution of the camera calibration problem.

The determination of an initial value of the distortion parameters by a linear least squares problem lead to a semi-linear formulation of the camera calibration problem. The semi-linear approach introduces an error function with at most eleven degrees of freedom, no matter how many distortion parameters are to be determined. The experiments have shown that this approach leads to a non-linear optimization with less iterations and better results.

Since we consider the reconstruction error as the ultimate goal of camera calibration, we additionally investigated some constraints introduced by a stereo camera setup. In particular, we incorporated the epipolar constraint into the calibration of the stereo camera with distortion. This improves the reconstruction tasks which actually depend on the epipolar constraint.

As a central topic of this work we showed that the standard pinhole camera model is limited when objects have to be observed in a great variety of depth. In a first approach we introduced a correction term for the residual distortion of a standard pinhole camera with distortion. The new term extends the standard in-plane distortion by a term which depends on the depth of the observed object. We presented an implementation of this correction term as a tensor spline. The calibration algorithm w.r.t. this new distortion model consists of two steps: The first step is a calibration w.r.t. the pinhole camera model with standard in-plane distortion. The second step determines the parameters of the residual depth-dependent distortion. This determination can be performed by standard linear least squares fitting. Since we determined the correction spline in an extra step after the standard camera calibration, the overall calibration remains stable.

A second approach to introduce a dependency on depth in distortion is defined by the two-plane distortion model. The two-plane distortion model treats the camera in a re-projective way. Thus, we were able to express the camera mapping as a point to line assignment. This allows us to weaken the pinhole assumption by introducing a second plane to determine the re-projected ray by two points which are located in those planes, instead of one point in a plane and the fixed focal point. The two-plane distortion model extends the pinhole camera model, since the mapping of an observed point to its representation in both planes is determined by a classic calibration algorithm w r t the pinhole camera model and does not change when the two-plane distortion mapping is estimated. Although we applied the re-projected viewing ray to formulate the two-plane distortion model, we resembled the standard projective error by measuring a projection of the Euclidean distance. The experiments show that a two-plane distortion model based on a polynomial space provides a significant improvement in high precision camera calibration.

Bibliography

[AAK71] Y. I. Abdel-Aziz and H. M. Karara. Direct linear transformation into object space coordinates in close-range photogrammetry. In *Proc. of the Symposium on Close-Range Photogrammetry*, pages 1 – 18, Urbana, Illinois, 1971.

[AB91] E. H. Adelson and J. R. Bergen. The plenoptic function and the elements of early vision. In *Computational Models of Visual Processing*, pages 3–20. MIT Press, 1991.

[AFM98] N. Asada, H. Fujiwara, and T. Matsuyama. Edge and depth from focus. *International Journal of Computer Vision*, 26(2):498 – 503, 1998.

[AJN05] A. Agarwal, C. V. Jawahar, and P. J. Narayanan. A survey of planar homography estimation techniques. Technical report, Centre for Visual Information Technology, International Institute of Information Technology, Hyderabad, India, 2005.

[Ali01] D. G. Aliaga. Accurate catadioptric calibration for real-time pose estimation of room-size environments. In *International Conference on Computer Vision (ICCV)*, pages 127–134, 2001.

[Asl03] V. Aslantas. Estimation of depth from defocusing using a neural network. *Internation Journal of Computer Intelligence (IJCI)*, 1(2):305 – 309, 2003.

[Atk96] K.B. Atkinson, editor. *Close Range Photogrammetry and Machine Vision*. Whittles Publishing, 1996.

[AW92] E. H. Adelson and J. Y. A. Wang. Single lens stereo with a plenoptic camera. *IEEE Transactions on Pattern Analysis and machine Intelligence*, 14(2):99–106, 1992.

[BAOM02] M. Baba, N. Asada, A. Oda, and T. Migita. A thin lens based camera model for depth estimation from defocus and translation by zooming. In *Proceedings of the 15th International Conference on Vision Interface*, pages 274 – 281, Calgary, Canada, 2002.

[Bar03] J. P. Barreto. *General central projection systems, modeling, calibration and visual servoing*. PhD thesis, University of Coimbra, 2003.

[BBHM+06] C. Brauer-Burchardt, M. Heinze, C. Munkelt, P. Kuhmstedt, and G. Notni. Distance dependent lens distortion variation in 3d measuring systems using fringe projection. In *British Machine Vision Conference (BMVC)*, volume 1, pages 327 – 336, Edingburgh, 2006.

[BD95] T. Blaszka and R. Deriche. A model based method for characterization and location of curved image features. In *ICIAP*, pages 77–82, 1995.

[BD05] J. P. Barreto and K. Daniilidis. Fundamental matrix for cameras with radial distortion. In *IEEE International Conference on Computer Vision (ICCV)*, pages 625–632, 2005.

[BKH07] P. Barth, M. Kellner, and T. Hanning. PoCoDeR: Device control by pointing gesture. In *International Conference on Artificial Intelligence and Applications (AIA)*, pages 643 – 648, Innsbruck, 2007.

[BLM90] J. Biemond, R.L. Lagendijk, and R. M Mersereau. Iterative methods for image deblurring. *Proceedings of the IEEE*, 78:856 – 883, 1990.

[Bra02] G. R. Bradski. OpenCV: Examples of use and new applications in stereo, recognition and tracking. In *Vision Interface*, page 347, 2002.

[Bro71] D. C. Brown. Close-range camera calibration. *Photogrammetric Engineering*, 37(8):855 – 866, 1971.

[BW93]   T. E. Boult and G. Wolberg. Local image reconstruction and subpixel restoration algorithms. *CVGIP:Graphical Models and Image Processing*, 55(63), 1993.

[Can86]   J. Canny. A computational approach to edge detection. *IEEE Transactions on Pattern Analysis and Machine Intelligence*, 8(6):679 – 698, 1986.

[CF05a]   D. Claus and A. W. Fitzgibbon. A plumbline constraint for the rational function lens distortion model. In *Proceedings of the British Machine Vision Conference (BMVC)*, pages 99–108, 2005.

[CF05b]   D. Claus and A. W. Fitzgibbon. A rational function lens distortion model for general cameras. In *Proceedings of the IEEE Conference on Computer Vision and Pattern Recognition (CVPR)*, pages 213–219, 2005.

[CR99]   S. Chaudhuri and A. Rajagopalan. *Depth from defocus: a real aperture imaging approach*. Springer Verlag, 1999.

[Cri01]   A. Criminisi. *Accurate visual metrology from single and multiply images*. Distinguished Dissertation Series. Springer, London, 2001.

[CRZ99]   A. Criminisi, I. Reid, and A. Zisserman. Single view metrology. In *The 7th International Conference on Computer Vision*, pages 434–442, 1999.

[CZZF97]   G. Csurka, C. Zeller, Z. Zhang, and O. Faugeras. Characterizing the uncertainty of the fundamental matrix. *Computer Vision and Image Understanding*, 68(1):18–36, Oktober 1997.

[dB78]   C. de Boor. *A Practical Guide to Splines*. Springer, New York, 1978.

[DF01]   F. Devernay and O. Faugeras. Straight lines have to be straight: automatic calibration and removal of distortion from scenes of structured environments. *Machine Vision and Application*, 13(1):14 – 24, 2001.

[Die93]   P. Dierckx. *Curve and Surface Fitting with Splines*. Clarendon Press, Oxford, 1993.

[DM97] P. E. Debevec and J. Malik. Recovering high dynamic range radiance maps from photographs. *Computer Graphics*, 31:369 – 378, 1997.

[Dol97] J. Dold. *Ein hybrides photogrammetrisches Industriemesssystem höchster Genauigkeit*. PhD thesis, Universität der Bundeswehr, München, 1997.

[DS74] J. C. Dainty and R. Shaw. *Image Science: principles, analysis, and evaluation of photographic-type imaging processes*. Academic Press, 1974.

[Fau93] O. D. Faugeras. *Three-dimensional computer vision. A geometric viewpoint*. MIT Press., 1993.

[FB92] J.G. Fryer and D.C. Brown. Lens distortion for close-range photogrammetry. *Photogrammatic Engineering and Remote Sensing*, 52(1):51 – 58, 1992.

[Fit97] A. W. Fitzgibbon. *Stable Segmentation of 2D Curves*. PhD thesis, University of Edinburgh, 1997.

[Fit01] A. W. Fitzgibbon. Simultaneous linear estimation of multiple view geometry and lens distortion. In *Proceedings of the International Conference on Pattern Recognition*, 2001.

[För00] W. Förstner. Image preprocessing for feature extraction in digital intensity, color and range images. *Geomatic Methods for the Analysis of Data in the Earth Sciences*, 95:165 – 189, 2000.

[FP02] D. A. Forsyth and J. Ponce. *Computer Vision: A Modern Approach*. Prentice Hall, New York, 2002.

[FS92] C. S. Fraser and M. R. Shortis. Variation of distortion within the photographic field. *Photogrammatic Engineering and Remote Sensing*, 58(6):851 – 855, 1992.

[FS98] J. Flusser and T. Suk. Degraded image analysis: An invariant approach. *IEEE Transactions on Pattern Analysis and Machine Intelligence*, 20(6):590–603, 1998.

[FSG95] C. S. Fraser, M. R. Shortis, and G. Ganci. Multi-sensor system self-calibration. *Videometrics IV*, 2598:2 – 15, 1995.

[FT87] O. D. Faugeras and G. Toscanini. Camera calibration for 3d computer vision. In *Proceedings of the International Workshop on Industrial Applications of Machine Vision and Machine Intelligence*, pages 240 – 247, Silken, Japan, 1987.

[GCP02] P. Gurdjos, A. Crouzil, and R. Payrissat. Another way of looking at plane-based calibration: The centre circle constraint. In *ECCV '02: Proceedings of the 7th European Conference on Computer Vision-Part IV*, pages 252–266, London, UK, 2002. Springer-Verlag.

[GD02] Christopher Geyer and Konstantinos Daniilidis. Paracatadioptric camera calibration. *IEEE Transactions on Pattern Analysis and Machine Intelligence*, 24(5):687–695, 2002.

[GH05] S. Graf and T. Hanning. Analytically solving radial distortion parameters. In *Conference on Computer Vision and Pattern Recognition (CVPR)*, volume 2, pages 1104 – 1109, San Diego, 2005. IEEE.

[GN01] M. D. Grossberg and S. K. Nayar. A general imaging model and a method for finding its parameters. In *International Conference on Computer Vision (ICCV)*, pages 108–115, 2001.

[Goo96] J. W. Goodman. *Introduction to Fourier Optics*. McGraw-Hill, New York, 1996.

[Gra08] S. Graf. *Kamerakalibrierung mit radialer Verzeichnung - die radiale essentielle Matrix*. PhD thesis, Universität Passau, 2008. to appear.

[Gro87] P. Grossmann. Depth from focus. *Pattern Recognition Letters*, 5(1):63 – 69, 1987.

[GvL96] G. H. Golub and C. F. van Loan. *Matrix Computations*. John Hopkins University Press, Baltimore, 3 edition, 1996.

[Haa00] Jürgen Haas. *Echtzeit-Korrespondenzprobleme in Bildsequenzen und Subpixelgenauigkeit*. PhD thesis, Universität Passau, 2000.

[Han06]   T. Hanning. Re-projective calibration of a stereo camera system. In *International Conference on Visualization, Imaging and Image Processing (VIIP)*, pages 7 – 12, Palma de Mallorca, Spain, 2006.

[Har97]   R. Hartley. In defense of the eight-point algorithm. *IEEE Transactions on Pattern Analysis and Machine Intelligence*, 19(6):580–593, Juni 1997.

[HBK06]   T. Hanning, P. Barth, and M. Kellner. Segmentation of quadrangles for calibration purposes. In *International Conference on Signal and image processing (SIP)*, pages 181 – 187, Honolulu, Hawaii, 2006.

[Hec87]   E. Hecht. *Optics*. Addison-Wesley, Reading, 2. edition, 1987.

[Hei97]   J. Heikkilä. *Accurate camera calibration and feature based 3D reconstruction from monocular image sequences*. PhD thesis, University Oulu, Finland, Passau, 1997.

[Hei98]   J. Heikkilä. Moment and curvature preserving technique for accurate ellipse boundary detection. In *Proceedings 14th International Conference on Pattern Recognition*, pages 734 – 737, 1998.

[Hei00]   J. Heikkilä. Geometric camera calibration using circular control points. *IEEE Transactions on Pattern Analysis and Machine Intelligence*, 22(10):1066–1077, 2000.

[HF98]   R. Halir and J. Flusser. Numerically stable direct least squares fitting of ellipses. In V. Skala, editor, *Proc. Int. Conf. in Central Europe on Computer Graphics, Visualization and Interactive Digital Media*, pages 125 – 132, 1998.

[HGP04]   T. Hanning, S. Graf, and G. Pisinger. Extrinsic calibration of a stereo camera system fulfilling generalized epipolar constraints. In *International Conference on Visualization, Imaging and Image Processing Conference (VIIP)*, pages 1 – 5, Marbella, Spain, 2004.

[Hor86]   B. K. P. Horn. *Robot vision*. MIT Press, Cambridge, MA, USA, 1986.

[HS92]   R. M. Haralick and L. G. Shapiro. *Computer and Robot Vision*, volume 1. Addison-Wesley, 1992.

[HS97]   J. Heikkilä and O. Silven. A four-step camera calibration procedure with implicit image correction. In *Conference on Computer Vision and Pattern Recognition (CVPR)*, pages 1106 – 1112, San Juan, Puerto Rico, 1997. IEEE.

[HS07a]   T. Hanning and R. Schoene. Additional constraints for Zhang's closed form solution of the camera calibration problem. Technical Report MIP-0709, Fakultät für Informatik und Mathematik, Universität Passau, 2007.

[HS07b]   T. Hanning and O. Smirnow. On the point spread function introduced by first order optics. Technical Report MIP-0710, Fakultät für Informatik und Mathematik, Universität Passau, 2007.

[HSG06]   T. Hanning, R. Schöne, and S. Graf. A closed form solution for monocular re-projective 3d pose estimation of regular planar patterns. In *International Conference of Image Processing (ICIP)*, pages 2197 – 2200, Atlanta, Georgia, 2006.

[HZ00]   R. Hartley and A. Zisserman. *Multiple View Geometry in Computer Vision*. Cambridge University Press, 2000.

[Jah96]   J. Jahn. *Introduction to the Theory of Nonlinear Optimization*. Springer, 2 edition, 1996.

[Jai89]   A. K. Jain. *Fundamentals of Digital Image Processing*. Prentice-Hall, 1989.

[Jän93]   B. Jäne. *Digitale Bildverarbeitung*. Springer, 3. edition, 1993.

[KSH06]   J. Kannala, M. Salo, and J. Heikkilä. Algorithms for computing a planar homography from conics in correspodence. In *British Machine Vision Conference (BMVC)*, volume 1, pages 77 – 86, Edingburgh, 2006.

[Lau06]   V. Lauren. *Semi-lineare Approximation*. PhD thesis, Universität Passau, 2006.

[LF96]   Q. Luong and O. Faugeras. The fundamental matrix: theory, algorithms, and stability analysis. *International Journal of Computer Vision*, 17(1):43–76, 1996.

[LRWW98] J. C. Lagarias, J. A. Reeds, M. H. Wright, and P. E. Wright. Convergence properties of the nelder-mead simplex algorithm in low dimensions. *SIAM Journal on Optimization*, 9:112–147, 1998.

[LT88] R. K. Lenz and R. Y. Tsai. Techniques for calibration of the scale factor and image center for high accuracy 3-d machine vision metrology. *IEEE Transactions on Pattern Analysis and Machine Intelligence*, 10(5):713–720, 1988.

[Lüc06] P. Lücke. *Mikrooptische Sensoren nach dem chromatisch konfokalen Messprinzip*. PhD thesis, Universität Karlsruhe (TH), Karlsruhe, 2006.

[Luh03] T. Luhmann. *Nahbereichsphotogrammetrie*. Wichmann, 2. edition, 2003.

[Lüt97] H. Lütkepohl. *Handbook of Matrices*. Wiley, New York, 1997.

[MBK81] H. A. Martins, J. R. Birk, and R. B. Kelley. Camera models based on data from two calibration planes. *Computer Graphics and Image Processing*, 17:173 – 180, 1981.

[Mel94] T. Melen. *Geometrical Modelling and Calibration of Video Cameras for Underwater Navigation*. PhD thesis, Norwegian University of Science and Technology, Trondheim, Norway, 1994.

[MLK+06] P. Mengel, L. Listl, B. Koenig, C. Toepfer, M. Pellkofer, W. Brockherde, B. Hosticka, O. Elkahili, O. Schrey, and W. Ulfig. Three-dimensional cmos image sensor for pedestrian protection and collision mitigation. In *Advanced Microsystems for Automotive Applications 2006*, pages 23 – 39, Berlin, 2006. Springer.

[MP04] W. Matusik and H. Pfister. 3d tv: a scalable system for real-time acquisition, transmission, and autostereoscopic display of dynamic scenes. *ACM Transactions on Graphics*, 23(3):814 – 824, 2004.

[NLB+05] R. Ng, M. Levoy, M. Bredif, G. Duval, M. Horowitz, and P. Hanrahan. Light field photography with a hand-held plenoptic camera. Technical report, Stanford Computer Graphics Laboratory, 2005. Computer Science Tech Report CSTR 2005-02.

[NM65]   J. A. Nelder and R. Mead. A simplex method for function minimization. *The Computer Journal*, 7:308–313, 1965.

[PH07]   G. Pisinger and T. Hanning. Closed form monocular re-projective pose estimation. In *International Conference of Image Processing (ICIP)*, volume V, pages 197 – 200, San Antonio, Texas, 2007.

[Pis05] G. Pisinger. Model based ellipse fitting for the estimation of the cross sectional area in MR images. In *Proceedings of the 3rd IASTED International Multi-Conference on Biomedical Engineering*, pages 231–235, 2005.

[Pis06] G. Pisinger. Estimating the sensor model parameters of a CCD camera. In *International Conference on Visualization, Imaging and Image Processing (VIIP)*, pages 1 – 6, Palma de Mallorca, Spain, 2006.

[PKH05] G. Pisinger, R. Kickingereder, and T. Hanning. A ray-based subpixel edge detection algorithm for contour pixels of a circle. In *International Conference on Visualization, Imaging and Image Processing (VIIP)*, pages 197 – 201, 2005.

[PST97] F. Pedersini, A. Sarti, and S. Tubaro. Estimation and compensation of subpixel edge localization error. *IEEE Transactions on Pattern Analysis and Machine Intelligence*, 19(10), 1997.

[PTVF92] W. H. Press, S. A. Teukolsky, W. T. Vetterling, and B. P. Flannery. *Numerical recipes in C: the art of scientific computing*. Cambridge University Press, New York, NY, USA, 2 edition, 1992.

[PWH97] T. Pajdla, T. Werner, and V. Hlaváč. Correcting radial lens distortion without knowledge of 3-d structure. Technical Report K335-CMP-1997-138, Czech Technical University, Center for Machine Perception, Praha, 1997.

[RB98]   P. Rademacher and G. Bishop. Multiple-center-of-projection images. In *SIGGRAPH '98: Proceedings of the 25th annual conference on Computer graphics and interactive techniques*, pages 199 – 206, New York, NY, USA, 1998. ACM Press.

[SA96]   S. Shah and J. K. Aggarwal. Intrinsic parameter calibration procedure for a (high-distortion) fish-eye lens camera with distortion model and accuracy estimation. *Pattern Recognition*, 29(11):1775 – 1788, 1996.

[SCS94]   M. R. Shortis, T. Clark, and T. Short. A comparision of some techniques for the subpixel location of discrete target images. *Videometrics III*, 2350:239 – 250, 1994.

[SG87]   M. Subbarao and N. Gurumoorthy. Depth recovery from blurred edges. In *IEEE Conference on Computer Vision and Pattern Recognition (CVPR)*, pages 498 – 503, Ann Arbor, Michigan, 1987.

[SGN01]   R. Swaminathan, M.D. Grossberg, and S.K. Nayar. Caustics of catadioptric cameras. In *International Conference on Computer Vision (ICCV)*, pages II: 2–9, 2001.

[SHZ06]   R. Schöne, T. Hanning, and A. Zimmermann. Approximation mit quadratischer Nebenbedingung. Technical Report MIP-0605, Fakultät für Mathematik und Informatik, Universität Passau, 2006.

[Sla80]   C.C. Slama, editor. *Manual of Photogrammetry*. American Society of Photogrammetry & Remote Sensing, Virginia, 4. edition, 1980.

[SM99]   P. F. Sturm and S. J. Maybank. On plane-based camera calibration: a general algorithm, singularities, applications. In *Proceedings of the IEEE Conference on Computer Vision and Pattern Recognition (CVPR)*, volume 1, pages 432 – 437, Fort Collins, Co., 1999.

[Smi08]   W. J. Smith. *Modern optical engineering*. McGraw-Hill series on optical and electro-optical engineering. McGraw-Hill, New York, 4. edition, 2008.

[Spe93]   P. Spellucci. *Numerische Verfahren der nichtlinearen Optimierung*. Birkhäuser, 1993.

[SR04]   P. Sturm and S. Ramalingam. A generic concept for camera calibration. In *Proceedings of the European Conference on Computer Vision, Prague, Czech Republic*, volume 2, pages 1–13. Springer, May 2004.

[SZH05]   R. Schoene, A. Zimmermann, and T. Hanning. Level curve cutting of nurbs-approximated freeformed surfaces. In W. J. Blau, D. Kennedy, and J. Colreavy, editors, *Proceedings of the SPIE*, volume 5824, pages 277 – 284, Dublin, 2005. SPIE.

[TL00]   W. Tecklenburg and T. Luhmann. Kameramodellierung mit bildvariaten Parametern und finiten Elementen. *Publikationen der Deutschen Gesellschaft für Photogrammetrie and Fernerkundung*, 9:140 – 149, 2000.

[TM84]   A.J. Tabatabai and O.R. Mitchell. Edge location to subpixel values in digital imagery. *IEEE Transactions on Pattern Analysis and Machine Intelligence*, 6(2):188 – 200, 1984.

[TMHF00]   B. Triggs, P. McLauchlan, R. Hartley, and A. W. Fitzgibbon. Bundle adjustment – A modern synthesis. In W. Triggs, A. Zisserman, and R. Szeliski, editors, *Vision Algorithms: Theory and Practice*, LNCS, pages 298–375. Springer Verlag, 2000.

[Tsa87]   R. Y. Tsai. A versatile camera calibration technique for high-accuracy 3d machine vision metrology using off-the-shelf tv cameras and lenses. *IEEE Journal of Robotics and Automation*, 3(4):323 – 344, 1987.

[TYO02]   T. Tamaki, T. Yamamura, and N. Ohnishi. Unified approach to image distortion. In *International Conference on Pattern Recognition*, volume II, pages 584–587, Quebec, Canada, August 2002.

[WCH92]   J. Weng, P. Cohen, and M. Herniou. Camera calibration with distortion models and accuracy evaluation. *IEEE Transactions on Pattern Analysis and Machine Intelligence*, 14(10):965 – 980, 1992.

[WH05]   Y. Wu and Z. Hu. A new constraint on the imaged absolute conic from aspect ratio and its application. *Pattern Recognition Letters*, 26(8):1192–1199, 2005.

[WLD99]   R. Wagner, F. Liu, and K. Donner. Robust motion estimation for calibrated cameras from monocular image sequences. *Computer Vision and Image Understanding*, 73(2):258 – 268, 1999.

[WM91] G.-Q. Wei and S. D. Ma. Two plane camera calibration: A unified model. In *Conference on Computer Vision and Pattern Recognition (CVPR)*, pages 133 – 138, Hawaii, 1991. IEEE.

[WM93] G.-Q. Wei and S. D. Ma. A complete two-plane camera calibration method and experimental comparisons. In *Proceedings of the 4th International Conference on Computer Vision*, pages 439 – 446, Berlin, 1993.

[WM94] G.-Q. Wei and S. D. Ma. Implicit and explicit camera calibration: Theory and experiments. *IEEE Transactions on Pattern Analysis and Machine Intelligence*, 16(5):469 – 480, 1994.

[YH04] X. Ying and Z. Hu. Catadioptric camera calibration using geometric invariants. *IEEE Transactions on Pattern Analysis and Machine Intelligence*, 26(10):1260–1271, 2004.

[Zha96a] Z. Zhang. Determining the epipolar geometry and its uncertainty: A review. Technical Report 2927, INRIA, 1996.

[Zha96b] Z. Zhang. On the epipolar geometry between two images with lens distortion. In *Proceedings of the International Conference on Pattern Recognition*, volume I, pages 407 – 411, Vienna, Austria, 1996.

[Zha98] Z. Zhang. A Flexible new technique for camera calibration. Technical report, Microsoft Research, 1998. Technical Report MSR-TR-98-71.

[Zho86] G. Zhou. Accurate determination of ellipse centers in digital imagery. In *Annual Convention of the American Society for Photogrammetry and Remote Sensing*, volume 4, March 1986.

[Zim01] A. Zimmermann. Fast least squares approximation using tensor products of functions and linear forms. *Approximation, Optimization and Mathematical Economics*, 383-393, 2001.

[ZZW05] H. Zhang, G. Zhang, and K.-Y. K. Wong. Camera calibration with spheres: Linear approaches. In *International Conference of Image Processing (ICIP)*, volume II, pages 1150 – 1153, Genova, Italy, September 2005. IEEE.

Index

$D(g)$ 114
I 23
$\Delta_{P,n}$ 161
$\Delta_{r,D}$ 19
B^{-1} 24
Π_z 13
δ^* 24
$\tilde{\delta}^*$ 24
$S_{n,U}^d$ 137
$S_{n,U}^{k,d}$ 137

angle error 173
aperture 11
astigmatism 15

B-spline base 136
back focal length 7
BFGS algorithm 38

calibration matrix 25
camera calibration 27
camera coordinate system 13
CCS 13
center ray 8
central projection 13
chromatic aberrations 16
circle of confusion 8
coma 15
correspondence problem for contours .. 101
corresponding points 92

decentring distortion 22
depth of field 8

depth-dependent correction
   w.r.t. the Euclidean error 138
   w.r.t. the projective error 135
   w.r.t. the re-projective error 135
   with splines 137
direct linear transformation 47
distortion 16
   decentering 22
   division model 21
   elliptical 22
   field of view 20
   fish-eye 20
   radial 19
   tangential 22
   thin prism 22
distortion mapping 17
distortion model 17
   w.r.t. the two-plane distortion 147
distortion parameters 17
DLT 47

elliptical distortion 22
epipolar constraint 92
epipolar line 92
epipole 93
essential matrix 92
Euclidean error 29
   w.r.t. the two-plane distortion 149
extrinsic camera parameters 14, 17

FET 20
field curvarture 15
first order optics 7

fish-eye camera 20
fish-eye transformation............... 20
focal length 8
focal plane 7
focal point 7
front focal length 8
fundamental matrix 92

Gauss-Newton algorithm 38
generalized epipolar constraints 95

homography 40, 51

ICS 13
image coordinate system 13
image of the camera mapping 23
image plane 8
image sensor 9
image transformation 14
　　w.r.t. the plane $\{z = -1\}$ 145
in-plane correction 162
intrinsic camera parameters 14, 17

lens maker's equation 7
Levenberg-Marquardt algorithm 38
local plane coordinate system 156

multi-plane camera 156

normalized Euclidean error 29
　　w.r.t. the two-plane distortion 151

one-plane distortion model 148
optical axis 5
optical center 8

paraxial 7
Petzval fied curvarture 15
PFET 20
pinhole camera 14
pinhole camera with distortion 17
pinhole equation 25

point spread function 9
point to point error 162, 173
pose estimation 64
principal plane 7
principal point 13
projected Euclidean error 150
projective error 28
prototype reconstruction 37
PSF 9

radial alignment constraint 42
radial distortion 19
radial essential matrix 94
rational function lens distortion 94
re-projection 23
re-projective error 28
reduced parameters calibration function 78
root mean square error 35

Seidel aberrations 15
self-calibration 52
semi-linear problem 77
sensor input function 8
skewness 14
spherical aberrations 15
steepest descent 38
stereo camera system 91
stereo reconstruction 37

tangential distortion 22
tensor product 135
thin lens 7
thin prism distortion 22
third order optics 15
two-plane distortion model 147
two-plane re-projection 148

un-distortion 23

MIX
Papier aus verantwortungsvollen Quellen
Paper from responsible sources
FSC® C105338

If you have any concerns about our products,
you can contact us on
ProductSafety@springernature.com

In case Publisher is established outside the EU,
the EU authorized representative is:
**Springer Nature Customer Service Center GmbH
Europaplatz 3, 69115 Heidelberg, Germany**

Printed by Libri Plureos GmbH
in Hamburg, Germany